The Golden Calf

Economism and American Policy

Howard Brody

Brody, Howard.
The Golden Calf: Economism and American Policy
239 p. Includes index.

ISBN 1463762755
ISBN-13 9781463762759

Table of Contents

Acknowledgments 4

Chapter 1. Introduction 6

Chapter 2. One Family's Story 23

Chapter 3. From Economics to Economism:
    The Rise of Market Worship 36

Chapter 4. Economism's Origins: Evangelicalism in England 59

Chapter 5. Economism's Origins: Puritanism in America 83

Chapter 6. The Reverse Robin Hood Rule: Economism
    as Stealth Policy 108

Chapter 7. Economism and Intelligent Design:
    Religion Masquerading as Science 137

Chapter 8. Layoffs 159

Chapter 9. Economism and the Great Recession of 2008 178

Chapter 10. Conclusion: What Next for America? 202

About the Author. 228

Index 229

Acknowledgments

Figures 10.2, 10.3, and 10.4 are reprinted from *The Spirit Level: Why Greater Equality Makes Societies Stronger,* by Kate Pickett and Richard Wilkinson. ©2010 by Kate Pickett and Richard Wilkinson. Reprinted by permission of Bloomsbury Press. Figure 10.1 is a modification of another figure from Wilkinson and Pickett's *The Spirit Level.*

I am grateful to my colleague, Dr. Harold Y. Vanderpool, for reading chapters of the manuscript and for advising me on the accuracy of the religious history, especially in Chapters 4 and 5. Subsequently, Drs. Jan C. Heller and John H. Carrier also offered excellent suggestions for revisions.

In a work like this, as you see what recent incidents are mentioned and which are not, it is helpful to know the dates for the completion of the manuscript. I completed most of the work on this manuscript in January-February, 2011. I then made some further revisions in June and July, 2011.

So the people stripped themselves of their gold earrings and brought them to Aaron. He took them out of their hands, cast the metal in a mould, and made it into the image of a bull-calf. "These," he said, "are your gods, O Israel, that brought you up from Egypt." Then Aaron was afraid and built an altar in front of it and issued this proclamation, "Tomorrow there is to be a pilgrim-feast to the Lord." Next day the people rose early, offered whole-offerings, and brought shared-offerings. After this they sat down to eat and drink and then gave themselves up to revelry. But the Lord said to Moses, "Go down at once, for your people, the people you brought up from Egypt, have done a disgraceful thing; so quickly have they turned aside from the way that I commanded them."

--Exodus 32, 3-8, New English Bible

Chapter 1.

Introduction

How the Snake Became Beloved

Once upon a time there was a snake. Everywhere he went, people shrieked, "Snake! Snake!" and beat him with rocks and sticks. Being called "snake" did not hurt much, but the rocks and sticks certainly did. Besides, he was terribly depressed because he knew that he could never look forward to being treated any better.

The snake had heard that the raven was the wisest of the birds, and so he went into the forest to consult the raven about his self-esteem issues.

"Hey, snake," said the raven. "What's happening?"

"Life stinks," said the snake. "Everywhere I go, people shout, 'Snake! Snake!' and then beat me with rocks and sticks. Now, I know that I have some problems. It's true that I'm poisonous. Plus I occasionally eat small infants and pets."

"Ah, yes," observed the raven severely. "It has also come to my attention that you include birds' eggs in your diet."

"I haven't eaten any recently," objected the snake. "Not yet today, anyway."

"Well, you certainly have a PR problem," said the raven. "Remember that the best defense is a good offense. Don't think about being a snake and how you can get people to stop beating you. Instead think of what people love, and figure out how to be one of those."

"I don't get you," replied the snake.

"Okay, people love ponies, right?" said the raven. "Remember a few years back they had those obnoxious plastic things in pastel colors, My Little Pony or something? Little girls could not get enough of them. Or there was that book about Misty of Chincoteague—must've sold a gazillion copies."

"That's very well to talk about," moaned the snake. "But how in the world would I ever get people to think I'm a pony?"

"Attend to me carefully," said the raven.

The snake went back among the people. The people, as before, shrieked, "Snake! Snake!" and ran to get the rocks and sticks.

"Hold on there," commanded the snake. "I'm not a snake. I'm a Pretty Little Pony."

The people at first were puzzled. "How can you be a pony? A pony has four legs. You don't have any legs."

"Aha! You thereby demonstrate your ignorance. Ordinary ponies have four legs. But you are obviously unaware that the very best ponies get by with no legs at all."

The people scratched their heads over this. "Well, ponies also have manes and long hairy tails. You have no mane, and you are pretty much all tail, but not a hair in sight."

"There you go again," and the snake shook his head. "Sure, ordinary ponies have those things. But the best ponies these days have become much more advanced."

The people persisted. "Ponies eat oats and hay. You eat small infants and pets and birds' eggs."

"Look," said the snake, "have you figured out how much energy there is in oats and hay? It might get you by till two in the afternoon but there's no way you'd make it to five p.m. If you really want that late burst of energy, you'd better go with something with more vitamins and protein."

So the people finally were persuaded, and the snake started to enjoy life. People came by and stroked it regularly. They did not seem to mind that small infants and pets regularly disappeared from the vicinity. As for birds' eggs, the people went around robbing the nests to be sure that their Pony had a generous supply.

All went well until one day when some people from the next county over happened to come through the village. As soon as they saw the snake, they shrieked, "Snake! Snake!" and reached for the rocks and sticks.

"Stop!" shouted the local people, aghast. "That's not a snake. That's our Pretty Little Pony."

The out-of-towners snorted. "What do you mean, Pretty Little Pony? That's clearly a snake."

"He said he was a Pretty Little Pony."

"Nonsense. Just look at it. What part of 'snake' don't you understand?"

The local people were perplexed and came to the snake for advice. "Pretty Little Pony, you said you were a pony and we believed you. But now these other people have come along and they say you are really a snake. How do we know you haven't been fooling us all this while?"

"Ah," said the snake sagely. "The Time of the Big Test has finally arrived."

"What do you mean, Pretty Little Pony?"

"Look," replied the snake, "You agree that there's an afterlife, right?"

"Of course," chorused the people.

"And that in the afterlife, people are rewarded or punished?"

"Of course," the people said again.

"There you go," said the snake. "Whether you are rewarded in the afterlife, or not, depends on your Unwavering Faith."

"What does Unwavering Faith have to do with this?" asked the people.

"It's simple," replied the snake. "You have declared that I am your Pretty Little Pony. Now these unbelievers have shown up from a foreign place, claiming that I'm something else. You show your Unwavering Faith by sticking to your convictions that I am your Pretty Little Pony."

"But," the people protested, "what if they show us proofs that you really are a snake?"

"Proofs, schmoofs," sneered the snake. "If nobody ever tried to talk you out of your Faith, how could you ever pass The Test? It's only in the face of adversity and pressure that you can really demonstrate your Unwavering Faith in my Ponyhood. These outsiders who are causing you to doubt, they are part of The Test. You must surmount their unbelief to show that you truly have Unwavering Faith and deserve to be rewarded in the next life."

"Well, we don't know," said the people. "Now that they have called our attention to it, you really do look like a snake."

"Who are you going to believe?" replied the snake. "Your Pretty Little Pony, or your lying eyes?"

And so the people stood steadfast in their belief that the snake really was their Pretty Little Pony. When the people from the next county over saw the Unwavering Faith of the local people, they started increasingly to doubt their own doubts. "Maybe it's the Pretty Little Pony, after all," they began to say.

When the people from yet a farther-away county happened by some time later, they found an even bigger crowd of people declaring that the snake was their Pretty Little Pony. The more people who declared this, the easier it became to convince any future doubters.

And so the snake finally became beloved by all, and could consume small infants and pets and birds' eggs to his heart's content. Eventually he became very fat, and people began to wonder how he could be the Pretty Little Pony and yet be so fat. But that is a story for another time.

Why the Fable?

The fable of the snake depicts a group of people being misled about an object of worship, somewhat akin to what happened with the followers of Aaron in the Old Testament story about the Golden Calf. They were fooled, in effect, into worshiping a false god. What's important to us is the particular way they were misled. They became confused about what sort of beast was in front of them. Nor were they misled simply by mistake. The snake had an agenda; he wanted people to treat him in a certain way. The snake was quite willing to use deception to convince people that he was a different sort of beast than he really was.

Were the people in the fable at fault because their religious faith made them gullible? My goal in this book is not to denigrate religion. So from my standpoint, the problem is not the people's felt need to have faith in their lives. Rather it was the cynical way that the snake took advantage of that need. Since religious impulses can be a powerful force for good, those who manipulate those impulses for selfish ends deserve special condemnation.

So now we have two animals before us, the snake and the calf. What are we to make of the story of the Golden Calf? What were Aaron and his followers thinking when they constructed their idol? Their timing, after all, was atrocious. Their leader, Moses, believed devoutly that the Israelites had a special covenant with (the real) God. And God had come through for them handsomely—rescuing them from bondage in Egypt and destroying Pharaoh's pursuing army, just to mention the highlights. What could have possessed them, at this critical moment, to start violating the chief among the Commandments that God had just sent down?

If we try to imagine their thoughts, one possibility seems to go like this:

There's something really scary about this God that Moses keeps talking about. For one thing, you can't see him. Maybe he's by our side, or maybe he's abandoned us—how could we be sure? I want to be *certain* that I can *see* my god right in front of me. I want to see my god right here and now, glittering in the sun.

And while I know that this is starting to get me into dangerous territory, there's this omnipotence thing as well. If Moses' God could do what he did to Pharaoh, what might he do to me, if he decided that I had messed up? Maybe, just maybe, if I can make my god with my own hands, then perhaps I can *control* him. Maybe, just maybe, I can feel safe that if I give in to temptation—say, to greed or covetousness—then *this* god will cut me some slack.[1]

What does any of this have to do with economics and public policy in America?

Americans today have a general idea about what economics is. We know what species of animal we are talking about when we discuss economics. We imagine that it is a science. It is not physics, and so we cannot expect the precision and the degree of certainty from economics with which laws of physics can be expressed. The subject matter of economics is human social behavior, which is by nature a messier subject than what physicists study. Still, we expect that economics will be conducted in a scientific matter. Economists construct theories, and we expect those theories not to be merely for the sake of imagination. We expect that the theories will help us in some way better understand the real world in which we live. In particular, we expect economists rigorously to test their theories against the facts of the world, and to jettison any theories that cannot meet the test.

By contrast, we have very different ideas about religion. We think of religion as a different species of animal from economics. We know that religion is not a science. It is about what we humans aspire to be, not about the details of what actually is. Different religious belief systems engage the facts about the real world in different ways, but in general, we don't expect religious accounts to be subjected to the same sorts of tests to which we put scientific theories.

What would we think, then, if it turned out that theories that are actually religious theories were being promoted among us as if they were economics? What if the advocates of these theories (the majority of whom, we might discover, are actually not properly trained economists) were in effect selling us a snake by claiming that it was a pony? What if they proposed their theories as hard-headed descriptions of the real world, so that anyone who refused to hew to those theories was being irrational? But what if we discovered, on the other hand, that these theories were not about the real world at all, but described a fantasy world of how these people devoutly believed human society ought to be? And finally, what if we discovered that these advocates were (at least some of them, and at least part of the time) quite aware that the pony was really a snake, but had no compunction about lying to us in order to advance their *religious* cause?

"Over the Top"—or Not?

If you have won the Nobel Prize in economics, you might think that you had won the right to express yourself in just about any way you thought proper. But Paul Krugman, writing his economics column for the *New York Times* of August 19, 2010, was clearly worried about what he was going to say. "As I look at what passes for responsible economic policy these days, there's an analogy that keeps passing through my mind," he began. "I know it's over the top, but here it is anyway..."[2]

For a number of months, Krugman had been writing mostly the same message over and over. He had been recounting how in 2008, the entire world teetered at the edge of a financial depression of a magnitude to match the Great Depression of the 1930s. At first, leaders resolutely reversed the policies that had gotten us into that mess. President George W. Bush began by ordering a massive bailout of U.S. financial institutions, and newly-elected President Obama followed with a government stimulus package. Krugman had been a leading voice among those fearing that the stimulus package had been too small, and the events of the summer of 2010, as economic recovery sputtered and as unemployment remained at record levels, seemed to bear him out. Far from heeding Krugman's call for even more government stimulus, however, leading policy opinion had done a one-eighty. The same policies that had gotten us to the brink of the precipice were somehow back in fashion. Instead of more economic stimulus, policy gurus called for austerity and deficit reduction. The "apostles of austerity," as Krugman called them, now included not only the Republican Party, but enough moderate Democrats to kill most chances of aggressive government action to diminish lingering unemployment.

And so, to describe this worsening situation, what analogy came to Krugman's mind, that he feared readers would judge "over the top"? "[T]he policy elite—central bankers, finance ministers, politicians who pose as defenders of fiscal virtue—are acting like the priests of some ancient cult, demanding that we engage in human sacrifices to appease the anger of invisible gods."

Krugman continued, "Hey, I told you it was over the top. But bear with me for a minute." He then went on to discuss, in the remainder of his column, how all the facts about the state of the economy proved these "austerians" wrong, yet being proved wrong by all the facts seemed to diminish the fervor of their arguments not one iota. Krugman justified the claim about "human sacrifice" by citing the consequences of slashing government spending on critical services in Greece and Ireland, as well as the human toll of unemployment in the U.S.

What the rest of this book is basically about is to reassure Krugman that he was wrong about one thing only. He was wrong in regarding his own analogy as being "over the top." I will demonstrate that there is nothing over the top at all in regarding today's apostles of this particular brand of "economics" not as social scientists explaining reality, but as priests of some religious cult. Even

Krugman, for all that he disagrees with the "austerians," seems to have been seduced by their claim that their snake is actually a pony—thereby making him think he was somehow exceeding a limit of good taste by calling it the snake that it really is. As to the claim that the priests of this bizarre religion are quite willing to resort to human sacrifice, the historical exploration in this book will show that this is hardly new, either. Indeed, one of the locations Krugman mentions is eerily reminiscent of one of the most infamous earlier acts of human sacrifice to appease the economic gods—the Irish potato famine of 1846.

Because Krugman, for all his incisive analysis of the present state of the economy and what it needs to set it right, hasn't quite realized that the people he is criticizing are calling a snake a pony, and are getting away with it, he seems willing to talk as if he is debating with them about *economics*. He has not realized that it is not economics at all, but rather a completely different species of animal. Continuing to call it "economics" just further muddies the waters. I will explain in this book why the better name for this religious cult that disguises itself as economics is *economism*.

Later Chapters

A good part of this book consists of historical inquiry—into the roots of some of today's economic theories, and into the recent history of the U.S. and of the economic plight of the middle class. To help guide us through this history, it will be useful to think of the impact of all these events on a single American family. I'll tell the story of this family in Chapter 2. Until we grasp what *economism* is, it will be impossible to understand what happened to this family between the end of World War II and the present day.

Chapter 3 will go into depth about economism, and why it represents a sort of market worship or idolatry rather than true economic science. Chapters 4 and 5 trace the historical sources of economism in America today. Chapter 4 tracks some of the origins back to evangelicalism in England in the first half of the 19th century. Chapter 5 suggests that we also must look closer to home, to the Puritan or "Protestant Ethic" that developed in America starting in the late 17th century. I will show why we need evangelicalism to see why so many today believe that government policies that help the poor are bad. We need the Protestant ethic, and its Calvinist and Puritan origins, to see why so many believe that policies that help the rich are good.

Chapter 6 looks at one particular application of economism to the American policy debate, which I call the "Reverse Robin Hood Rule." By this rule, any time we implement a policy that privatizes something that was previously paid for out of tax dollars, we effectively rob the poor to give to the rich. The Reverse Robin Hood Rule also helps us see why and how economism operates in the American political debate by stealth. No one would win a political argument by saying frankly, "We should take money from the poor and give it to the rich." But it has become very easy to win the debate by claiming that one is on the side of "private enterprise" and "shrinking big government" and "cutting taxes"–even though all those terms amount to the same thing.

Chapter 7 compares economism to intelligent design. I will review the reasons why many have decided that despite the assertions that intelligent design is science, it really is religion masquerading as science. I will show that economism is analogous to the case of intelligent design.

Chapter 8 addresses layoffs and their consequences. I explore how we came to accept layoffs as a sensible way for corporations to do business, and how the actual costs and consequences of layoffs are usually kept off economism's balance sheet. I also explore what might have to happen for workers in the U.S. to regain sufficient bargaining power to avoid unnecessary layoffs.

Chapter 9 brings the story up to date by considering the Great Recession of 2008-9. At first, it might seem that the failure of some of our nation's largest and most trusted financial institutions–and the failure of the economic wise ones to predict this possibility–made this book unnecessary by exposing all the glaring flaws of economism. Yet—as Krugman has tried to show—later events demonstrated that economism's ideas still had remarkable staying power, and that many people would go to great lengths to deny obvious truths about what factors caused the crisis.

Chapter 10 offers concluding thoughts and addresses the future. The U.S. public, in the 2010 elections, responded to economism's failure in the previous decade by electing precisely that group most likely to do economism's bidding.

Instead of seeing that the snake was a snake, even more people jumped onto the "pretty little pony" bandwagon. Careful thinking is needed today more than ever to prevent economism from seducing us into adopting misguided policies. And even more careful thinking is needed to detect economism's stealth campaign, and to realize when fringe religious viewpoints are being shoved down our throats as unquestioned scientific truths. We need, in short, to stop worshiping the Golden Calf.

Why Am *I* Writing This Book?

At first glance, I would appear to be completely unsuited for the sort of work that this book undertakes. I am trying to trace certain ideas through the history of religion to see if they have affected modern economics and policy, and yet I am neither a historian, nor a theologian, nor an economist. My formal training has been in medicine, and also in philosophy and ethics. I seem to have no expertise whatever for even beginning to think about these issues.

So what *do* I have to bring to this work? In order to do work in the ethics of health care, I studied ethics as a branch of philosophy. A related branch of philosophy is social and political philosophy, which addresses the theories and values that ought to underlie government and public policy. More generally, however, philosophy gives one certain tools to study the logical structure of ideas.

Philosophers speak of something called a *category mistake*. A category mistake is something that is wrong because of what you know about the logical structure of thought. You don't have to consult any facts about the world to know that it is wrong. If I wanted to know whether my favorite baseball slugger hit a home run yesterday, I have to watch the TV sports report, or consult the box scores in the newspaper. But, if I wanted to know whether the Pythagorean Theorem hit a home run yesterday, I do not need to consult any facts at all. I already know that the Pythagorean Theorem did not hit a home run yesterday, because the Pythagorean Theorem is *logically* not the sort of thing that can hit home runs. There is no need to look at the box scores.

My qualifications for writing this book, such as they are, make it clearer just what sort of book this is. I am going to explore the logical structure of ideas–some ideas related to religion and other ideas related to economics and economic policy. I will ask in each case whether the logical structure of ideas conforms to the structure that is appropriate for a set of religious beliefs on one hand, or for a social science like economics on the other. If we find that ideas that have one logical structure seem to have slipped over into the other arena–that religious-type ideas have sprung up where one would expect to find economic ideas–then perhaps we have a problem. Perhaps we even have a category mistake. Perhaps our future thinking about these matters is going to be messed up until we put the different sets of ideas back in their proper places.

There is one point on which I must again be very clear. The purpose of this book is not to criticize or to disagree with any set of religious beliefs. I believe in the freedom of religion and of each person's right to believe whatever she wants in that area of life. If (for example) some people happen to believe that sick children in the U.S. whose families do not have health insurance, and who die because they cannot get timely, quality medical care, deserve to die because they are being punished by God, I fully grant their right to hold those beliefs, as much as I personally find them repugnant. The problem with the people in the snake fable was not that they felt the need for faith. The snake cynically used their legitimate need for faith against them. (I would, however, modestly submit that had they read this book, they might have known better than to trust the snake and his twisted logic.)

The only thing this book is about is whether you can hold certain religious beliefs, but call them economics or economic policy. So far as I am concerned, you are welcome to hold those beliefs. All I ask is that you call them by their right name.

The Origins of This Book—Further Background

If you wish, you can turn to the next chapter and dive into the contents of the book. The remainder of this introductory chapter is simply a bit more about the story of how I came to write it.

This book began with my puzzlement over many different things. I have spent a good deal of time studying the arguments over health reform. I have become convinced (as are many health policy experts, and a goodly percentage of the U.S. public) that a so-called single payer system would be the most sensible way to promote real health reform in the U.S.[3] I joined the organization, Physicians for a National Health Program, which is dedicated to promoting a single-payer health system.[4] Why, then, were we told that a government-run, single-payer health system simply could not be talked about? Sen. Max Baucus, holding hearings on one reform bill in 2009, went so far as to have single-payer advocates arrested when they tried to speak before his committee.[5] Why is discussing a plan, that has been proven in many places to work well to achieve the basic values favored by the American people, politically impossible?

Most people are probably aware that there is a lot of research linking poverty to ill health. Poor people generally have worse health than rich people, and that happens no matter what society they live in. Fewer, however, are aware of a growing body of evidence about income inequality and health (a topic we'll read more about in Chapter 10). Briefly, the research shows that people enjoy better health in a society where the income gap between rich and poor is relatively small. This is true when you compare nations to other nations, and also when you compare states to other states within the U.S.

The U.S. is rapidly becoming one of the most unequal countries in the world in terms of personal income. We therefore should not have been surprised to read a recent study of the health of different social classes in Britain and the U.S., to find that even poor Britons enjoy better average health, by a number of measures, than do well-off Americans.[6] But even if the details about health are not widely known, I would have thought that the more basic fact–that the rich in the U.S. are getting richer while the average person is not–would have attracted attention and prompted some general sense of outrage.

I was, therefore, much puzzled as years went by and the U.S. public seemed resolutely uninterested in those facts about income inequality. What most astounded me was reading an opinion poll comparing U.S. and European attitudes, and learning that *rich Europeans were more likely to think that income inequality was an important political issue than were poor Americans.*[7]

I was puzzled by the attitude toward poverty that seemed prevalent among many Americans who call themselves Christians. If one approaches the Gospels with an open mind, it is hard to ignore a consistent message about the poor and the rich. Jesus seems to be teaching that the Christian, on approaching the gates of heaven, will be judged first and foremost by how well he treated the poor and less fortunate. The duty to look out for the poor seems a much stronger duty than any obligation to accumulate wealth: "Ye cannot serve God and mammon" and "It is easier for a camel to go through the eye of a needle, than for a rich man to enter the kingdom of God." When I spoke with Christian clergy who worked in the same academic medical centers where I did, I found that they agreed with this basic understanding of Jesus's teaching. I therefore wondered why, apparently, a large segment of the U.S. Christian community has adopted a political stance that seems frankly to be allied with the rich against the poor.

Finally, I was puzzled by the nation's response to the Great Recession in the fall of 2008. I had thought there was a sort of folk wisdom in the U.S. about what happened during the Great Depression. Franklin Roosevelt, with his New Deal, greatly increased government spending, and that economic stimulus was critical in putting people back to work (at least until the next economic stimulus, the run-up to World War II).

So I was puzzled when John McCain gave a series of campaign speeches in which he urged cutting taxes *and reducing government spending* as the best way to right the economy. McCain lost, of course, but he nevertheless garnered 46 percent of the popular vote. Admittedly, many people may have voted for him for other reasons. But it still seemed strange that a significant proportion of the American public could be swayed to vote for the candidate who called for reducing government spending, in exactly the sort of crisis in which our collective historical wisdom argues for increasing government spending.

I stopped being puzzled, and decided instead to write this book, after I made three discoveries.

First, I read a book called *Medicine and the Market: Equity v. Choice*, by Daniel Callahan and Angela A. Wasunna.[8] Dan Callahan is a very distinguished senior bioethicist, and both he and Wasunna were affiliated with the Hastings Center, a premier bioethics "think tank" in New York. Their book offered a survey of the health financing systems of most of the developed countries of the world as well as some Third World health care systems. They conclude that the world-wide experience so far shows that the market, all by itself, cannot assure that a country's health care system will provide access to health for the entire population, high quality outcomes, and efficiency. The most successful health care systems have heavy doses of government regulation even if they are not "socialized" in the strict sense.[9]

Callahan and Wasunna then surveyed what various economists and policymakers around the world thought about this state of affairs. They found that some advocate turning over more of health care to market forces. But these people continue to advocate reasonable amounts of government regulation, and base their advocacy of market solutions on specific facts. Another group, however, whom Callahan and Wasunna call the "politicals,"[10] simply claim that all of health care should be a function of the private marketplace, and don't seem to care whether there are any facts to support their claims or not. What most struck me about Callahan and Wasunna's account is that they found that the "politicals" exist *almost solely within the U.S.* If you do find "politicals" in other nations, they are almost always inspired by American models or mentors.[11]

The second thing that I discovered was a magazine article by Gordon Bigelow, a professor of English at Rhodes College in Memphis. What most struck me at first was the article's subtitle: "The evangelical roots of economics." As Professor Bigelow's ideas form a good deal of the content of Chapter 4, I'll postpone any more discussion of them for now. But it was eye-opening to see two things. First, Bigelow seemed to be backing up what Callahan and Wasunna had hinted at--that today's economic-policy theories in the U.S. were functioning more like a religion and less like a science. Second, Bigelow claimed that one could see how this had come about by studying the historical record--in his case, England in the first half of the 19th century.

Finally, for my third discovery, I owe a debt to my bioethics colleague at Michigan State University, Judy Andre, who had also first alerted me to Bigelow's article. Judy taught a course on the ethics of international development, and argued that the topic of development was one to which we in bioethics ought to pay more attention. Reading something that Judy had written on this subject, I came first across the word *economism*.[12] I decided I needed to learn more about what economism was; and that led me on the present journey that has resulted in this book.

If you want to turn immediately to what *economism* is, you can go to Chapter 3. However, as I promised earlier, I want to lay out the story of a fairly typical (if fictional) American family. The history of this family will later offer us a reference point as we try to figure out various historical events and their significance.

Notes

1. I am indebted to Dr. John H. Carrier for this interpretation of the Biblical Golden Calf narrative.

2. Krugman P. Appeasing the bond gods. *New York Times*, Aug. 19, 2010, http://www.nytimes.com/2010/08/20/opinion/20krugman.html (accessed July 2, 2011).

3. Depending on the specific poll and the way the questions are worded, between 44 and 65 percent of the American public can be shown to support a single-payer health care financing option; Geyman J. *Hijacked: the road to single payer in the aftermath of stolen health care reform.* Monroe, ME: Common Courage Press, 2010:105-20.

4. For background on PNHP and single-payer, see www.pnhp.org. An excellent comparison between the characteristics of a single-payer health plan with the health reform plan that was actually approved by Congress in 2010 can be found in Geyman, *Hijacked.*

5. "The Ed Show" for Thursday, May 9, 2009 (transcript), http://www.msnbc.msn.com/id/30641022/

6. Banks J, Marmot M, Oldfield Z, Smith JP. Disease and disadvantage in the United States and in England. *JAMA* 295:2037-45, 2006.

7. Kawachi I, Kennedy BP. *The health of nations: why inequality is harmful to your health.* New York: New Press, 2006:26; citing in turn Lipset SM. *American exceptionalism: a double-edged sword.* New York: Norton, 1997.

8. Callahan D, Wasunna AA. *Medicine and the market: equity v. choice.* Baltimore: Johns Hopkins University Press, 2006.

9. Today in the U.S. the term "socialism" and especially "socialized medicine" is used incredibly loosely. Properly, a socialized medical system is one in which the government owns all hospitals and clinics and all health workers are government employees. By this definition, for example, neither Canada nor Great Britain has socialized medicine.

10. Callahan and Wasunna, *Medicine and the market*: 39.

11. Callahan and Wasunna credit the original distinction between who they call the instrumentalists and the politicals, however, to the Canadian

health economist Robert Evans (whom we'll see more of in Chapter 6). And it is telling for our purposes that Evans refers to the "politicals" instead as the *fundamentalists*. Evans RG. Going for the gold: the redistributive agenda behind market-based health care reform. *Journal of Health Politics, Policy and Law* 22(2):427-465, 1997.

12. Andre J. Learning to listen: second-order moral perceptions and the work of bioethics. In: Eckenwiler LA, Cohn FG, eds. *The ethics of bioethics: mapping the moral landscape.* Baltimore: Johns Hopkins University Press, 2007: 220-28.

Chapter 2.
One Family's Story

Carol Benson's family was proud of their long American heritage. They traced their name back to Josiah Benson, who had emigrated from England to the colonies in 1684 and had settled in Massachusetts. Another branch of the family were more recent arrivals; Patrick O'Ryan brought his young wife and baby daughter from Ireland in 1846. While in the 19th century many Americans looked down at the Irish, having Irish ancestors no longer seemed unfashionable in the more enlightened year of 1941.

Keep Josiah Benson and Patrick O'Ryan in mind. They will become important at a later stage of our story.

But we were speaking of Carol Benson's family's pride, and that was why her parents were initially dismayed when she seemed attracted to Stanley Wyzansky. America had just begun the military draft in the summer of 1941. The Army Air Corps had built a new base just outside of the Benson's home town in California's Central Valley. The local Women's Club sponsored a dance for the servicemen, and that's where Carol met Stan.

Stan's father and mother had come to Chicago from Eastern Europe in 1898. His father worked long hours selling vegetables from a pushcart while his mother raised their three sons. Stan's older brothers finished high school and then immediately looked for work to contribute to the family income, though jobs at the height of the Depression were hard to come by. But the family recognized Stan's intellect and vowed that he would go to college. They scraped up enough money to send him to the local junior college. In 1939 Stan managed to land a day job selling men's wear and a slot in a law school that offered evening classes. (Stan had done well in biology and chemistry and would have preferred to go to medical school, but the family's strained finances would not allow that luxury.) He was making decent progress in law school when in June of 1941 he was called up in the draft, assigned to the Air Corps, and shipped to California.

Carol's family had also lived in the Midwest but moved to California in 1912 when a doctor recommended the change for her mother's health. Carol's father owned a department store in their small Valley town. Carol's oldest brother was teaching school and preparing for a career as a college professor; her next brother had completed dental school in San Francisco. Carol also had enjoyed chemistry and biology, but medical school was not then usually thought of as a career option for women. So Carol ended up in a nutrition course at Berkeley, and was about to begin an internship in Los Angeles to train as a hospital dietitian. She was spending some time at home before the internship began when she met Stan at the dance.

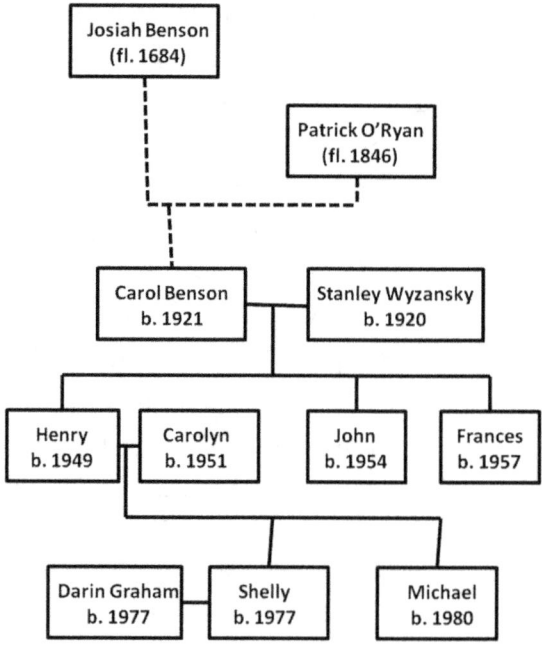

Figure 2.1. The Benson-Wyzansky family tree

Stan came to the Benson house frequently after that, and Carol's parents set aside their first impressions and came to like the well-mannered but dedicated young man to whom their daughter was becoming obviously more attracted.

Pearl Harbor, however, radically altered their courtship. Stan was soon shipped back East for officers' training, then was sent to the Pacific Theater where he worked as a supply officer at an air base on Fiji, and eventually was sent to join the forces establishing U.S. air bases on Iwo Jima. Carol finished her dietitian internship and enlisted in the Army Medical Corps, serving in hospitals for the war wounded first in Britain and then in France.

Carol and Stan wrote letters back and forth as often as they could, even though a month or more could easily go by before a batch of letters was received. When the war ended in 1945 and the troops were demobilized, they both returned to California, and were married by a justice of the peace. They then headed back to Chicago and had to move in for a while with Stan's mother before they could find an affordable apartment on the North Side.

Peacetime

Stan was able to resume law school quickly with the financial support of the new GI Bill that provided educational aid for returning servicemen. He graduated in 1948 and was able to land a job with a law firm in downtown Chicago. Carol worked as a dietitian in some Chicago hospitals to help make ends meet until their first child, Henry, was born in 1949. From then on she became a housewife and mother full time, giving birth to another son, John, and a daughter, Frances, over the next 9 years.

Stan, meanwhile, did general practice law and after a while began to build a practice around personal injury cases. His income from his law practice was never very great, but the family was able to afford one car, a Chevrolet Bel-Air, and (by 1955) a three-bedroom split-level house in the suburb of Glenview. Family summer vacations usually lasted three days and featured a site within a day's drive of home that had some historical significance—Stan was insistent on Henry, John and Frances being well educated. The children thought it a special treat if they got to stay at a motel that had a swimming pool.

Henry graduated from high school in 1967 and chose to attend the University of Wisconsin, managing to get a partial merit scholarship to pay the extra sum required for out-of-state tuition. He went on to make Stan proud by studying for the M.D. degree that Stan as a young man had been unable to pursue. Stan was a little disappointed that neither John nor Frances showed much interest in the law. Both attended the University of Illinois (paying the affordable in-state tuition), and both ended up with masters' degrees, John in journalism and Frances in library science.

As the kids became more independent, Carol went back to work part time in her old career as a dietitian, and for the first time the family had need for two cars. Stan, meanwhile, was appointed as a magistrate, the lowest-level judge in the state court system. From there he moved to an elected circuit judgeship. The family celebrated by upgrading the Chevrolet Bel-Air to an Impala.

By 1985, Stan decided to take advantage of the relatively generous retirement benefits accorded to Illinois judges. Less and less able to tolerate the Midwestern winters, he and Carol found a conveniently-sized home outside of Sarasota, Florida for their retirement, with a golf course close at hand.

Views of Life

Stan found many things about America to complain about during his life. He considered himself a political liberal—his great hero had been Illinois Gov. Adlai Stevenson—and he was upset at the unfair treatment of people of color that led to the civil rights movement of the 1960s. He also was concerned about the neglect of the environment, and the fact that rivers and lakes in the U.S. were routinely catching fire as a result of their heavy industrial pollution. The Cold War with the Soviet Union and the threat of all-out nuclear war provided constant anxiety. Conditioned by his own wartime service to support the military, Stan was slow to accept the possibility that the war in Vietnam might have been a policy mistake.

But if you asked Stan and Carol what they thought of one aspect of American life—economic opportunity—neither would have had many complaints. Both recalled vividly the hardships of the Depression. The life of their own generation, by contrast, had been very comfortable. Both of them worked hard, and hoped that they had raised their children to be hard workers too. But at the same time they took pride that their children all seemed poised to have greater success in life than they had, and that their grandchildren would start off with benefits that Stan and Carol had never dreamed of. They had done it all according to the accepted American middle-class model, with Stan the breadwinner earning the salary and Carol the housewife and mother cooking the meals, doing the laundry, and providing the family's emotional stability.

Meanwhile, Henry Wyzansky graduated from the University of Wisconsin medical school in 1975, luckily with only a small amount of debt. It helped greatly that his wife, Carolyn, whom he married in 1971, worked a variety of office jobs. He began his pediatrics residency at the University of North Carolina hospital in 1975, and their daughter, Shelly, was born in 1977.

During his residency, Henry became interested in academic medicine and research, so he next took a job as a junior faculty member at the University of Minnesota medical school. In the late 1970s, it was generally understood that physicians working in universities would be paid less than the typical income in private practice. But Henry and Carolyn were both used to frugal living, having each been raised by parents heavily marked by the Depression— and in those times, the medical school and residency lifestyle was far from affluent. It seemed quite feasible that Carolyn could stay home and raise Shelly (and Michael, who was born three years later) and that they could survive comfortably on Henry's salary.

When Shelly was ready for college in 1995, Henry's and Carolyn's planning seemed to have paid off. Henry's career had advanced, and medical schools now paid their physicians closer to the market value in the community. The Wyzanskys had paid off their debts and were close to owning their home mortgage-free. Shelly looked around, and decided finally on her parents' alma mater, Wisconsin, where she majored in interior design.

The Third Generation

Shelly now becomes our focus of attention. She's a tall, attractive woman who resembles both of her parents. Shelly loves both her parents and her grandparents, but sometimes feels that they don't give her enough credit. Her parents, especially, imagine that since she grew up during a time when it seemed you could just take out a credit card and buy whatever you wanted, their daughter must have missed out on some of the lessons about frugality and the work ethic that was drummed into the previous generation. Shelly feels that she's a reasonable blend of both worlds. On the one hand, she sees how her parents (and even more, her grandparents) sometimes engage in foolish stinginess, bringing considerable trouble on themselves by failing to spend a small sum up front. On the other hand, Shelly feels that she was raised with the same basic values that shaped her parents. She helped to pay her college expenses by working part-time as a waitstaff. She learned to expect to work hard and to deliver value to her employer in exchange for what she earns. And her mother taught her to be a smart shopper and to look out for bargains. She's a far cry from some of the kids she met in college who seemed to feel that the world should just hand them a living.

Shelly's first move after graduation didn't seem very smart to Henry and Carolyn, however. During one spring break in college, she and some of her girlfriends spent a few days in San Diego, and fell in love with the city. Henry had once looked at a job at the medical school there—and had turned it down when he found out how expensive local housing was. Shelly argued that she planned to go there with several of her college girlfriends and they could share the cost of an apartment. And she was really tired of the upper Midwest.

There were no openings with the interior design firms she applied to, and she ended up with a string of part time jobs, mostly (again) as waitstaff. Rent, as well as gas and insurance for her Ford Focus were more expensive than she had planned for. She was often maxed out her credit cards and Henry and Carolyn continued to help her out—which bothered all of them as they had all assumed Shelly would be on her own by now, even as they tried not to talk about it.

Then things seemed to look up. She found a job with a small firm that designed residential bathrooms and kitchens. Soon after she started with the firm, she met Darin Graham, who worked as a manager for one of the contractors with which Shelly's firm often collaborated on home improvement projects. Darin, like Shelly, enjoyed running and hiking in the nearby mountains. They dated for a year and then married in a quiet ceremony. Darin had a small house, and the financial advantages of Shelly not having to pay rent any more was one of the factors that pushed them into an earlier commitment than she might otherwise have chosen.

One immediate problem was that neither Shelly's nor Darin's employer offered health insurance. Henry as a physician knew what happened to uninsured people who developed health crises, and he and Carolyn leaned on Shelly to try to get some sort of coverage. She started to look for other jobs, but soon found that interior design jobs were hard to come by in San Diego, and most wanted more experience than she had.

Even without the apartment rent to pay, Shelly and Darin seemed always to be at their credit card limit. Darin had had to take on some debt to finish college and he was still paying off his student loans. All it seemed to take was one thing going wrong, like one of their cars needing a $500 repair, and they were way over budget. Shelly was embarrassed that she still sometimes had to beg a quick loan from her mother (and suspected that Carolyn often didn't tell Henry about it).

Despite these problems, Shelly and Darin were really not prepared for the burst of the California housing bubble in 2008 and the start of the recession. The first thing to go was Shelly's design job when the small firm she worked for went under. Darin held onto his job, but the contractor had much less work coming in as yesterday's millionaire McMansion owners discovered they could hardly keep up the payments on their homes, let alone afford remodeling.

Shelly and Darin had assumed that the occasional bouts of abdominal pain that Darin experienced were probably just due to stress. But they could not ignore the time that the pain was accompanied by bloody diarrhea, even after their health insurance had lapsed. Darin had a full medical workup and was found to have Crohn's disease, an inflammatory disease of the bowel caused by an immune system problem. The doctor explained to them that Darin could probably look forward to a normal life span and could maintain a stable weight, and that Crohn's disease has a natural course of flare-ups followed by long quiescent periods. But to gain control over the symptoms and the inflammation at the beginning, he'd need an intensive course of drug treatment with close monitoring and repeated testing. When Shelly called her dad for advice he agreed with all that the doctor in San Diego was saying.

As Shelly and Darin looked at the bills that had already come in as a result of Darin's medical work-up, and the bills that threatened to come in for the intensive treatment he needed for the next six months to a year, they started to wonder whether they would be among those Americans who had to file for bankruptcy due to medical expenses—a group that, at least in the days before health reform, accounted for just about half of all personal bankruptcies in the U.S.

The Benson-Wyzansky Family and the American Dream

In the story of this small offshoot of the Benson family, from Stanley Wyzansky to Shelly Graham, we've seen the virtual unraveling of the American dream within three generations. Stanley lived in a world where the dream was possible. He worked hard, sacrificed, and got to enjoy the fruits of his labors. The son of a pushcart peddler, he rose to become an attorney and eventually a judge. Personally, he was able to enjoy some years of retirement in Florida and a chance to play golf whenever he wanted. Stanley would be the first to say that those pleasures counted much less to him than the success of his children—his eldest son a physician, all his children having advanced degrees and earning a solid living. The duty that had driven his father and brothers to be sure that Stanley got to go to college was passed along to Stanley as a duty to assure that his children and grandchildren had a better start in life than he did. That duty, he could say in his old age, he had been able to fulfill.

By the time Stan's granddaughter Shelly graduated from college, things had changed dramatically. Here we need to turn to statistics to be sure that Shelly's and Darin's story is not simply a fluke. What changed the world in which Stan and Carol Wyzansky had been able to raise three children and send them all to college on a single income, to the one where Shelly and Darin seemed hardly able to get by on two incomes—before Shelly lost her job?

Jacob S. Hacker offers us some clues in his important book, *The Great Risk Shift*. First, he reminds us that the American middle class has seen little if any rise in real income between Stanley's time and ours. More than three-quarters of the rise in middle-class income between 1979 and 2000 is attributable to women's increased work hours.[1] Many people imagine that today, Shelly and Darin both work so that they can afford nicer cars, bigger homes, and fancier vacations, things that Stan and Carol were happy to do without. Not so, replies Hacker, in a day when basic household expenses such as rent or mortgage, education, and health care have all become drastically more expensive: "Families haven't been working more hours to get ahead..... *They've been working more hours just to break even.*"[2]

Many people are aware that while the American middle class has been struggling, the wealthy have it much better. Even as recently as 1975, the year a proud Stan attended his son's medical school graduation, the richest one percent of U.S. households earned twelve times the income of the average middle class family. At the time, that seemed sufficient for the wealthiest Americans to enjoy a lifestyle that was certainly adequate for all their needs and that set them apart as privileged. By 2003, shortly after Shelly and Darin's wedding, the richest one percent of families earned 18 times as much as the average middle-class family.

Larry M. Bartels, a professor of Public and International Affairs at Princeton University, would add that these figures actually understate the incredible concentration of wealth. He notes that between 1981 and 2005, the real income of the top 1 percent of earners doubled. The real income of the top one-tenth percent nearly tripled. The real income of the top one-hundredth percent (the top 13,000 taxpayers in the U.S.) increased five-fold. Bartels informs us, "more than four-fifths of the total increase in Americans' real pre-tax income between 1980 and 2005 went to the top 1% of taxpayers."[3]

Hacker comments further that the American dream did not go off track merely because middle-class incomes remained stagnant while the wealthy got wealthier: "The gap between Richie Rich and Joe Citizen is a lot larger than it used to be, but it's actually grown less quickly than the gap between Joe Citizen in a good year and Joe Citizen in a bad year."[4] Again, common wisdom says that income instability is mainly a problem among the poor and uneducated; certainly Stan and Carol's grandchildren, all with college educations, must be immune. Not so, replies Hacker. The new income instability in America crosses all education levels.

The real underclass of the permanently poor, Hacker reminds us, is probably less than we imagine—fewer than one in ten Americans experience five consecutive years of poverty during adult life. The flip side is that many more Americans, including many who think of themselves as solidly middle class, are at risk of churning in and out of poverty. Right now having children seems the farthest thing from Shelly and Darin's minds; but if they were to consider, it would be a sobering statistic that more than half of U.S. children spend at least one year living in poverty by age 18. (In Germany it is less than a quarter.)[5]

And what do Shelly and Darin have to look forward to as they get older? Is golf and a retirement home in Florida part of their future? Hacker compares the prospects for Henry and Carolyn Wyzansky, now going back only one generation instead of two, with those of their daughter. Henry and Shelly are both apparently in the middle class, and yet their prospects look quite different.[6] Henry and Carolyn made it through their early years when housing and their kids' college education were still quite affordable. They were therefore able to set aside a reasonable sum for their own retirement. (As a university professor, Henry also had access to one of the best retirement programs in the country, so that even in the Great Recession, his fund lost relatively little of its value.) By the time Shelly and Darin came onto the scene, however, basic costs had skyrocketed. Darin is still trying to pay off his college loans at a time in his life when he's facing the possibility of medical bankruptcy. Setting aside a reasonable sum for retirement is at this point as impossible a dream for Shelly and Darin as is having children. Ironically, if anything were to threaten the comfortable retirement prospects that Henry and Carolyn now anticipate, it would be a need to dip into their own retirement savings to come to their daughter and son-in-law's aid.

Moral Decay?

In short, something has changed drastically in America during the last three generations of the Benson-Wyzansky family. Conventional wisdom might add here that it obviously is a matter of individual initiative and responsibility. Stan and Carol, World War II vets both, represent the so-called "greatest generation." They worked hard, sacrificed, and never complained. Each succeeding generation has become lazier and has felt more entitlement. With the moral fiber of America unraveling in that way, how can we be surprised that Shelly is not doing as well as her father or grandfather?

There are several people who would be highly offended by this argument. Their names are Stan, Carol, Henry, Carolyn, and Shelly. Stan and Carol knew that they did a decent job of instilling in their own children the same values of hard work and family caring that they had themselves. Henry and Carolyn knew that they heard those messages loud and clear from their own parents all the while they were growing up, and that they accepted their duty to pass the same values along to their own children. Shelly compared her own life in college to those of some of her peers who never seem to have gotten those messages, and felt secure that she had also been raised in the proud tradition of the Benson and Wyzansky families. Who, they would all demand, knows so much about what's in their hearts and minds to say different?

Hacker, for his part, argues that all the members of Benson-Wyzansky family are probably right. There's no evidence that the American work ethic has changed enough to explain the income instability that he describes. The only way to explain the sea changes he's charted is that the basic social contract between the nation and the individual has undergone a profound shift.[7] To take just one example, the social contract seemed to say one thing when Stan was helped to finish law school by the benefits of the GI Bill. It said something profoundly different when Darin, who had gone to college, held a job, and paid his taxes, was told that he had to fend for himself in finding the money to pay for his Crohn's disease. (The health reform legislation that passed in 2010 was a move toward restoring a bit of the old social contract, but it came several years too late to help out Darin. Moreover, as I write this, powerful political forces have pledged to repeal health reform entirely, to fight its key provisions in court, and to starve it of needed funds.)

By "social contract" we don't just mean the relationship between an individual and the government. Hacker emphasizes that the spirit of Stanley and Carol's post-war days was a product equally of government and the private sector.[8] To highlight the private-sector aspect of the shift, Hacker notes that in the late 1960s, when Henry was in college and Stanley was considering switching careers from attorney to magistrate, the nation's largest employer was General Motors. The average GM worker was paid $29,000 a year in current dollars, and received generous health and retirement benefits. In the year that the California housing bubble burst, the biggest U.S. employer was

Wal-Mart. They paid their employees $17,000 a year in those same dollars, offered no guaranteed pension, and provided health benefits for only half of their workforce.[9] (We'll talk more about that typical General Motors worker in Chapter 8.)

This book is about what changed in America during these last three generations of the Benson-Wyzansky family, and where the change came from. A major part of what changed, I will claim, is the capture of American economic policy by a peculiar idea. That idea is called *economism*. It's peculiar because it claims to be one thing and is actually something quite different—like a snake claiming that it's a pony. To see what it really is, we have to explore its history. We have, indeed, to go back to the days of those forebears that Carol Benson and her parents were so proud of—Josiah Benson in Boston in the late 17th century, and Patrick O'Ryan in Ireland in the middle of the 19th. And finally, when we understand where economism came from and what sort of thing it really is, we will have a sense of what we can do about it.

Notes

1. Hacker JS. *The great risk shift: the new economic insecurity and the decline of the American dream.* Revised and expanded edition. New York: Oxford University Press, 2008:86-89.
2. Hacker, *Great risk shift*: 96.
3. Bartels LM. *Unequal democracy: the political economy of the new Gilded Age.* New York: Russell Sage Foundation/Princeton University Press, 2008: 11-13, quote p. 13.
4. Hacker, *Great risk shift*: 27.
5. Hacker, *Great risk shift*: 32.
6. Hacker, *Great risk shift*: 98.
7. Hacker, *Great risk shift*: 42-80.
8. Hacker, *Great risk shift*: 43-46.
9. Hacker, *Great risk shift*: 80.

Chapter 3.

From Economics to Economism:
The Rise of Market Worship

What, exactly, is *economism*? The term appears to have come into use among a group of scholars who address the *ethics of development*. It may therefore help if we first figure out who those people are and what their agenda is.

The Ethics of Development

During the 19th century, cholera epidemics regularly swept through Europe and the U.S. As public health experts became aware that cholera was spread predominantly by sewage-contaminated water, and as Western cities improved their sanitation and water supply systems, these epidemics faded into history. Today, public health people say that if there is an outbreak of cholera in a certain place, you can bet your money that there's a war (or, as in Haiti in 2010, a natural disaster) and the setting up of emergency refugee camps. Therefore, when in 2000-1 a cholera outbreak occurred in an area of Kwazulu-Natal, far from any war or refugee problems, epidemiologists took notice and inquired into the causes.[1]

The government in that region had been loaned money by the International Monetary Fund and World Bank. As a condition for the loan, the international agencies had imposed strict conditions that included cost-containment measures. In particular, the agency demanded that many public services previously supplied for free now had to be covered by user fees. This was supposed to assure a sound economy, and the eventual ability of the government to repay the loans.[2]

One service that the government had previously provided in this region was clean drinking water. As part of the Western-imposed economic "reforms," the local government started charging a fee for this water use. The local residents could not afford the fee, so they went back to their previous habits of taking their drinking water directly from a nearby river–which happened to be contaminated with sewage. The cholera outbreak that followed resulted in 260 deaths.[3]

This anecdote about a cholera outbreak illustrates the subject matter that has spawned books and university courses on the ethics of development. Bodies such as the IMF and the World Bank portray themselves as doing good work because they are stimulating economic development in poor nations. Economic development is taken to be a good thing in itself, and even more, a necessary step toward whatever other advances these countries and their people may wish to make in the future. For those reasons, the work of these international bodies would appear to be immune from criticism.

Critics have, however, emerged, energized by examples such as the cholera outbreak. They ask a number of questions. Is it truly the case that these "development" programs help the poorer nations, as opposed to rich Western nations, and multinational corporations based primarily in the West? Is it true that the economic development that occurs affects people in the nation equally, or does only a small group benefit, while the poverty of the masses is unchanged? Do the various measures that the IMF and World Bank employ, to see how well and how fast economic development is occurring, actually reflect the well-being of all the people in the poorer nations, or do the measures shine a light only on economic exchanges that are beneficial to the West?

The more extreme critics might say that we imagine that we have advanced because these poorer nations are independent, freed from the bonds of colonialism. But in fact those nations have simply traded one sort of bondage for another. "Development," to these critics, means an economic relationship that largely mirrors the abuses of the old colonialism–what is "developed" will always be what serves the interests of the rich Western nations disproportionately. The colonial states of olden times sent their armies into the poorer countries to impose their will. Now, these critics charge, they send in multinational corporations and the IMF.

People concerned about the ethics of development ask, first, if any of these criticisms have merit; and second, how we would know. What would tell us the difference between a type of economic development that truly aided the people of the poorer nations, and a different type that amounted to neocolonialism? Which measures of economic activity and productivity ought to be used by those who seriously want to help the people of the poorer nations, and why?

These questions seem to me to be worth asking. In the process of asking such questions, however, scholars have encountered resistance. One source of this resistance has been labeled *economism*.

Economism's Features

Des Gasper of the Institute of Social Studies in The Hague, in his monograph, *The Ethics of Development*, cites as an early source for the term "economism" a book edited by Paul Ekins and Manfred Max-Neef, *Real-Life Economics*, published in 1992.[4] The term later appeared in the title of a volume by Teivo Teivainen, *Enter Economism, Exit Politics*, in 2002.[5] Different authors, however, use the term in somewhat different ways, so Gasper tried to assemble various separate strands into a unified definition.[6]

Gasper suggests that economism consists of five separable, but closely connected ideas:

- "The economy" is a separate and distinct sphere of society. The rest of society has only tenuous and occasional ties to the economy. Therefore, we can develop policies and plans for the economy without worrying about the rest of society.
- Even if only a part of society, the economy is the primary part. It makes perfect sense, for example, to talk about countries in the developing world as "transitional economies" or "emerging economies," as if each nation simply and solely *was* an "economy."
- People are, at core, economic beings. The laws of the marketplace describe virtually all of their behavior and the reasons for it. People are beings of economic exchange, driven first to make money and then to spend it on the goods obtainable in the marketplace. They are not motivated by concerns for rights, or justice, or the meaning of what they do, in any terms other than economic ones.

- Economic calculation is the best way to understand, value, and manage human life. It is appropriate that every aspect of our lives be thought of and analyzed in terms of economic calculations. For example, if we want to know how a country is doing overall, we simply have to know what is happening to its GDP or some similar index of overall economic productivity.

- The economy, above all else, must be managed solely with an eye toward its own internal technical requirements–that is, what economists study. There ought to be no interference from politicians, or policymakers, or moralists, or anyone else.[7]

Economism vs. Economics

One of the best ways to draw out the differences between economism, according to the definition we have just laid out, and legitimate economics is to consult an economist. Uwe Reinhardt of Princeton University is one of the most prominent and respected health economists in the U.S. I assume that even those who might disagree with Reinhardt's views on any particular topic would still recognize his credentials.

In 1996, Reinhardt contributed a short paper on economics to the *Journal of the American Medical Association.* He warned his audience of physicians that some of his colleagues, or at least people who acted like his colleagues, would readily give them advice as to what sort of health care system the U.S. ought to have. He then proceeded to explain, first, why this advice was bogus, and second, why no "scrupulous" economist would offer any such advice.[8] He listed a variety of concepts commonly appealed to in economics, such as efficiency, showing why each was too limited, and depended on too many assumptions, to serve as a foundation for sweeping policy proclamations.

Reinhardt then gave some examples of questions where the tools of economists are highly useful. Let us suppose, for example, that someone proposes to lower health care costs by putting a ceiling on the fees that physicians are allowed to charge. What would be likely to happen? How would physicians then behave differently? What other consequences would this have for patients and other parties? Economics as properly applied is a perfectly sound means of addressing these questions and could offer some quite reasonable answers. The answers, Reinhardt added, would tend to be based principally on the facts, and would be unlikely to reflect the ideological views of the individual economist.

Reinhardt summarized:

> In short, properly trained and scrupulously practicing economists appreciate that their ability to offer normative [that is, value-laden] pronouncements on health policy is much more limited than seems widely supposed among policymakers. Normative economics seeks to prescribe what "ought" to be done. Because public health policy almost always redistributes economic privilege among members of society, such prescriptions almost always involve moral judgments best left in the political arena.[9]

People who have been won over by economism would say the opposite. They would have no trouble telling us very broadly what sort of health system the U.S. ought to have. It would be one that is governed by the laws of the market, and that treats all aspects of health care as consumer goods. How much any person "needs" health care would be determined by one thing only–what that person is willing to pay for the care on the open market. Anything else would be denounced as an illegitimate interference with the market by politicians, policymakers, and other do-gooders.

Reinhardt, who allies himself with the "trained and scrupulous" brand of economics, points out that no economic theory or formula can give us a final answer on anything as big as the design of an entire health care system. In any plan for a health care system, there are bound to be some winners and some losers. There is no economic law that dictates who those winners and losers ought to be. That is unavoidably a moral decision; and given that the public at large is footing the bill for at least some health care, it is unavoidably a political decision as well. (If we chose in the U.S. to get the government completely out of health care, and turn it all over to the so-called free market without exception, that would also be a moral and political decision, and politicians would have to be involved in implementing it.) Reinhardt is far from accusing the politicians of illicitly interfering with the operations of the market for health care. Instead he turns the tables on his less "trained and scrupulous" colleagues, and accuses them of inappropriate interference with the politicians and moralists.

Economism's Attractions

Gasper gives us a number of reasons to regard economism as a flawed guidance system for public policy. He notes, "The market calculation of a businessman is not an appropriate or sufficient method in other spheres [of social life], including for much of the determination of public choices."[10] Yet he also admits that there is a surface attraction to economism: "[My view] contrasts with the perspective of many mainstream economists, for which the further we can extend market evaluation and calculation the better, since the market is seen as a unique combination of ethical liberalism, systematic calculation, and relative administrative simplicity."[11]

Thinking about all of human life and society as one grand marketplace therefore has a number of attractive features. The first Gasper calls "ethical liberalism," by which he means "liberalism" in a technical philosophical sense, according to which the Declaration of Independence (for example) is a "liberal" document. Liberalism in this traditional sense values individual human freedom. The market seems an exquisite example of valuing human freedom. Everyone comes into the marketplace and engages in whatever exchanges he or she freely desires. Amartya Sen is an economist and philosopher whose position on most issues is as far away from economism as one can get. He has a well-developed view of human rights and human dignity, and he believes that our policies of international development ought to be driven by those considerations. Yet even Sen insists that if, for whatever reason, we were to take away a person's freedom to make economic exchanges in the marketplace, we would have lost a very basic element of human dignity. It is important to honor the freedom to take whatever you own, go to the market, and exchange it for something else in hopes of bettering yourself.[12]

The second attractive feature Gasper calls "systematic calculation." Thanks to decades of work by smart economists, we have developed elegant and reliable measures of what the market as a whole is up to at any given time. Millions of people may make millions of exchanges, yet we can figure out the sum total of all of them. When we listen to the evening news on TV, we hear a number of "stories," but probably will hear only one number–at least that we can anticipate consistently hearing from one day to the next. That number is the Dow Jones average. We should not be surprised if in the U.S. we pay inordinate attention to what happens to the stock market. There is no other comparable number that can be reported daily, that all of us can keep track of and generally understand what it means, that represents any other measure of other sorts of social success or failure. Since unemployment numbers are generally reported only monthly, but the Dow is reported daily, we tend to be lulled into the impression that stock market value is much more important to all of us that the employment rate. There is a clear attractiveness about making even more of human life calculable by such elegant mathematical approaches.

Finally, we have "relative administrative simplicity." In the ideal model of economics, the market basically runs itself. Any administration, any bureaucracy, is an example of the dreaded interference in the market. None of us likes bureaucracy and all of us are attracted to the idea of a way that society might run all by itself without the need for bureaucrats. The more we explore this idea, the more we find it to be illusory. The market never runs itself, and to the extent that it approaches that ideal state, we often see consequences that we do not like–the recent subprime mortgage bubble being only one example, or the possibility that Shelly and Darin Graham might face bankruptcy over Shelly's unemployment and Darin's medical bills another. Yet, as an ideal, administrative simplicity without bureaucracy remains highly attractive.

Economism's Flaws

Freedom, precise calculation, and lack of bureaucracy all sound like good reasons to think of human life as completely an extension of economics and the market, making economism appealing. But the tradeoff is unacceptable. Gasper lists several dire consequences of viewing the world the way economism recommends.

First, economism pays attention only to those things to which a price tag can be applied. It appreciates, for instance, only work that is paid for. Sometimes this problem is easy to get around. If you volunteer for Habitat for Humanity and spend your weekends helping to build houses for the poor, the market value of the home that is built reflects the contribution of your volunteer labor, so the fact you did not get paid does not detract from our regarding what you did as valuable. But things get more serious when we consider the relationship between men and women. In most societies, by tradition, women do a lot of the unpaid work that is essential to keeping families and communities together. Some of it, like cooking and cleaning, would allow us if we wished to calculate a dollar value of hiring somebody to do it. Other aspects of "women's work," such as child rearing, is much harder to calculate according to monetary figures. Economism systematically devalues (and indeed in effect denies the reality of) the work that cannot easily be valued in dollar terms. Economism therefore helps make women and their contributions less visible within society.

Second, to economism, a paid economic input is a cost. If I work for a living and am paid a wage, then the wage is what I gain, and the hours of labor are what I have lost. If two workers work all day and each one is paid $150, then the two cases are identical. The fact that one worker hates his job and would get out of it in a blink of an eye if only he could, while the other worker loves her work and would do it gladly even if it paid her nothing, is not considered to be of any importance. The fact that people in the community, if asked, would see one worker's job as contributing vastly to the well-being of the entire community, while the other worker's job is just something to do to make money and might even degrade the community and its values, is similarly dismissed as unimportant.

In Chapter 8 we will talk more about layoffs and explore the tremendous costs in human capital attributable to our present system of work insecurity. To economism, hardly any of that matters. Imagine that I am working at a job that pays $80,000 a year. I am laid off. I spend nine months looking for a new job, perhaps undergoing some retraining in the process, and end up taking a job that pays $65,000 a year. From an economism perspective, what I have lost can be precisely calculated–it is $15,000 a year, plus whatever losses occurred during my time of unemployment. What this does to me as a person, to my willingness to invest myself in the new job, to be creative and to take risks in the future, and all the other major psychological and social consequences of being laid off, becomes invisible according to economism.

Finally, Gasper mentions the way economists treat future costs and benefits. According to economic practice, these must be discounted according to some formula to reflect the greater uncertainly as one moves farther out into the future. Because a dollar that you have in your hand today is, the economists tell us, worth so much more than a dollar that you might have ten years from now, the result is the systematic devaluing of long-range planning and caring about future generations' well-being. When we think, for example, about energy policy, we are confronted with very serious questions about the extent to which we can take risks with our childrens' and grandchildrens' lives, in order to save costs in the short run (for example, by continuing for many more years to rely on carbon fuels, in the face of environmental risks). Economism, Gasper observes, "treats [the] problem . . . as if it were a technical calculation by a single selfish businessman seeking to maximize profit by comparison of his options over time in a growing economy."[13] Trying to reduce the magnitude of this issue (which philosophers call justice between generations) to calculations of discounted future earnings misses all the major dimensions of the problem.

We see a part of what is wrong with economism when we look at how it addresses issues such as unemployment, women's role in society, or planning for the future. To see what is most seriously wrong with it, we have to grasp how it depicts human beings and human society.

Economists today like to invoke Adam Smith (1723-1790), the Scottish philosopher who is often considered a sort of father of economics. The part of Smith's huge work, *The Wealth of Nations*, that they like to quote is the part about the "invisible hand." This was Smith's metaphor for the way that a well-functioning marketplace transforms almost like magic thousands or millions of seemingly independent and random exchanges between buyers and sellers, each one out only to better herself, into a grand scheme that ends up benefiting all of society. By contrast, if anyone set out to rationally plan out all those exchanges—as the Russian and Chinese communists found to their dismay in the 20th century—the result would almost certainly be a social disaster.

There is, however, another part of Adam Smith. He was a social and political philosopher. A good part of his book consists of straightforward ethical statements about how people ought to behave and how society ought to be arranged so that human beings flourished, and so that virtue would triumph over vice. Smith saw very clearly that the marketplace, however wonderful it might be, was nevertheless a human social institution. For the marketplace to work well, the entire society within which it was embedded had to work well too. And it never occurred to Smith even for a minute that any "invisible hand" would suffice to make human society overall function for human betterment. Only good government and good ethics could do that, and only if people constantly attended to the lessons and requirements of both.[14]

Advocates of economism never get this second half of Adam Smith. They somehow imagine that the marketplace is everything, and so the rules of the market are sufficient to govern every aspect of human life. They fail to see, as was clear to Smith, that rather than glorify the market, this actually undermines the market, by stripping away the social practices that are necessary for the market to function. To take an extreme example, if I am to enjoy all the benefits that the "invisible hand" provides through the marketplace, I must be reasonably sure that when I go to trade in the market, the people with whom I interact will not pull out guns and knives and rob me of my money. But the ethical and social rules that prohibit violence cannot themselves be derived from marketplace rules. If it were up to the market, completely unfettered, it would simply be a matter of the person who has the most money being able to buy the biggest guns and knives.

By extolling the wonders and beauties of the so-called free market, economism trades on a form of nostalgia. For many of us, the word "market" conveys a down-home, small-town aura, reminding us of things like farmers' markets in the suburbs, where the vegetables are fresher than what you can buy at the supermarket. Philosopher Alan Wolfe noted that as late as the early 1800s, markets were almost exclusively local. They helped to build community solidarity, respect for one's neighbors, and stronger interpersonal ties. For example, a person who got a reputation for sharp trading and taking advantage of others would soon find himself suffering the social consequences of his behavior, while his neighbor who was known to treat others fairly and generously reaped the rewards of his enhanced reputation. This marketplace was not an impersonal mechanism of economic exchange and efficiency; it was face-to-face, up close and personal.[15]

People did not begin to take for granted that when somebody said "market," they meant one standardized, impersonal system that organized all economic life within the country (or the world) until the last years of the nineteenth century. But when they called this distant, impersonal system a "market" they neglected to ask whether it lacked those very features that had made the old-time, local, face-to-face market work so well as a community resource.[16] Compare, for example, how all the participants the local market were well known to each other, with the relationship between the buyer of goods in a big box store, and the workers halfway around the world who work under bad conditions for low wages to produce those goods. As we will discuss more in Chapter 6, even applying the same term, "market," to both situations amounts to a degree of subterfuge.

Economism paints the individual as effectively isolated from all important social networks and looking out only for his own good. Other people, even his spouse and children, are not intimates about whom he cares deeply; they are simply instruments by which he can get his own needs and desires met. When he approaches any situation, he does not ask what love, or compassion, or virtue, or justice, or any other human value or meaning requires. He simply asks how he can maximize his own desires, by giving up something he wants less in exchange for something that he wants more. This individual, moreover, sees no value in cooperation. Even if a group of people, by cooperating, can create some grand project that brings great value to all of them but that none could have accomplished alone, economics has a hard time figuring out a formula to divide up precisely what is actually indivisible–what *each* person contributed *by himself* to the cooperative effort. Since economics cannot calculate it precisely, the value of cooperation is taken to be zero, and disappears from anyone's thinking. Once we have figured out the dimensions of the human being that are open to purely economic analysis, we know all that is important. All the rest can be jettisoned from our theories and our formulas.[17] Arthur Okun wrote, "Everybody but an economist knows without asking why money shouldn't buy some things."[18] Apparently the economist Okun has in mind is a devotee of economism, and not a "scrupulous" economist as Reinhardt would describe one.

Gasper uses a particularly gruesome example to develop one of his central points about economism–that a summative measure like GDP is a very poor way to tell the actual quality of life within a developing nation. He asks us to imagine a jobless man who robs and murders a retiree. He uses the money he has stolen to entertain, and then to rape, a series of women. A policeman becomes suspicious of the rapist and starts to dog his tracks. The rapist then murders the policeman, cuts out his organs, and sells them on the international black market. Gasper notes that every transaction in this series of crimes contributes positively to the GDP. From the perspective of economism, the activities of this murderer-rapist are highly productive. Gasper's point is that this extreme scenario shows that there is no necessary connection between what stimulates the economy and what actually improves the quality of life within the nation. Yet economism is blind to this possibility, and simply assumes that when the GDP goes up, everyone must be better off.[19]

The distinguished philosopher Martha Nussbaum argues that our schools and universities must return to teaching students about the arts and humanities, because without such training, the graduates can never be effective citizens in a democracy. She believes that being such a citizen involves both knowing oneself as a person with a "soul" and also realizing that the other citizens of one's nation have souls too. (Nussbaum invites her readers to imbue "soul" with religious significance, or not, as each chooses.) Speaking of the sort of training that focuses only on technical skills and that is aimed at getting employment, Nussbaum writes:

> But we seem to be forgetting about the soul, about what it is for thought to open out of the soul and connect person to world in a rich, subtle, and complicated manner; about what it is to approach another person as a soul, rather than as a mere useful instrument or obstacle to one's plans; about what it is to talk as someone who has a soul to someone else whom one sees as similarly deep and complex.[20]

Economism, by contrast, encourages us to see both ourselves and other people precisely as "mere useful instrument[s] or obstacle[s] to one's plans." In Nussbaum's terms, economism is a soulless way to depicting human society and the world around us.[21]

To summarize: If we want to live in a society that reflects basic human values, including acceptable moral rules, economism is a very poor guide. Yet economism is blind to its own deficiencies. It claims to be able to tell us the definitive answer to any problem in any aspect of human life, and accuses us of being irrational if we disagree with its proposals. If a powerful elite takes over control of a society, wedded to economism as their belief system, then the results for that society could be disastrous.

Economism, Market Fundamentalism, or Market Populism?

While I will use the term economism in the remainder of this book, other authors have used different terminology for what appears to be the same phenomenon. A quick review of these other terms will highlight some additional features of economism.

In 1998, George Soros introduced the term *market fundamentalism* to describe a system of beliefs very similar to economism.[22] Margaret R. Somers, a historian and sociologist, characterizes Soros's meaning of the term as "the fervent conviction that all social life should be organized according to market principles" and then goes on to suggest that it operates in the world in three distinct ways:

- As a story about how the world ought to be, which can take the form of an ideology or a political narrative
- As an organized, well-funded political and social movement, aggressively promoting that story
- As a set of techniques and practices that dictate specific legal and policy solutions to various problems[23]

Somers is especially interested in an aspect of economism that Gasper does not emphasize—the effect it has on our views of citizenship, and ultimately of democracy. She explains:

[T]hree decades of what has become market-driven governance are transforming growing numbers of once rights-bearing citizens into socially excluded internally rightless and stateless persons. A political culture that tolerates, even legitimates, these brute disparities in life chances has a corrosive effect not only on citizenship and human rights, but equally on perceptions of what we owe each other as fellow humans.[24]

Somers characterizes the end result of this corrosion as the "contractualization of citizenship": "Contractualizing citizenship distorts the meaning of citizenship from that of shared fate among equals to that of conditional privilege....earned privileges that are wholly conditional upon the ability to exchange something of equal value."[25] In a democratic society, we are supposed to be citizens because we are human beings who belong here; we are not supposed to have to prove our right to be citizens. Under economism or market fundamentalism, she claims, we are at risk of losing our equal citizenship if powerful people decide that we are not contributing enough economic value to the society.

Somers explains further that economism, or market fundamentalism, acts as an ideology and not as anything resembling a science:

> [O]n the one hand, its ideology of absolute market freedom is almost totally at odds with actually existing successful market societies, which rely heavily on social institutions (e.g. laws and tax codes) to protect the rich from the full market exposure while forcing market 'freedoms' on the rest of us. On the other hand, this distance from reality seems to matter not at all, but even to contribute to the beguiling notion that prosperity is associated with complete market freedom... The visibility of so much wealth, coupled with the invisibility of poverty and the poor, seems only to lend credibility to the market as the arbiter of moral authority.[26]

Historian Thomas Frank, writing earlier about the decade of the 1990s, preferred the term *market populism*.[27] He viewed economism, in the decade before the dot-com bubble burst, as primarily a cultural phenomenon, and saw it as originating in the populist political movements of earlier times—though amounting to a strange inversion of populism since those previous movements were generally directed by the common people against the privileged, and this new market populism seemed to treat the wealthy as just like the common people and their critics as some arrogant, insufferable elite. He agreed with Somers that a critical aspect of economism was the threat that it posed to democracy. Economism turned the tables on democratic institutions in our society by insisting that the market was democratic and they were not:

> The market and the people—both of them understood as grand principles of social life rather than particulars—were essentially one and the same. By its very nature the market was democratic, perfectly expressing the popular will through the machinery of supply and

demand, poll and focus group, superstore and Internet. In fact, the market was *more* democratic than any of the formal institutions of democracy—elections, legislatures, government. The market was a community. The market was infinitely diverse, permitting without prejudice the articulation of any and all tastes and preferences. Most importantly of all, the market was militant about its democracy. It had no place for snobs, for hierarchies, for elitism....[28]

Frank went on to explain why this appealing picture of the market as the *real* democracy and the legitimate democratic institutions of our society as corrupt and as opposing the interests of the common person is completely bogus—an issue we will return to in Chapter 6, when we address how economism advances its cause by stealth.

Since it seems that these various authors are all, in fact, alluding more or less to the same thing, I will simplify by using the single term *economism* as we proceed.

How Widespread is Economism?

The theme that I will develop in this book is that economism is what philosophers call a category mistake–it is in fact religious faith, dressed up as if it were science. Nothing we have seen about the features of economism makes sense if we imagine that it is a science being practiced by scientists– as Reinhardt explained, it cannot pass the "trained and scrupulous" test. If, however, we shift gears, and imagine that its practitioners view economism as if it functioned more like a religious dogma, then a lot of things about it start to make much more sense. In the remaining chapters I will show, first, that it's no stretch to think of economism as religion, since that's exactly where its historical roots lie. Next, I will demonstrate further how it in fact functions like religion, at the same time as its practitioners insist that it is nothing but pure science.

Before turning to the historical account that will occupy us for the next two chapters, I wish briefly to address the question of who adheres to economism and just how widespread the practice is. The short answer is that I am not sure, even though Chapter 1 shows that it is very widespread among a prominent group of American policymakers and politicians. Recall that Gasper attributed such a view to "many mainstream economists."[29]

Gordon Bigelow, a literary historian, seems to equate economism with the practice of neoclassical economics.[30] (In the next chapter we will investigate Bigelow's theory that this school of economics had its origins in evangelical religious thought in England in the early 19th century.) The neoclassical school appears to be the most prominent approach to economics in most American and European universities. That would suggest that the vast majority of academic economists adhere to economism, and since they teach the courses that even non-academic economists have to study to learn the field, that gives economism great influence and scope.

On the other hand we have it from Uwe Reinhardt, who certainly from his perch at Princeton ought to be aware of what is happening in university economics departments, that "trained and scrupulous" economists will have no truck with economism. Even allowing for some exaggeration on Reinhardt's part—he might be reluctant to admit it if he were actually in a minority—it is hard to square the picture Bigelow paints with Reinhardt's observations.

One person who has studied the landscape with some care is Jonathan Chait, senior editor at *The New Republic*. He titled his recent book *The Big Con: The True Story of How Washington Got Hoodwinked and Hijacked by Crackpot Economics*, which seems to reveal how he feels about the matter and about the validity of economism.[31] What Chait means by "crackpot" economics is one particular variant of economism, the supply-side economics which has become a staple belief of the post-Reagan Republican Party. There are significant differences between supply-side economics and neoclassical economics. For example, it has traditionally been a staple of neoclassical economics that it is a bad thing for the government continuously to run a deficit. Supply-siders, by contrast, believe that government deficits don't matter, so long as the machine that produces them is tax cuts for the wealthy. Eventually, they claim, the tax cuts will stimulate the economy, which will increase overall productivity, which will raise tax revenues and erase the deficits. (At least Republicans thought this while a member of their own party was in the White House, running up the big deficits. As soon as a Democrat was elected, they suddenly became deficit hawks.) Neoclassical economists might be politically conservative and favor smaller government; but they do not share the belief of supply-side economics that the tax rate, all by itself, virtually determines the behavior of the economy.[32] As we will see, supply-side economics has a very close affinity with economism, and generally takes on characteristics that blur any distinction between science and religion.

Chait carefully studied the origins of supply-side economics, since he wanted to know where this theory that swept Washington off its feet came from. He concluded, drawing on the thoughts of liberal economist Paul Krugman, that supply-side thinking did *not* come from any discernible movement within U.S. academic economics. Chait first states that one can find virtually no supply-siders on the faculty of any American university economic department; later he admits that there may be a couple of them.[33] As one of his star examples of supply-side theory, Chait discusses the career of George Gilder, whose book *Wealth and Poverty* (1981) was incredibly influential among Reagan and his followers. Gilder, Chait recalls, had no discernible economic credentials prior to writing his book; his prior claim to fame had been restricted to writing tracts attacking feminism. In the mid-1980s, Gilder became a wholehearted advocate of computer technology, and grew wealthy publishing a newsletter that recommended stocks in various technology companies. In the 2001-2002 bursting of the dot-com bubble, his readers deserted him and he lost his fortune. Gilder today has switched causes and become an advocate of intelligent design–the topic we will take up in Chapter 7.[34]

The problem, as I said at the beginning of the chapter, is that the term "economist" is somewhat loose. There may be very few devotees of economism in university economics departments, even thought those departments might be bastions of political conservatism. But there may be many more adherents among policymakers and political commentators who focus primarily on economic issues. We will see in later chapters that economism functions best by stealth. It does not do, in politics, to say out loud, "I am going to shove my religious beliefs down your throat, but while doing so, I will deny that they are religious and claim instead that they are simply hard science, so that you cannot rationally dispute them." As part of this general stealth approach (which may be unconscious rather than deliberate), many believers in economism will claim that they are hard-headed, scientific economists.

In opposing economism, there are two possible arguments I might have resorted to but will not—the argument that all economics of the dominant neoclassical school is scientifically mistaken; and the argument that all economics is really theology and not science. The first of these arguments is proposed by an Australian economics professor, Steve Keen. Neoclassical economics, or at least the version of it commonly taught in the economics classroom, fails in two major ways, according to Keen. Its theories are internally contradictory; and it fails correctly to predict real world events.[35]

The second argument is made very effectively by economics professor Duncan K. Foley. Writing about Adam Smith as the founding father of economics, Foley states:

> [A]t its most abstract and interesting level, economics is a speculative philosophical discourse, not a deductive or inductive science. ...The most important feature of Adam Smith's work is not what it tells us concretely about how the economy works (although it tells us a great deal about that), but its discussion of how we should feel about capitalist economic life and what attitudes it might be reasonable for us to take toward the complicated and contradictory experience it affords us. These are discussions above all of faith and belief, not of fact, and hence theological.[36]

To use a crude and now outdated distinction, science is about facts and ethics or religion is about values. Foley is claiming that whether it likes to admit it or not, economics is really mostly about values—at least "at its most abstract and interesting level" (a level that Reinhardt would probably refer to as non-scrupulous). It is not, at its core, a mere description of how the world operates; it instructs us what we ought to think about that operation, whether it is good or bad for us.

If my goal is to dismiss economism as religion masquerading as social science, I could get there quicker by dismissing all neoclassical economics as unscientific (following Keen) or by labeling all economics as religion (following Foley). But I am not sure to what extent these more sweeping claims can be defended, so I prefer a more modest course. I am not worried if much of today's economics is actually "scrupulous" science and of good quality. All that I need to demonstrate is that a peculiar and extreme spinoff of this body of thought, that I am calling economism, has the characteristics that I attribute to it. As this extreme variant seems to have captured the minds of many powerful individuals within American society, whose dedication to this idea has already wreaked considerable havoc (as I shall document in later chapters), it is only that variant that I need to confront here.

Besides the elements that we have already identified, economism (as it is commonly practiced in the U.S.) appears to have two articles of faith–government policies that favor the poor are bad; and policies that favor the rich are good. We will see where the first of these beliefs comes from in the next chapter.

Notes

1. Mugero C, Hoque A. Review of cholera epidemic in South Africa, with focus on Kwazulu-Natal Province. 11 April 2001; http://www.kznhealth.gov.za/cholerareview.pdf (accessed December 28, 2010).

2. Ka-Min L. Water charges blamed for cholera outbreak in South Africa. Third World Network, November 2000; http://www.twnside.org.sg/title/2114.htm (accessed December 28, 2010).

3. Hemson D, Dube B. Water services and public health: the 2000-1 cholera outbreak in Kwazulu-Natal, South Africa. February 2004; http://www.hsrc.ac.za/Research_Publication-17977.phtml (accessed December 28, 2010).

4. Gasper D. *The ethics of development.* Edinburgh Studies in World Ethics. Edinburgh, UK: Edinburgh University Press, 2004; Ekins P, Max-Neef M. *Real-life economics: understanding wealth creation.* New York: Routledge, 1992. The entry, "Economism" in Wikipedia, apparently put up in 2007, is superficial and incomplete, and itself signals the degree of controversy surrounding the term—two commentators have suggested trashing the entire entry, while a third argues that the term is important and should be included. (The entry suggests "economic reductionism" as a synonym for economism; that term would be philosophically sound, but I have never encountered it anywhere else.) The entry also notes that the term 'economism' was initially used by Lenin and other Marxists, who apparently used it derisively against their opponents and never defined it carefully. Today's usage of the term implies no commitment to Marxism; http://en.wikipedia.org/wiki/Economism (accessed December 28, 2010).

5. Teivainen T. *Enter economism, exit politics: experts, economic policy and the damage to democracy.* New York: Zed Books, 2002.

6. Gasper, *Ethics of development*: 80-81.

7. Gasper, *Ethics of development*: 80-81; originally Gasper listed six key elements, but I have combined two that seemed repetitious.

8. Reinhardt U. Economics. *JAMA* 275: 1802-4, 1996, quote p. 1803.

9. Reinhardt U. Economics. *JAMA* 275: 1802-4, 1996, quote p. 1803. Reinhardt continues to warn about this unscrupulous (as he would put it) brand of economics today; see for example his entry in the *New York Times* economics blog, "When Value Judgments Masquerade as Science," August 27, 2010;

http://economix.blogs.nytimes.com/2010/08/27/when-value-judgments-masquerade-as-science/ (accessed December 27, 2010).

10. Gasper, *Ethics of development*: 72.

11. Gasper, *Ethics of development*: 72.

12. Sen A. *Development as freedom*. New York: Anchor Books, 2000: 26-27.

13. Gasper, *Ethics of development*: 72.

14. See for example Muthu S. Adam Smith's critique of international trading companies: theorizing "globalization" in the Age of Enlightenment. *Political Theory* 36:185-212, 2008. Muthu focuses especially on Smith's account of the international joint stock trading companies of his day, the equivalent of today's multinational corporations. Smith was harshly critical of these companies, not merely because they often were monopolies, but because he thought that by their very form, they tended to be unjust, inefficient, and cruel to those over whom they had power, and also tended to corrupt civil governments by gaining political ascendency. Muthu notes that Smith's criticism of these companies is profoundly moral: "Given Smith's belief in the fundamental sociability of human beings, the sociability of commerce both within and across societies simply puts into practice a core feature of what it means to be human. Thus, when commerce becomes thwarted, subjected to the power of a few, and restricted to a wealthy elite, the consequences are not only materially damaging for domestic economies and international markets, but they are also, in a fundamental sense, dehumanizing" (192).

15. Wolfe A. *Whose keeper? Social science and moral obligation*. Berkeley, CA: University of California Press, 1989: 19. Wolfe's view is summarized in Coontz S. *The way we never were: American families and the nostalgia trap*. New York: Basic Books, 2000:100.

16. Coontz, *Way we never were*: 100.

17. Gasper, *Ethics of development*: 81.

18. Okun A. *Equality and efficiency: the big tradeoff*. Washington, DC: The Brookings Institution, 1975: 13; quoted in Churchill LR. The hegemony of money: commercialism and professionalism in American medicine. *Cambridge Quarterly of Healthcare Ethics* 16:407-414, 2007.

19. Gasper, *Ethics of development*: 125-6.

20. Nussbaum MC. *Not for profit: why democracy needs the humanities.* Princeton, NJ: Princeton University Press, 2010: 6.

21. Since one of the main thrusts of this book is the claim that economism is not economics as a social science, but rather religious ideology disguised as social science, it may seem odd to charge economism with depicting humans as without souls. This might be a problem if economism were to claim openly to be a religion, and if theologians were to study it to see if it were internally consistent as a belief system. But economism escapes this sort of scrutiny precisely by denying its own nature. It is this denial, I will argue in the remainder of this book, that makes economism so dangerous as a way of thinking.

22. Soros G. *The crisis of global capitalism: open society endangered.* London: Little, Brown, 1998: xx, xxii, 126. As we saw in Chapter 1 (note 11), health economist Robert Evans anticipated Soros by a year when he used the term "fundamentalist" to describe a similar ideology in 1997.

23. Somers MR. *Genealogies of citizenship: markets, statelessness, and the right to have rights.* New York: Cambridge University Press, 2008:73-74. UN economists Richard Kozul-Wright and Paul Rayment define 'market fundamentalism' in very similar terms, though they say nothing about its origin: "the tendency ... to give overriding importance to the pursuit of economic efficiency and to regard political and social demands to influence the level or content of economic growth as an irrational and unwarranted interference with the free market which, left to itself, can be relied upon to generate the best of all possible outcomes for all members of society"; and the "refusal to admit to doubts about the agenda and to alter course" even in the face of strong evidence of policy failures; Kozul-Wright R, Rayment P. *The resistable rise of market fundamentalism: Rethinking development policy in an unbalanced world.* New York: Zed Books, 2007: 13-14, 20.

24. Somers, *Genealogies of citizenship*: 2.

25. Somers, *Genealogies of citizenship*: 3.

26. Somers, *Genealogies of citizenship*: 4. Somers distinguishes between market fundamentalism and what she calls "the far more nuanced theories of neoclassical academic economists" (75n).

27. Frank T. *One market under God: Extreme capitalism, market populism, and the end of economic democracy.* New York: Anchor, 2001.

28. Frank, *One market under God*: 29.

29. Gasper, *Ethics of development*: 72.

30. Bigelow G. Let there be markets: the evangelical roots of economics. *Harper's Magazine* 310 (1860): 33-38, May 2005.

31. Chait J. *The big con: the true story of how Washington got hoodwinked and hijacked by crackpot economics.* Boston: Houghton Mifflin, 2007.

32. Chait, *The big con:* 18-20.

33. Chait, *The big con:* 21.

34. Chait, *The big con:* 23-26.

35. Keen S. *Debunking economics: The naked emperor of the social sciences.* New York: Zed Books, 2001. Keen goes on to insist however that some critical economists have avoided these mistakes and have constructed alternative approaches that are more scientific, but these approaches are not taught in standard economics classroom: "Clearly, then, my target in this book is not economics in general, but the dominant school of thought within economics. This school is technically known as neoclassical economics..." (10).

36. Foley DK. *Adam's fallacy: A guide to economic theology.* Cambridge, MA: Harvard University Press, 2006: xiv-xv.

Chapter 4.
Economism's Origins: Evangelicalism in England

Patrick O'Ryan shivered as he lifted another shovelful of earth that late January day in 1846. The temperature in County Cork was just above freezing, but the dampness made the cold more penetrating. "Now don't be complaining about the dank air, my boy," he said to himself. It was Ireland's damp climate, the elders of the village said, that made potatoes grow so well here.

The English might defeat the Irish and then treat the island as a conquered colony. The British landlords might take most of the best land for grazing cattle and sheep, and other cash crops they could profitably export back to England. They might restrict the Irish tenant farmers to just a few acres of the least fertile land for their own use, making them work on the landlord's land five or six days out of the week to pay their rent. Yet still the Irish could manage to feed their families, with the potatoes they could grow on their small plots of acreage.

The system would work, that is, if the crop was healthy. Crop failures were common; Patrick remembered the severe losses in 1839. And now there was talk of a new kind of blight, even more serious, that had already destroyed much of the potato crop in Europe.

The elders had also taught him how to pick the autumn days when the soil temperature and moisture were just right, and bury portions of the newly harvested potatoes at the proper depth. Sound potatoes would then be preserved as good as new for use in the winter and spring months. Patrick was now digging into one of those storage hills, as he, Kate, and little Bridget had just about exhausted the last batch of potatoes.

Patrick knew practically to the shovelful just how deep he had buried the potatoes, and it took him a while to realize that the reason he was going deeper than he thought he needed to was that he was digging up not soil, but rotten vegetation. The potatoes had seemed all right last fall when he had buried them. Only now did he realize that unseen, the blight had taken hold. Instead of being preserved, the potatoes had gradually rotted away underground.

For a moment, though, the reality was too terrible to contemplate. Patrick O'Ryan leaned on his shovel and stared down into the nothingness that was supposed to be his family's supply of food for the next two months.[1]

In the middle of 1846, the Whig party took control of the government of Great Britain.[2] The new Prime Minister, Lord Russell, and his assistant secretary of the treasury, Charles Trevelyan, inherited a crisis from the outgoing moderate Tory government of Sir Robert Peel. The potato blight in Ireland had wiped out the crop that the majority of peasants relied on for their sustenance. The Peel government had responded to the threats of widespread starvation by purchasing several shiploads of corn meal from America and distributing it as emergency food relief.

Russell and Trevelyan knew what they needed to do. They immediately put an end to the food-relief program. The result of their policies is what we know today as the Irish Potato Famine. About a million Irish starved to death and another million emigrated.

Russell and Trevelyan chose their policies carefully and deliberately. Though no doubt a number of practical and political considerations guided their choices, their fundamental reasons were religious. Both were fervent adherents of the religious movement called evangelicalism.

In this chapter I show how evangelicalism in England in the first half of the 19th century forms one of the roots of today's economism. What is evangelicalism? Why did it gain so much power at that particular time? What, in particular, did it teach regarding treatment of the poor? How, finally, were those teachings embodied in government policies during the Potato Famine? What then led evangelicalism to lose favor? And, finally, how did key evangelical ideas then re-emerge in the form of neoclassical economics, when that discipline was introduced in the 1870s?[3]

The Nature of Evangelicalism

By stating that Lord Russell and Charles Trevelyan were fervent evangelicals (as the term was used in 19th century England), I mean to say that they held a set of religious beliefs that we could summarize as follows.[4]

They did not believe that humans were born innocent, to become sinners later on in life only if they did bad things. They thought that each of us is a sinner through and through from the very moment of birth. That is simply the human condition.

They believed that there was, however, good news. Fortunately for us, already at the moment of birth, our sins had been atoned for. Christ died on the cross to atone for our sins and for the sins of all mankind. Thanks to Christ's loving intervention on our behalf, all of humankind can be saved, and after death can go to Heaven. Had Christ not given us this gift with his own life, our only option would have been everlasting hellfire, which we would all have deserved, being sinners by nature.

They believed that when they died, each would face a personal Day of Judgment and be sent to Heaven, a place of eternal joy and peace, or to Hell, a place of eternal suffering and torment. (Boyd Hilton, an authority on evangelicalism, stresses that these descriptions of Heaven and Hell were accepted by evangelicals quite literally–whatever pictures we paint of what we imagine Heaven and Hell to look like, was exactly what people of Russell and Trevelyan's time expected to encounter.[5]) One thing and one thing only will determine what happens to each–*his or her deep, abiding, and sincere faith in Jesus Christ as savior*, or the lack of that faith.

They understood that in the course of a lifetime, each might become a highly virtuous person and do many good works. Those deeds would not, however, gain one a place in Heaven. They were important only indirectly as a sign of faith. People of deep faith can be expected to be virtuous and to do good works. But it is the faith and not the works that is the key to their eternal salvation.

They also assumed that people of faith might go regularly to church, and participate in religious ceremonies and rituals. But like virtuous deeds and good works, religious practices on earth were totally useless as a way of gaining entry into Heaven. Their faith was not in anything on earth (not even a church), but in God and Christ. Salvation was a matter directly between them and God. No clergy and no church could effectively intercede on their behalf.

Finally, they could be thankful to God for his kindness. God has been kind to us by arranging matters so that this earthly life is full of trials and suffering. If things on earth were easy, we could fall into the trap of imagining that we were not sinners by nature after all–that we did not have to do anything special or difficult to gain entry into Heaven. If we fell into that trap, of course, we would never develop the abiding faith in Christ that was needed to preserve us from eternal damnation. Fortunately, earthly life is much more likely to remind us at every turn of the need to apply ourselves to the task of rising above our sinful natures and of finding true faith. Ironically, earthly suffering is one of our truest reminders of God's love.[6]

If I were going to provide a detailed history of evangelicalism, I would have to add a number of refinements to this summary view. As you can readily imagine, there were differences and strains within evangelicalism. Factions disagreed on matters such as how far off in the future the millennium was likely to be, and how likely or unlikely it was that humankind would actually learn its lessons from the trials of earthly life.[7] We also would have to put evangelicalism in its proper place by contrasting it to the various strains of belief and practice within the official Anglican church, as well as its relationships with dissenting faiths such as John Wesley's Methodism developed during the previous century. However, for the purposes of this chapter—identifying the historical antecedents of economism—we can dispense with these details.[8]

Why Then?

Through much of the 18th century, the average Englishman had become quite blasé about matters of religion, and saw no reason to avoid earthly pleasures out of religious concern. The dominant worldview of the day was the philosophy of the Enlightenment. On this view, God had set the world working in accord with his laws of nature, and then probably did not take much interest in what happened afterward–certainly not in whether individual human beings were sinful or had faith. This view of God-as-watchmaker who wound up the watch and then let it run on its own was, as we now understand, the general religious attitude of leading American thinkers of the day such as Washington, Franklin and Jefferson.

Things changed, Hilton suggests, with the French Revolution in 1789. The natural world order--at least as represented by the French monarchy, and the power of the landowning upper classes--seemed to have been turned inside out. Evil and disorder were now abroad throughout the land.[9] If the reigning order could so quickly be turned topsy-turvy in France, who was to say that England might not be next? The question was how to reconcile the existence of a powerful and loving God with this new ascendence of suffering and social dislocation. The answer, for many in England, was evangelicalism:

> In other words, the moderate evangelicalism which developed after 1789 represented a shift in natural religion from *evidences* to *paradoxes*, that is, from examples of benign contrivance in the natural world to demonstrations of how superficial misery may work inner improvement. Those who found it impossible to point to the obvious harmonies of nature as evidence of the goodness and good sense of the deity had to argue instead that *apparent* nastiness, like war and famine, was–to those who understood the divine economy–a blessing in disguise.[10]

Thomas Robert Malthus published the first edition of his *Essay on the Principle of Population* in 1798, thereby adding another note of pessimism to the social upheaval already created by the French Revolution. Malthus's famous theory was that population always increases faster than the food supply, suggesting that cycles of plenty and starvation (the fat and lean years of the Old Testament) were inevitable. Evangelicalism, as we will see later on, tends to be a popular belief in a time when the history of the world is seen as cyclical, and is generally incompatible with a world in which we can look forward to steady progress. The Enlightenment of the 18th century had seemed a time for faith in reason and progress. If Malthus was right, that same exercise of reason showed us in the end that progress was illusory. It was only in the next world that we could expect any real improvement.[11]

Evangelicalism and Poverty

The main focus of this chapter is how evangelicalism created ideas about poverty that took such deep root in the Anglo-American culture that they still persist today under the guise of economism. How, exactly, did evangelicalism view poverty? Gordon Bigelow summarizes:

[Evangelicals] regarded poverty as part of a divine program. Evangelicals interpreted the mental anguish of poverty and debt, and the physical agony of hunger or cold, as natural spurs to prick the conscience of sinners. They believed that the suffering of the poor would provoke remorse, reflection, and ultimately the conversion that would change their fate [in the afterlife]. In other words, poor people were poor for a reason, and helping them out of poverty would endanger their mortal souls.[12]

One evangelical authority, James Stevens, explained in 1831:

To prevent the possibility of death from famine, to prevent the possibility of actual want, may appear a desirable object. But we forget that it is in this very possibility, that the efficiency of those laws of God by which society is governed, consists. From observations on the state and order of the world, we are fully authorized to infer, that it is the will of God, as expressed in the laws of nature, that the life of man should depend upon various contingencies; as upon his own exertions and character, the good will of others, advantages of situation, and so forth. . . . We find that upon this very contingency and uncertainty of subsistence, upon this very possibility of utter destitution (and if there is a possibility,–there are likely to be instances) the integrity of the social compact, the prevention of actual vice, the industry and happiness of man, the peace and security of the political body, are made to depend. Physical evil, it is a well-known fact, is necessary for the promotion of moral good.[13]

It is perhaps worth noting Stevens's use of the term "efficiency" to justify the suffering of the poor–a remarkable bit of prescience regarding the language one often hears from economists and conservative policymakers today.

There are two distinct senses in which trying to relieve the suffering brought about by poverty directly challenges the will of God. First, as we have already noted, evangelical theory holds that God has designed this world to work in a certain way, and has determined the behavior of the world through his natural laws. One aspect of his design of the world is that because Christ atoned for the sins of all mankind by dying on the cross, but only a devout faith in Christ will assure each person's salvation, the earth has been created as a sort of training ground or obstacle course to lead to eternal salvation through faith. Suffering, whether brought about by poverty or any other means, is God's plan to encourage atonement and faith among weak and sin-ridden humanity.

A second aspect of the design of the world is that (as Thomas Chalmers, a leading evangelical, insisted), "working-class poverty did not come suddenly like an epidemic, nor did it come 'undivined'. It was the necessary and inescapable consequence of licentious habits, which could only be cured by 'sustained evangelical tuition', emphasizing the eternal retribution that awaits all reprobates."[14] The poor were poor because of who they were, where they came from, and how they behaved. That was as much a facet of natural law as the fact that oak trees grew from acorns. In short, God had created the poor for a reason, and he made them suffer for a reason. Messing with God's divine plan was ill-advised.

In Chapter 1, I expressed my own puzzlement as to why so many self-proclaimed Christians today seem little moved to follow Jesus's own example in addressing the needs of the poor. Apparently this puzzlement also cropped up in 19th century England, for Chalmers took considerable pains to explain why his ultimate teachings on poverty deviated so far from the message of the Gospels. Chalmers argued that while Jesus may have often preached about the importance of how one treats the poor, an accounting of his actual behavior reveals him very infrequently dispensing charity or giving aid. For example, Chalmers offered the opinion that in John 6:26-27, we see an example of Jesus actually refusing to give bread to the poor. The incident occurs immediately after the miracle of the loaves and the fishes, and the miracle of Jesus walking on water. Jesus had left the crowd behind when he saw that they meant to proclaim him king. Some of the people followed him and asked him why he had fled, He answered, "In very truth I know that you have not come looking for me because you saw signs, but because you ate the bread and your hunger was satisfied. You must work, not for this perishable food, but for the food that lasts, the food of eternal life."[15]

Admittedly this passage seems to reinforce the evangelical teaching that earthly existence is but a training ground for the next world. But it seems quite a stretch to claim that it depicts Jesus refusing to give bread to the poor, as nothing is said anywhere in John 6 about the crowd of people being impoverished. Even so, Jesus did not refuse to give them either bread or fish; he merely chastised them later for placing too high a value on their stomachs being full in comparison to other signs of God's grace. For Chalmers to claim that this passage negates Jesus's very clear statements, on other occasions, that how one treats the poor will determine a good portion of God's judgment regarding eternal life seems a considerable stretch. For whatever reasons, the evangelicals discounted the teachings of the Gospel about the goodness of charity and of the worthiness of the poor in the eyes of God.

The Poor Law

Evangelicalism reached its greatest policy success in the Poor Law Amendment of 1834. The old Poor Law system, dating back to Elizabethan times, was based on the idea of "outdoor relief," an odd way of saying that the recipients of welfare could remain in their own homes while receiving aid. The recipients of aid were presumed to be for the most part widows and orphans and the disabled. The giver of the relief was the local parish, collecting funds by a sort of property tax.

The new Poor Law provided "indoor" relief–no one could remain at large while receiving aid. If you wanted to be helped by the system, Bigelow summarized, you had to agree to be effectively incarcerated in the district workhouse:

> The Poor Law [Amendment of 1834] nationalized and monopolized poverty administration. It forbade cash payments to any poor citizen and mandated that his only recourse be the local workhouse. Workhouses became orphanages, insane asylums, nursing homes, public hospitals,

and factories for the able-bodied. Protests over conditions in these prison-like facilities, particularly the conditions for children, mounted through the 1830s. But it did not surprise the evangelicals to learn that life in the workhouse was miserable. These early faith-based initiatives regarded poverty as a divinely sanctioned payment plan for a sinful life. The first anti-poverty program in the first industrial economy was not designed to alleviate suffering, nor to reduce the number of poor children in future generations. Poverty was not understood as a problem to be fixed. It was a spiritual condition. Workhouses weren't supposed to help children prepare for life; they were supposed to save their souls.[16]

By using the phrase "faith-based initiative," Bigelow obviously intends to create a parallel between the evangelical policies of England in the 1830s and the U.S. of the first decade of the 21st century. His suggested parallel is significant in one other way. One criticism commonly aimed at anti-big-government conservatives today is inconsistency. When it comes to using the power of the state to promote their ideological beliefs, suddenly they are all in favor of big government. In a similar way, evangelical policy-makers were distrustful of giving government too much power to interfere with the workings of the market. As we will see below, the evangelical minister of the treasury, Charles Trevelyan, was quick to denounce the only effective program for easing the Irish potato famine as "monstrous centralization."[17] But apparently no one in the evangelical movement denounced the creation of the workhouse system as a "monstrous centralization."

Besides the belief that doing anything serious to reduce poverty would violate God's law, another thought underlay British policy toward the poor during this time. Policymakers influenced by Malthus had one further, utilitarian reason to avoid giving any aid to the poor. According to Malthus's theory, if you fed the poor, they would multiply, outstrip the food supply, and later starve in even greater numbers.

In one way, evangelicals concerned themselves a good deal with the duty of the rich to give alms to the poor. They did so, however, in a very constrained and limited fashion. Recall the basic teaching that good works could never assure one of salvation, but might indirectly hint that one had arrived at a sufficient level of faith and atonement. Ironically, many evangelicals worried more about the ultimate salvation of the rich than of the poor. This was not because they agreed with Jesus that "it is easier for a camel to pass through the eye of a needle than for a rich man to enter the kingdom of God."[18] Rather, they assumed that the rich were in greater danger of damnation because of their own *lack* of suffering. The poor, presumably, were daily brought into obvious contact with the wages of sin and thus were given numerous incentives to repent. The rich, who had easier lives, and whose sins were perhaps of a more subtle nature, might fail to take heed until it was too late.

The rich therefore had to be encouraged both in their underlying faith, and in the good works that might be reflective of that faith. Giving alms to the poor was one such type of good work. But to be effective in preparing one for the next world, an act of charity had to have very specific features. Above all, it had to be heartfelt and spontaneous. That meant that no legalized or institutionalized charitable giving could pass muster. Had there been a United Way in England back then, it would not have had many donations from evangelicals. The more organized, the less (truly) charitable was the activity. This, of course, meant that no state-sponsored poor relief could ever be acceptable.

In short, evangelical concerns about charity focused almost completely on what it said about the state of salvation of the giver. Whether it had any impact on the recipient was important in only one way. If the charity was so directly contrary to the will of God as to seriously jeopardize the other person's salvation, then it became sinful in itself. For that reason, the devout evangelical giver was abjured always to distinguish carefully between the deserving and the undeserving poor. To give alms to the latter would only perpetuate sinful behavior and no doubt lead to their eternal damnation.[19]

The Irish Potato Famine

What did it really mean to leave home? Patrick O'Ryan wondered. It had little to do with a place, let alone a building. Of the ramshackle cabin they were leaving behind in County Cork, he thought: good riddance. He had never dared to put any effort, let alone money, into fixing it up. The O'Hallorans had tried to improve their shack, and the middleman that the Earl of Eastham had hired to manage the estate immediately raised their rent, and then evicted them when they could not pay.

No, it was only the people who mattered—and the knowledge that while the younger relatives might someday follow them to America, they were seeing the older ones for the last time in this world. It had wrenched his heart to say his farewells to his own mother and father, and old Uncle Mike. It was even harder to watch his dear Kate's tears as she parted from her mother and grandmother.

The ship bound for Boston that they had boarded in Cork Harbor had certainly no cabins, and not even bunks, for the 280 poor emigrants. It was basically a matter of roaming amongst the cargo in the hold and finding a corner in which to lie down. At least, from what he had heard, the American shipmasters were more reliable than the British about providing a modicum of food and water during the month-long voyage. Kate had heard fearful stories about the Irish who fled to Liverpool and other cities in England being herded onto the ships side by side with the cattle, and having to stand, covered with urine and manure, for the entire passage.[20]

Patrick was also glad that Kate had seen the letter that the O'Donnell family had received from their cousin who had settled in Wisconsin. Tell everyone, she had written, to be sure to bring enough money over and above the ship's passage to pay for travel inland once they had reached America. Most of the Irish were flooding into the large ports, taking all the menial jobs and driving down wages. There were many better chances for advancement in the interior states. But first one had to survive the passage. Patrick looked around him at his fellow passengers and saw the majority so weakened by hunger that a fever could spread through the whole ship in an eyeblink. He shuddered to think of little Bridget and how quickly a child of her age could succumb.

Between 1846 and 1849, the potato crop in Ireland massively failed due to the blight. The bulk of Irish rural residents depended on potatoes and had no money to buy other food. (The problem was *not* an absolute shortage of food, as all during those years Ireland continued to export food to England.) About a million people starved and about another million emigrated, reducing the population of Ireland by about one-fourth.

The basic causes of the famine had nothing to do with religion and were rooted instead in colonial oppression. Much of the productive land in Ireland was owned by absentee English landlords. The peasants had to work the landlord's land and produce cash crops for export, in exchange for being granted a small plot of land with which to supply their own needs. Potatoes were the only food crop that could be grown on these small plots and produce sufficient nutrition to sustain them.

Looking through racist lenses, many English decided that the Irish peasants lived in a state of primitive savagery. Their preferred method for cultivating potatoes, in specially designed, elongated mounds of earth, was translated from Gaelic into English as "lazy beds." Contrary to the impression this term created, it was actually a very sophisticated and labor-intensive way of maximizing the yields of the small plots the Irish peasants were granted. The dominant English view, however, was that the Irish would be done a huge favor if they could be prompted to give up their savage ways, move to the cities, and seek honest and useful employment in factories. It did not escape the English that this effective clearing-off of the rural population would open up more English-owned land for the profitable grazing of cattle, to serve the English beef market. It would also supply a cheap labor pool for the factories in the cities that the English capitalists would own and profit from.

The first governmental reaction to the famine also had nothing to do with evangelicalism. The administration of the moderate-conservative (Tory) Sir Robert Peel was in power when the famine began. (Peel was famous for creating the modern metropolitan London police force, and it is in his honor that London policemen are still known as "bobbies.") Peel responded to reports of the famine as if it was a secular humanitarian crisis. He initiated two actions. First, corn meal could be purchased quickly and at a decent price from America, and Peel arranged for a supply to be procured and sent to Ireland. Corn meal formed no part of the traditional Irish diet, and the meal was very rough and difficult both to mill and digest, but at least it would prevent starvation.

Peel also attempted a local repeal of the Corn Laws, the tariffs that artificially raised the price of bread. (In England, "corn" refers to the grain that Americans call "wheat.") But that effort split his own conservative party and Peel lost support. In mid-1846, his administration was replaced by the opposing party, the Whigs, among whom evangelicalism was especially influential. As we saw, the new prime minister, Lord Russell, and his assistant secretary of the treasury, Trevelyan, were fervent evangelicals. Immediately the humanitarian-relief model was scrapped, to be replaced by policies that were aimed at saving the souls of the Irish in the next world, regardless of what fate befell them in this one.

Trevelyan steered Britain's Irish policy toward the removal of all "monstrous centralization," as he labeled government aid to the poor.[21] He sought to dismantle the supposedly primitive Irish agricultural system, relocate the populace from the countryside to the cities, and eventually create a productive manufacturing economy (as if this exercise in government social engineering on a grand scale did not amount to a "monstrous centralization" of a different stripe). He was certain that food aid of any sort would simply prop up the backward status quo and ultimately lead to even greater misery. Only the complete elimination of all poor relief would serve as a sufficiently powerful prod to bring about the needed changes.

A part of Trevelyan's agenda for Ireland seems eerily modern in its reliance on racial stereotypes. Trevelyan, it appears, was taken in by the misleading term "lazy beds." He interpreted this as suggesting that the reason why the Irish persisted as a savage race, instead of becoming civilized and accepting their role as willing cogs in the English industrial machinery, was the role of the potato. He assumed that hardly any labor was needed to grow potatoes in the Irish way, so that the availability of this crop encouraged a natural laziness and discouraged industry. Only if the potato were displaced from its central role as an article of diet would the Irish have any hope for improvement, in this world as well as the next. Blaming the potato and the Irish, instead of British colonial policies that robbed the Irish of their land and forced them to rely on the single crop that could be grown on what they had left, simply illustrated how little Trevelyan—in company with most of his fellow Englishmen--understood the true situation.[22]

Trevelyan's aim to be sure that no poor person would get food aid was taken to the extreme degree by a legal measure implemented in Ireland, prohibiting anyone who had a quarter-acre of land or more for his own use from getting any assistance under the poor law relief system. A quarter-acre was completely insufficient for growing enough food to support a household, potato blight or no. The local poor relief system was supported by local taxes, paid primarily by the landowners, who therefore had a financial incentive to reduce the availability of relief. The incentives of the landowners led to wholesale evictions which in turn hastened Irish emigration.

In one regard, Trevelyan and his colleagues failed. The situation was so dire that eventually public works projects had to be created to provide some income for Irish willing to work. However, the Whig administration demanded that these work projects be designed so nothing of any use resulted. Workers were paid to dig holes or to destroy existing roads. The supposedly primitive and savage Irish, as if anticipating Barack Obama's later economic stimulus ideas, requested that the government create works projects to build much-needed infrastructure such as railroads. Their requests were ignored. It seems that the evangelicals were petrified by the possibility that their public works programs might actually produce benefits, and thus serve as a precedent for future projects of the same type. Any precedent of the central government interfering with the market to give relief to the poor had to be nipped in the bud.

Aftermath of the Famine: Evangelicalism Loses Influence

By mid-century, evangelicalism's grasp on British political and economic policy was weakening. The potato famine was one factor. The policies of Russell and Trevelyan may have saved many souls in the next world, but in this one they were widely perceived as embarrassing failures for England.

Writers such as Charles Dickens were at the same time chipping away at public acceptance of evangelical doctrine. It was an important article of evangelical faith that most people who suffered economically deserved what they got due to their own sinfulness. The fiction of the day increasingly depicted sympathetic characters who suffered poverty due to circumstances beyond their control and despite lives of blameless virtue. Some were the proverbial widows and orphans at whom the original Elizabethan poor laws had been aimed. Others were the innocent victims of speculation, who lost their meager life savings in the periodic upheavals of the financial markets. The same novels that depicted the lower classes sympathetically placed evangelical doctrines in the mouths of the most self-righteous and hypocritical characters. While Scrooge in *A Christmas Carol* is not specifically depicted as a proponent of evangelicalism, Dickens seems to put his own sentiments into the mouth of Scrooge's nephew Fred when the latter says that he appreciates Christmas because it is the "only time I know of, in the long calendar of the year, when men and women seem by one consent to open their shut-up hearts freely, and to think of people below them as if they really were fellow-passengers to the grave, and not another race of creatures bound on other journeys."[23]

William Rathbone Greg struck near the heart of evangelism in his *The Creed of Christendom* in 1851. He rejected the evangelical depiction of God as "cruel, short-sighted, capricious, and unjust, punishing with infinite and endless torture men whom He had created weak, finite, and ephemeral,–nay, whom he had fore-ordained to sin."[24] Such a picture of God was not Christian, Greg protested, but rather blasphemous. The evangelical notion of earthly life as divinely-designed trial was now seen in a new light. Who, Greg seemed to be asking, could be asked to worship a God who had the power to create the human race in whatever form he wished; decided to design the race basically as children who loved to play with toys; sent them to live their mortal lives in a house filled with toys; and then consigned them to everlasting hellfire because they succumbed to temptation and played with the toys? Other commentators objected to a "tyrannical, arbitrary, and cruel" God who similarly punished with eternal damnation those who did not accept Christ as their Savior because they had never even heard of Christ.[25] Purely on its own terms, as an expression of *Christian* theology, evangelicalism was found wanting by these newly emboldened critics.

Another factor in the rejection of evangelical thought at mid-century lay with science and industry. The Enlightenment of the 18th century had believed firmly and optimistically in inevitable human progress fueled by humankind's rational powers. Optimism was replaced by pessimism with the French Revolution and Malthusian thought. By 1850, optimism was in the air again. Evangelicalism was most at home in a cyclical world, in which no long-term progress is possible. The scientific world that was making way for Darwin's evolutionary theory was for the most part dispensing with cyclic models. Similarly, it now seemed that industrialization, even granted its human and environmental costs, was capable of expanding the economy indefinitely. Belief in progress was back in vogue, and that in turn undermined the conditions favorable for evangelicalism.

The Rise of the New Economics

When evangelicalism waned, political economy, its companion philosophy in the public policy sphere, weakened along with it. But the new scientific tenor of the times would soon provide an opportunity for its rebirth.

William Stanley Jevons, who published *The Theory of Political Economy* in 1871, is generally credited with putting modern economics on its mathematical and scientific footing. It would be nice to be able to report that Jevons had been reared in a strict evangelical environment, but in fact he was brought up with, and remained true to, Unitarian beliefs in a benevolent God.[26] Hilton, for one, thought that Jevons was less influenced by religion and more by his studies of physics. He seemed to view economic transactions as like energy transfers, which could be described by mathematical laws even where they could not be directly observed (as is the case, for example, with potential energy).

However, in order to lay the groundwork for a "scientific" rebirth of evangelical ideas, one did not have to set out to create an economic theory that would directly blame the poor for poverty. Jevons recapitulated and improved upon half of Adam Smith's philosophy from *The Wealth of Nations*. The half of Smith that was of interest (as explained in Chapter 3) involved the idea that the activities of thousands or millions of individuals, each transacting exchanges in the marketplace to his own personal advantage, could be summed into a grand scheme that took on an apparent life of its own (as if guided by the famous "invisible hand") and whose behavior could be predicted with mathematical certainty.

As Jevons had it, the market was the ideal instrument for determining what people truly, actually wanted–in technical terms, for precisely measuring utility. The unit of the marketplace, the so-called *homo economicus*, is the ideal of the perfectly autonomous self, the unconstrained chooser. If you offer in the marketplace something that *homo economicus* does not want, he will not buy it. If you offer something that he does want, but set the price so high that he can buy something he wants more with the same money, he will also spurn it. If on the other hand you offer some good in the marketplace, and *homo economicus* buys it, then that thing is exactly what he wants, and the price he paid is exactly to the very penny how much he wants it. It makes no more sense to insist that he really wanted something else more, than to say that light travels at some speed other than 186,000 miles per second.

Bigelow argues that Jevons's economics was simply the moralistic evangelical view of the market in a new guise. Since the term 'political economy' had taken on such a negative connotation at the hands of Dickens and others, Jevons and his followers ditched that term in favor of *economics*. The now-disfavored 'political economy' had seemed mostly to be about politics and ideology. By contrast, the developers of the new field stressed its purely scientific nature. Jevons's overriding goal was to construct precise mathematical models of the marketplace, similar to the laws of Newtonian physics and mechanics. Bigelow stresses the analogy to Newtonian mechanics by using the example of the supposedly frictionless plane. Physicists were able to develop such elegant, simple mathematical laws by assuming ideal conditions and putting aside real-world complications like friction. But worse things happen when the same approach is used for a science of human activity:

> In conceiving their discipline as a search for mathematical laws, economists have abstracted to their own ideal conditions, which for the most part consist of an utterly denuded version of man himself. What they consider 'friction' is the better part of what makes us human: our interactions with one another; our irrational desires. Today we often think of science and religion as standing in opposition, but the 'scientific' turn made by Jevons and his fellows only served to enshrine the faith of their evangelical predecessors. The evangelicals believed that the market was a divine system, guided by spiritual laws. The 'scientific' economists saw the market as a natural system, a principle of equilibrium produced in the balance of individual souls.[27]

Economics–Religion or Science?

Let's look in more detail at the claim that neoclassical economics, as it developed in the 1870s and after, thought of itself as a science akin to physics, but actually embodied many of the religious views it inherited from evangelical political economy. Bigelow gives us a helpful case study by describing a rebellion among graduate students in the top French university economics departments in 2000.

The students demanded that their professors teach them economic theory that actually had something to do with the reality of human social life. Essentially the students accused the professors of living in an imaginary world, because that was the world in which their theories exactly predicted interesting phenomena. If they were to come out of their ivory tower and deal with the real world, the students suggested, they might find two things to be true. First, their pet theories would not work nearly as well, and would require a lot of modification. But any observations that they did manage to make would be about something real and important.[28]

When neoclassical economists encounter criticisms such as these students raised, they usually respond by explaining that the complainers are simply too stupid to grasp the mathematical elegance of the dominant economic theories. And indeed, the leaders of economics quickly attacked these students for daring to question the economic orthodoxy. But as Bigelow observed, the problem could not have been the lack of mathematical ability among the French students. These students had passed every test needed to be admitted into their country's finest economic graduate programs.[29]

Let's push the comparison between physics and economics a bit farther. Why did the students in the physics departments in France not join their economic counterparts in 2000, and complain about their own field of science? One possible answer is that it's because physics is a "real" science and economics is a social science, which we realize are very primitive sciences if they are sciences at all. But that answer is unsatisfactory. Sciences can only be as precise and as elegant as their subject matter allows; and there are many ways in which the physical world of objects is a great deal simpler and more straightforward than the world that economics seeks to explain. The French graduate students did not complain that economics needed to be more like physics. They complained because it needed a greater degree of input from the other social sciences, that perhaps do a better job than economics does of accounting for *real* human behavior, even if they lack the mathematical elegance and precision of neoclassical economic theories.

The world of theoretical physics might be as much removed from real human experience as is the imaginary world that the graduate students accused their economics professors of inhabiting. But in the world of applied science, engineers and architects have to design bridges and buildings that will stand up in the real world, not in some ideal one. And overall they seem to do a good job. If so, several things must be true about the way that the laws of physics and mechanics are applied. First, the differences between real-world conditions and the idealized world described by Newton's laws must, in practice, be understood and taken into account. We don't have starry-eyed engineers roaming about imagining that real-world planes are frictionless. Second, there must be additional laws and formulas that allow applied scientists to make the adjustments required by the real-world conditions. Maybe it is necessary at any given step of the process to make some simplifying assumptions; but then, at a later step, one can go back and correct for that simplification.

Third, and most important, the engineers and architects seem to have a firm grasp of where human beings are constrained by inviolable physical laws and where human beings have leeway and can take responsibility. Human beings and their actions are constrained by the laws of gravity. Engineers would simply shake their heads if somebody claimed to be able to set aside gravitation by mere human willpower (magicians who perform feats of levitation to the contrary). But human beings, and not the laws of nature, build bridges. If a bridge collapses, the bottom line is that somebody did something wrong, and the engineers set out to find out what and why.

Bigelow and the French graduate students are accusing neoclassical economics of being unlike physics (or engineering) in all of these three important ways. They claim that neoclassical economists have talked to each other about their ideal world, that is precisely predictable by the use of their mathematical theories, for so long, that they have virtually convinced themselves that their world *is* the real world–or at least that the differences between their ideal world and the real world are minor and easily dismissed. Because they think their ideal world is the real world, they see no need to develop further formulas that bridge the messy gaps between the ideal and real worlds. Finally, they seem to have thoroughly mixed up what is the working-out of natural law and what is a set of human choices for which humans need to take responsibility. When the economic equivalent of a bridge collapse occurs, we are not told that somebody has messed up; we are told by many so-called experts that this is simply the market working itself out according to its laws, and that no mere human beings should be so bold as to imagine that they could tinker with the laws of the marketplace.

Let's assume for now that this is an accurate depiction of how at least some neoclassical economists see the world. The next question is why one science (economics) has gone off in such a different direction from the other (physics). If we tried to answer that question by treating *each science solely as a science*, we would remain perplexed. If, on the other hand, we consider the possibility that *one of the sciences has incorporated into it some of the ideas and assumptions of religion*, then the perplexity might dissolve.

Suppose that you believed that your ideal world was not merely the outgrowth of the limits of human knowledge–the fact that in order to come up with a general, mathematical law, we usually have to simplify the way we think about the problem, focusing on some features and of necessity ignoring others. Suppose instead that you considered that world to be ideal because it seemed to embody important aspects of God's will. You thought that in that world, good people were rewarded and evil people were punished, just the way God wanted the world to be. It would then be natural that you would avoid trying to refine your theories and formulas to take into account less-than-ideal circumstances. It would also be natural for you, when critics pointed out the differences between the real world and your ideal world, to respond impatiently that that simply meant that the real world had better change its ways and act more like your ideal world does. Finally, it would seem natural if you regarded the elegance of your mathematical theories that predict behavior in your ideal world, as further proof that that must be the way that God meant the world to be. In sum, if you were swayed just as much by religious conviction as by an urge to develop a scientific field, we'd expect to find you behaving pretty much the way neoclassical economics has behaved (if its critics are correct).[30]

Real-world markets commonly reward the rich much more than the poor. One possible reason for this is that markets are human contrivances, and people with more power get to design human institutions more in their own favor. As the rich are generally a lot more powerful than the poor, they design markets to maintain their own wealth and power. Another possible reason is that markets follow laws that function very much like the laws of physics; humans are silly to think that they can interfere with those laws and make things come out the way they want to without eventually paying a very high price for their meddling. If you regard the market as a construct to be studied scientifically, then either explanation would appear to be worth considering at first blush–though most of us, knowing what we know about human societies, would probably think the first reason is the more plausible. If, on the other hand, you regard the market as God's creation designed especially to reward the good and to punish sinners, the first reason does not recommend itself at all and is likely to be dismissed out of hand.

From Evangelicalism to Economism

We have therefore traced the logic of an argument that starts with the role that evangelicalism assumed in influencing public policy in Britain in the first half of the 19th century, and that ends with the form that neoclassical economics has assumed since its creation a couple of decades later. To the extent that neoclassical economics and its practitioners avoid any resemblance to economism, as we have described it in the previous chapter, then the practitioners can claim that they are not the sorts of persons we have been talking about here. To the extent that some practitioners of neoclassical economics have approached closer and closer to economism in their thinking, then this description of religion masquerading as science seems to hit much closer to home.

However, so far, we have told only half of the story. An economism rooted in evangelical thought would naturally tend to regard the poor as unworthy sinners, so that any policy designed to help the poor is viewed as misguided. But we have seen no reason, *within evangelical thought itself,* for the rich to be regarded as especially worthy or as chosen by God. The evangelicals thought that we were all sinners, and that all of us had to repent and atone, rich and poor equally. We saw how some evangelicals even agreed that the rich were in greater danger of damnation because their sins were more subtle and so less likely to awaken in them the awareness of the need for atonement.

If we are going to explain the second important strand of economism in today's world, the tendency to see the rich as especially worthy even as we view the poor as especially unworthy, then we are going to have to look elsewhere. The next chapter seeks a religious doctrine that could explain the second part of our equation.

Notes

1. The image of the farmer digging up a storage hill only to find rotten potatoes underneath is borrowed from Bigelow G. *Fiction, famine, and the rise of economics in Victorian Britain and Ireland.* New York: Cambridge University Press, 2007: 132.

2. The Whig party, in the 19th century, was generally dedicated to supporting the interests of the wealthy merchants and owners of factories, while the rival Tories supported the monarchy and the landed gentry; http://en.wikipedia.org/wiki/Whig_(British_political_party).

3. One of my main sources for the material in this chapter is an article by Gordon Bigelow; Bigelow G. Let there be markets: the evangelical roots of economics. *Harpers Magazine* 310 (no. 1860), May 2005: 33-38. Bigelow is professor of English at Rhodes College, Memphis, TN. His later book-length work, *Fiction, famine, and the rise of economics in Victorian Britain and Ireland*, New York: Cambridge University Press, 2007, is more focused on literary history and criticism and therefore is less useful for my purposes.

4. In particular, I do not mean to suggest that the meaning of 'evangelicalism' in England in the 19th century is the same as in the U.S. today. I am grateful to Jan C. Heller for this observation.

5. Hilton B. *The age of atonement: the influence of evangelicalism on social and economic thought, 1785-1865.* Oxford, UK: Clarendon Press, 1986.

6. Bigelow, Let there be markets, 35; Hilton, *Age of atonement*: 8.

7. Hilton, *Age of atonement*: 8-11.

8. I am grateful to Harold Y. Vanderpool for pointing out these nuances in the religious history of England in the 19th century, and generally for his thorough review and critique of this and the next chapter.

9. Hilton, *Age of atonement*: 17.

10. Hilton, *Age of atonement*: 21-2.

11. See for example Hilton, *Age of atonement*: 32, 66-67.

12. Bigelow, Let there be markets, 35.

13. Hilton, *Age of atonement*: 86.

14. Hilton, *Age of atonement*: 85.

15. John 6:26-7, New English Bible.

16. Bigelow, Let there be markets, 36.

17. Bigelow, *Fiction, famine:* 119.

18. Matthew 19:24, New English Bible.

19. Hilton, *Age of atonement*: 100-3.

20. Famine: migrants and economic refugees. Multitext Project in Irish History, University College Cork; http://multitext.ucc.ie/d/Famine#MigrantsandEco nomicRefugees (accessed Nov. 21, 2010).

21. Bigelow, *Fiction, famine:* 119.

22. Bigelow, *Fiction, famine:* 120-1. Bigelow adds that more recent historical research has put the lie to the claim of the "primitive, savage" Irish by showing that the Irish before the famine enjoyed a height advantage over the English, suggesting much better nutrition and living standards than had been attributed to them by the common stereotypes; Bigelow, *Fiction, famine:* 142.

23. Dickens C. *A Christmas Carol*, 1843; http://www.stormfax.com/dickens.htm (accessed December 28, 2010).

24. Quoted in Hilton, *Age of atonement*: 271.

25. Hilton, *Age of atonement*: 278.

26. Hilton, *Age of atonement*: 319-21.

27. Bigelow, Let there be markets, 37.

28. Bigelow, Let there be markets, 34. The idea that there is something amiss in the curriculum of traditional business schools has received further emphasis since the Great Recession of 2008. See for example Scheiber N. Upper mismanagement. *The New Republic*, Dec. 18, 2009, http://www. tnr.com/article/economy/wagoner-henderson (accessed Nov. 20, 2010). Scheiber addresses primarily the problems that occur when people trained in finance try to manage in the manufacturing sector. John Cassidy noted that even financial firms find that business school graduates are so full of useless theory that they make questionable employees. One economist at Morgan Stanley told Cassidy in 1996, "We insist on at least a three-to-four-year cleansing experience to neutralize the brainwashing that takes place in these graduate programs." Cassidy J. *How markets fail: the logic of economic calamities*. New York: Farrar, Straus and Giroux, 2009: 104.

29. Bigelow, Let there be markets, 34.

30. See Chapter 3 for Keen's criticisms of neoclassical economics; Keen S. *Debunking economics: The naked emperor of the social sciences.* New York: Zed Books, 2001.

Chapter 5.
Economism's Origins: Puritanism in America

Josiah Benson was seasick often enough on the voyage from England to the Massachusetts Bay Colony during the spring of 1684 to ponder seriously just why he was making this trip. In his native city of Poole, in Dorsetshire on the south coast, trading ships went back and forth often enough to the North American colonies to make such travel seem routine. It was a far cry from the days when the Plymouth colonists set sail in 1620, or when John Winthrop took his fleet of eleven ships to found the Massachusetts Bay Colony in 1630, when people seriously wondered if any of them would ever again be heard from. Still, for Benson, it was a huge step, to uproot himself from England and to take all his possessions with him to this unknown continent.

The answer, he quickly decided, was the church, and his family heritage. His father Samuel had been a devout member of his congregation among the English who referred to themselves as "the godly," and whom others, initially in derision, labeled the Puritans. Samuel had fought in the Civil War against the forces of King Charles I, and Poole all through the war had been a Puritan stronghold. When the Puritans were removed from power in 1660 and Charles II was restored to the throne, the Puritans became dissenters and were essentially evicted from the Church of England, even though their original intent had been to remain part of the Church and to reform and purify it from within. As dissenters, the Puritans no longer had a centralized program or authority, and individual congregations interpreted religious developments and doctrines in their own way.

Ezekiel Hawkins, the popular and articulate leader of Benson's congregation in Poole, had been becoming increasingly dissatisfied with the policies of the King and the Church authorities. Puritan emigration to Massachusetts had been at its peak in the decade 1630-40 and all emigration had ceased with the start of the Civil War. Occasionally, however, a congregation would take the plunge and decide to emigrate. Hawkins was now preaching that their religious beliefs were no longer secure in England. He had been in correspondence with associates in the town of Middleborough, Massachusetts. The village had been burned during the King Philip's War with the Indians in 1675-76, and the town fathers were looking to rebuild and repopulate. They would welcome an infusion of new blood from the old country. Hawkins preached that in Massachusetts, far from the prying eyes of the King and the Church establishment, they would have the freedom to worship as they chose.

Benson was unmarried, had completed his apprenticeship as a blacksmith, and after Samuel's death had few remaining relatives in Poole. It seemed most sensible to join the rest of the congregation in the journey to resettle in Middleborough. At least it had seemed the best thing to do before the seasickness took hold.

Max Weber and the Protestant Ethic

I've shown that we can trace important links between elements of evangelical religious thought in England in the early decades of the 19th century, and the economic thought that emerged in England during the later decades of that century. The strands of thought borrowed from evangelicalism are especially prominent when economists and policy-makers address personal responsibility, and consider measures that appear to them to threaten to undermine a sense of personal responsibility–no matter how many other good consequences might flow from those measures, such as preventing starvation in the midst of a major famine.

When we consider the form that economism assumes in the early 21st century in the U.S., we will find a good deal that seems to relate directly to the connection between evangelicalism and neoclassical economics. But we will also find elements that appear to have no origin in England in the 19th century. Simply put, the roots of economism in evangelicalism explain why policymakers today would favor policies that fail to help the poor, but not why they would favor policies that explicitly aid the rich.

We have seen in the development of evangelical thought a considerable worry about wealth. To the evangelical, a wealthy man was in more jeopardy of his immortal soul than a poor man. The poor were tempted by the obvious sins of the flesh; but the rich might be tempted in more subtle ways which were harder to detect and guard against.

In particular, the rich were tempted by an economic system based increasingly on credit, and what the evangelicals considered speculation. The old agrarian England, in which wealth was something solid–you either had gold or you had land, or both–had only recently been challenged by a new economic order based on manufacturing and trade. There was a very fine line, if any at all, between legitimate business practices and illegitimate "speculation," and woe to one's chances of eternal life if one crossed that line.[1]

The attitude of economism today in the U.S. is far different. Not only is wealth glorified, but a public policy is seen as especially wise and justified precisely to the extent that it favors the rich. According to this line of thought, the rich appear to be God's chosen people. Moreover, the policies that favor the rich are widely endorsed by the Christian fundamentalist leaders of the religious right. If one has read in the Gospels that a camel can more easily pass through the eye of a needle than can a rich man enter heaven, and that one cannot serve both God and Mammon, the present worship of wealth along with the "free market" seems to require some explanation.

I suggest that we can find that explanation only by tracing the historical origins of American thought back to its Puritan roots in New England in the 17th and 18th centuries. The idea that the rich are especially God's chosen people is not an evangelical idea; it is an idea with complex roots going back to Puritanism and that religion's origins in Calvinism. And to guide us on this historical exploration, I shall draw on the early 20th century German sociologist, Max Weber (1864-1920). Weber first published the essays that later were gathered under the title, *The Protestant Ethic and the Spirit of Capitalism*, in 1904-5.[2] The term we commonly use today, "Protestant ethic," is Weber's creation.

Weber had a specific agenda. He believed that the emergence of a vigorous capitalist economy in particular parts of the world, at particular times in history, could not be explained only by the local material conditions. He noted, for example, that the city of Florence in the 14th and 15th centuries had all the material wealth, trade, and scholarly and technical learning that one would think necessary for the emergence of a capitalist system. By contrast,

Pennsylvania at the beginning of the 1700s was a primitive, backwoods colony only a step above a barter economy. Yet, as Weber viewed the matter, capitalism found a firmer foundation and a more welcome home in the latter place and time.[3] The lesson he drew from this is that there had to be something about the *thought* of a people and of a period that created the conditions needed for capitalism to take root and to flourish. And he imagined that only *religious* thought got deep enough into peoples' psyches to do the job.

Weber's ideas in the history and sociology of religion and of economics have stimulated a good deal of controversy. Some claim that there are so many reasons why capitalism might or might not emerge, or take a certain form, in any country and at any time, that it is foolish to single out particular religious thoughts as having special importance.[4] Some claim that Weber is simply wrong in ascribing advanced capitalistic practices to Protestant countries–the U.S. and northern Europe–and ignoring similar practices in other parts of the world. In short, Weber, seen in his own time as a ground-breaking sociologist, is no longer in the sociological mainstream. Fortunately, for our purposes, we can ignore almost all of the controversy associated with Weber's thinking on the origins of capitalism.

Another criticism of Weber comes from the history of religion. When Weber wrote at the beginning of the 20th century, people widely ascribed to a certain stereotyped view of the Puritans in America. Later historical research has turned this stereotype on its head—revealing, for example, that the Puritans actually had nothing against sex (or dancing for that matter). Leland Ryken, a professor of English, has usefully assembled the more recent understanding of Puritanism in his book, *Worldly Saints: The Puritans as They Really Were.*[5] Ryken takes issue with Weber's account, accusing Weber of mixing up some undoubted elements of Puritan thought with later Protestant and secular beliefs.[6] But Weber, in many ways, would not disagree, especially since Ryken stops his account of Puritan thinking and practice at 1700, and Weber is concerned to trace the evolution of that thought to the present time, regardless of what name it falls under.

For our purposes, the best way to take advantage of Weber's insights into how ideas transform themselves over time while retaining important vestiges of their religious origins, and at the same time to recognize a historical understanding of the actual Puritan doctrines, is to divide our discussion into three phases—the original Calvinist doctrines, which both Weber and Ryken agree formed the basis for Puritan thought;[7] English and American Puritanism up till around 1700; and later developments.

Calvin and the Logic of Religion

In order to track American Puritan thought, Weber suggests that we first need to understand the origins of Puritanism in the doctrines of the French-Swiss theologian John Calvin (1509-64). Weber argues that Calvin's teachings were psychologically unstable in an important way, and that instability led to their morphing into the later stages of Puritan thinking. It is those later stages, more than the original Calvinist roots, that had the greatest impact on American thought today.

Calvin thought about God in a rigorous and coldly logical way. He began with the premise that God is all-knowing and all-powerful. Calvin figured that such a God would of necessity have dictated exactly what would happen in the world, throughout eternity, from the very first moment of existence--the doctrine of predestination. It follows logically from predestination that everything that happens to each of us, in this life and the next, was fully planned out by God long before we were born. It is quite silly to think that any action we could take today could alter God's plan. Imagine, for instance, that we pray to God to ask a certain favor. This is doubly mistaken. It is mistaken because it assumes that God might alter his plan, but if his plans can be altered, he is not all-powerful. It is also mistaken because it assumes that we, as humans, might alter God's will, but that assumes that humans are more powerful than God. That latter idea is both wrong and intolerably arrogant.

God is all-knowing and all-powerful, but we as humans are miserable sinners who deserve nothing but death and hellfire. It follows logically from that difference in our respective status, that just as it is in vain for us to imagine that we as humans could *alter* God's plan, it is similarly arrogant of us to imagine that we could even *understand* God's plan. God's plan for us and for the entire universe, set as in stone from the first moment of creation, is a closed book to the likes of us. As soon as we think that we can detect a pattern in the thinking of God, that seems to make sense to us, it is probably a sign that we are in over our heads and are sure to misunderstand God's will and design.

Despite the apparent logic of his own utter inability to understand God's plan, Calvin was pretty certain about one aspect of it. Calvin thought it very clear that God had predestined the vast majority of humankind to eternal damnation and only a relatively small minority to salvation. Those who were to be saved did not deserve it because of anything they were or had done; it was simply a part of God's plan. Those who were to be saved, similarly, could not know that they were saved, because God's plan was opaque to miserable, sinful humans. Christ had indeed died to atone for human sin, but on this doctrine, he had only died for the Elect–those who were predestined by God to be saved. There was nothing equal-opportunity about Christ's sacrifice and atonement; so far as the majority of humankind went, it made no difference and they were destined for hell.

Since being among the Elect is unrelated to what you happen to do or not to do in life, and has to do only with God's plan as predestined from the moment of creation, you can no more make yourself go to hell through your own bad behavior, than you could earn a place in heaven through your own good behavior (if you were not already one of the Elect). Calvin assumed that you were one of the Elect, God's grace would come out through your life and deeds, do whatever you will. You could not be bad; in effect you would be forced to be good. And this doctrine opened the door a tiny crack for the possibility that you could, after all, find out if you were of the Elect or not. If you, or anyone else, was seen acting in such a way as to suggest God's irresistible grace, then it might be a good bet that that person was among the Elect. The trouble was that it was easy to be mistaken in such a judgment. Consider, for instance, a person who appears to lead a long and blameless life, only to act in a terribly sinful way at the very end. The Calvinist theory is that this person was among the damned from the very beginning, and the appearances of grace that showed throughout the person's earlier life were all illusory.

As Weber summarized it, Calvin dispensed with the loving God of the New Testament, and even with the vengeful and wrathful God of the Old Testament.[8] His God was a logical construction, a completely transcendental God divorced from human understanding as well as from human contact. And, more to the point for our inquiry, it seemed a matter of complete indifference to this God whether anyone was rich or poor—except for the fact that one's state of wealth or poverty had been predestined along with every other detail of one's life.

One element of Calvin's teaching, however, turned out to be very important in later developments of this line of thought. Since God had created the world and everything in it—including riches and money—then it necessarily followed that there was nothing inherently sinful about wealth. Ryken notes that Calvin himself said, "money in itself is good," and further quoted the influential English Puritan Richard Baxter (1615-1691), "All love of the creature, the world, or riches is not sin. For the works of God are all good, as such."[9] We will see in a minute, however, that the Puritan descendents of Calvinism had definite views about when and how wealth was a good thing.

From Calvinism to Puritanism

Having gotten this far with Calvin's doctrines, Weber took off his historian's hat and undertook to be a psychologist. He concluded that any religion organized according to Calvin's doctrines simply could not last for any length of time. People, Weber thought, would not stand for any church that could not tell them whether or not they were saved. So the Puritan authorities who succeeded Calvin very quickly began backtracking on the rigorous logic of the initial doctrines.[10] Ryken depicts Puritanism as overall a much more hopeful religion than austere Calvinism, stressing the potential of God's grace and of salvation through faith, rather than the risk that one might not be among the Elect. In many ways the Puritans in England and the American colonies in the 17th century thought much as the 19th century English evangelicals that we encountered in the last chapter, stressing both the inherent, total depravity of mankind left to its own devices, and the possibility of salvation through faith in Christ.[11]

While he had been unable to address the human need to know one's own state of salvation, Calvin had left a number of building blocks out of which later Puritan thought could be assembled. First, Calvin shared with Luther and the other Protestant reformers the conviction that the truly Godly person was a person of this world, and not of some other. Since God had determined everything from the first moment, he had also determined the structure of everyday human society. This world existed for only one reason--to embody, to magnify and to proclaim the glory of God. To participate in that endeavor, one did not have to withdraw into a monastery or become a religious hermit. One could go about one's normal, everyday business. Indeed--and this was critical to Weber's argument on the later origins of "the spirit of capitalism"--one's normal, everyday business should be seen as one's religious *calling*. Weber thought it important to discern a subtle difference between the Lutheran and Calvinist views of this calling. On the Lutheran account, it was more or less a matter of fate. If you worked at a menial job for low pay, you simply had to accept it as God's will. To the Calvinist, your calling was a religious duty, not simply something you had to accept. If you worked at a menial job for low pay, you had to work hard at your job every day as if the future of the world depended on it. For that job was part of God's design for a society that accorded with his divine laws; and your working hard at your menial job was your way of magnifying the glory of God in keeping with his design of the world.[12] And–which will become very important later–if this was so for working for a menial job at low pay, it was also true of Bill Gates and Donald Trump. Moreover, if your work was a calling, then whatever natural talents you happened to have for any certain kind of work was God's gift, bestowed not because you deserved it, but as a matter of divine grace.[13]

It's easy to misunderstand what was going on here. We have to remember what Calvinism denied–that you could win yourself a place in heaven, if you were not predestined as one of the Elect, *by means of* your hard work in your "calling." No matter what happened, you could not accomplish that feat. The very idea of a "self-made man" would have been anathema to the Puritans, who would have seen such ideas as a serious risk to one's salvation.[14] Still, by doing your duty faithfully, you could magnify and reflect the glory of God on this earth, and in doing so (to go back to the earlier Calvinist concept) *indicate* your *probable* status as one of the Elect.

Since working hard at one's vocation in life was a way to glorify God, the Puritans believed that the primary rewards for such service were spiritual and moral, not material. Ryken again quotes Richard Baxter, "[W]hen two callings equally conduce to the public good, and one of them hath the advantage of riches and the other is more advantageous to your souls, the latter must be preferred."[15] An earlier English Puritan, William Perkins (1558-1602), instructed his followers on the priorities to be addressed in the proper distribution of one's wealth. Maintaining oneself came first, followed by aiding family and close friends. Next came, in order, "relief of the poor," maintenance of the Church, and "maintenance of the Commonwealth."[16]

Poverty was also a part of God's plan, but the Puritans did not consider it a sign of divine disfavor or a moral failing. The Puritans agreed with the later evangelicals that God might bestow poverty on a person as a divine gift, as a way to prompt one to search one's soul and correct moral failings. But in general poverty and wealth were equal—each could pose temptations of its own sort, distracting one from religious contemplation and concern for salvation by focusing one's attention on material things. The Puritans also agreed with the evangelicals that as a rule, the rich should have more concerns for their eternal souls than the poor. Wealth seemed to them to create more temptations to distract one from the duty to serve God, and one such threat was the very idea that Weber later stressed—the idea that one must deserve one's wealth because one had been especially worthy in the eyes of God.[17]

From Puritanism to the Protestant Ethic

In one way, things had not worked out in the New World as Josiah Benson had imagined they would. His congregation's sense of religious freedom had proven to be short-lived. In the decade after they had arrived, the British Crown had tightened control over the governance of Massachusetts. The Puritans, for instance, had demanded the right to banish Quakers from their midst, and to execute them if they would not leave. The new laws now demanded tolerance for the Quakers, and a new Royal governor had been sent over to enforce them. Hard upon that event came the witch trials in Salem, Massachusetts, which inaugurated a period of reaction against the heavy-handedness and power of the Puritan clergy. Ezekiel Hawkins, the fiery minister, had been marginalized within the Middleborough community.

But Benson was mildly surprised to realize how little most of this now mattered to him. He had been startled to arrive in Massachusetts, the cradle of Puritan religious freedom, to learn that fewer men were attending church, and that many congregations were made up mostly of women (even though women were still forbidden from speaking in the church service). Yet the little town seemed to be thriving, and Benson along with it. He quickly earned enough as an assistant to the town's only established blacksmith to open his own smithy, and from the start he had been successful. He had found favor in the eyes of Annabelle Richards, another member of the congregation, and they were to be married next April. The future, he decided, looked very bright indeed. The ocean voyage of 1684 had for him proved fortunate.[18]

Cotton Mather (1663-1728), one of the later American Puritan thinkers, wrote, "Religion begat prosperity and the daughter devoured the mother."[19] Mather had in mind something like what happened to Josiah Benson. If you indeed work hard every day, as if the whole world depended on it, then whether you start off rich or poor, after a while you're going to have more wealth than you had before. And if you are thrifty and cautious in how you spend your money, your wealth is likely to grow even more. In this way Puritanism seemed to work against itself. The habits of mind it instilled in its followers tended to produce material prosperity, but the original Puritan teachings warned that this very prosperity could cause one to turn away from a proper religious devotion and humility.

As we follow Josiah Benson out of the 17th and into the 18th century, we begin to part company with the mainstream Puritan thought, according to Ryken. He suggests that what comes later, even if it retains its Puritan roots, should be viewed as Protestant or secular, depending on the details.[20] Weber, writing earlier, seemed to view the evolution of these ideas more as a continuum. For our purposes, the exact label does not matter so long as we remember the religious origins of the core ideas. So we can follow Ryken and refer to the next stage as a "Protestant ethic" rather than as a direct continuation of Puritan thought.

So suppose that you work industriously, make money, and invest that wealth shrewdly in such a way as to make even more money. (And we will suppose, here and later, that you do so only in a legal and ethical fashion.) What are we then to make of this? According to Calvin, since God's laws and God's grand design were of this world as well as the next, wealth in and of itself had no sinful connotations. And later Protestant thinkers came to regard this savings, investment, and increase in wealth as a religious duty. They reasoned–if you had the opportunity to become wealthier, it could only have been because God willed it; so if you pass up that opportunity, you are acting as if you could thwart God's plan, which is hardly the right sort of attitude. As Weber noted,

> Wealth is thus bad ethically only in so far as it is a temptation to idleness and sinful enjoyment of life, and its acquisition is bad only when it is with the purpose of living merrily and without care. But as a performance of duty in a calling it is not only morally permissible, but actually enjoined. ... To wish to be poor was, it was often argued, the same as wishing to be unhealthy; it is objectionable as a glorification of works and derogatory to the glory of God.[21]

One step at a time, Protestant thought was creeping up on the idea, not only that material wealth and worldly success was a good thing in the eyes of God, but that seeing oneself become successful and wealthy was the strongest possible sign of God's grace and of one's status among the Elect.

Weber pointed out that among Protestant writers of this period, the Book of Job seemed to be a special Biblical favorite. He suggested that there were two reasons why this text should especially resonate. First, the story of Job reinforces the lesson that God's plan is too mysterious for humans to understand, and humans must accept this. Job initially feels emboldened to demand from God an account of why God has made Job suffer after he had led a life of holiness. God chastises Job for imagining that he could put his puny human intellect on a level anywhere near that of God's. But the second reason was that after Job has been appropriately put in his place, God rewards him in the end not only with spiritual, but *especially with material wealth.*[22] In short, the Book of Job was further reaffirmation, from scriptural authority, that one could find in one's accumulation of wealth on this earth a sure sign of God's favor.

Benjamin Franklin plays a special role in Weber's analysis of the Protestant ethic and its influence on the rise of American capitalism. Weber lists the homilies in Franklin's *Autobiography* that glorify a life of industriousness and thrift, and that see wasting money and wasting time as, between them, the deadliest sins. The result of living one's life in the service of thrift, according to Franklin, was very simple–one would make more money. Franklin seemed unconcerned to offer any reason as to *why* it was good to live one's life so that making more money was one's highest goal. When he felt pressed, he cited a Biblical quotation: "Seest thou a man diligent in his business? He shall stand before kings" (Prov. 22, 29). Weber feels that this quotation is especially emblematic of the process of the development of American popular culture. Franklin, he noted, was not himself a Puritan; he was, as Weber put it, a "colourless deist" in his own religious orientation.[23] Weber asserted that the quotation from Proverbs had been one "which his strict Calvinist father drummed into him again and again in his youth."[24] Nothing could better drive home Weber's main point–that whether today's Americans are Puritans or Calvinists in any sense of the term does not matter. These ideas were introduced into our culture at an especially formative period and have outlasted religious changes ever since: "[T]he idea of duty in one's calling prowls about in our lives like the ghost of dead religious beliefs."[25]

I suggest that since the time of Franklin, the exact nature of what Weber called the "Protestant ethic" has continued gradually to evolve. Weber, from his vantage point roughly a century ago, had already noted some changing features. We could begin with the idea that God's plan for the universe is as evident in this world as in the next, and so when we work industriously in our everyday occupations, we are serving God and carrying out his plan–so that our work represents a type of religious calling. We next go to the idea that if industrious work yields an increase in wealth, that outcome is something we can tolerate, since to refuse to become wealthy under those circumstances would seem to be thumbing our noses at God's plans for us and for society. We then make the big jump from an increase in wealth being something we can tolerate, to an increase in wealth being something that we avidly seek, because especially through that means we can find a clue that God considers us among the Elect and that our salvation is guaranteed.

The next step in the process is to find more room for seeking and glorifying comfort. Weber believed that this step in reasoning had been thoroughly completed in his day. Using his fellow Germans as his example, he imagined that his forebears had rejected the ostentatious wealth of the landed gentry in the old days of feudalism, and regarded that sort of wealth as leading to fleshly temptations that the godly citizen would avoid. But, in the minds of the German burgher, there was a clear distinction between that feudal (that is, pre-Protestant) display of wealth and "the clean and solid comfort of the middle-class home."[26] To seek sufficient wealth to assure that you and your family enjoyed that level of comfort did not seem, at least by Weber's day, to be in any way incompatible with the "ascetic" Protestant ethic:

> When later the principle 'to make the most of both worlds' [that is, the Earth and the hereafter] became dominant . . ., a good conscience simply became one of the means of enjoying a comfortable bourgeois life . . . . What the great religious epoch of the seventeenth century bequeathed to its utilitarian successor was, however, above all an amazingly good . . . conscience in the acquisition of money, so long as it took place legally.[27]

The final step in reasoning that Weber could discern a century ago brought the Protestant ethic into closer proximity to evangelical thought. After we have developed an easy conscience that accepts wealth and comfort as religiously commendable pursuits, what are we to make of our fellow human beings who do not achieve these ends? Weber concluded that the Protestant ethic "gave [the middle-class businessman] the comforting assurance that the unequal distribution of the goods of this world was a special dispensation of Divine Providence, which in these differences, as in particular grace, pursued secret ends unknown to men."[28] In sum, on this view of the Protestant ethic, we had become very selective in which parts of God's plan we could know and which we could not. We had found it psychologically intolerable (Weber argued) to imagine, along with the coldly logical Calvin, that none of us could be assured of our own place among the Elect who were predestined for salvation. So Protestant thought evolved to allow us both to enjoy wealth and luxury on earth, and also to see in those accomplishments a reassuring sign of God's grace. But when it came to addressing the plight of our neighbors who were less well off in material possessions, the supposed inscrutability of God's plan to us mere humans came back full force. Surely we were rich and they were poor so as to serve some Divine plan, but of course we humans could not understand just what that plan was, and we certainly had no business questioning it. In this fashion we were relieved of any sense of guilt for being well-fed while others were starving, and we were relieved especially of any sense of responsibility to aid our less fortunate neighbors—an idea that, we have seen, actually was quite foreign to the Puritans.

This, in sum, was how Weber saw the later developments of the Protestant ethic from his vantage point in the early years of the 20th century. We must remember that Weber intended here to pass no value judgments. He thought of himself as a social scientist simply telling us the facts. He thought that certain religious ideas had been prevalent among certain people at a certain time; that as a result of those ideas, those people tended to behave in certain ways; and that those ways of behaving helped to stimulate the full development of the capitalist economic system. Whether either those religious ideas, or capitalism itself, were good or bad, was simply beyond his purview.

But much has changed in the century since Weber completed his study, and we need to update the account in a few particulars. The comfortable middle-class German businessman might seem the pinnacle of the Protestant-capitalist culture when the economic system was heavily tilted toward manufacturing. That view of capitalism fit especially well with Weber's ideas about the Protestant ethic, which simultaneously encouraged hard work and discouraged economic consumption. If you work hard but do not spend much, you will eventually have a lot of capital to invest in new manufacturing ventures, and that will be very good for the economy of the time.

What happens when we enter increasingly into a service economy, and when we realize that to an increasing extent, the health of our economy depends on consumption? What happens, for example, when we are in the year 2008, and as part of George W. Bush's economic stimulus package, we receive our income tax rebate checks–and are told that the patriotic thing to do is to go out and buy things, while if we put the money in savings, we'd be failing to help the economy in its time of peril? I would offer the suggestion that it is pretty natural, in this evolving economy, to gradually loosen our commitment to a comfortable middle-class idea of comfort, and to gradually extend the "Godly" lifestyle to include more and more luxury and consumption. The rich who spend their wealth on fancy cars and yachts and big houses must be the favorites of God because they became wealthy in the first place; and by spending their money that way they are stimulating the economy to assure that the rest of us have jobs. So it would be very shortsighted to criticize their behavior on any religious grounds. No snide comments about the camel and the eye of the needle are welcome here any longer.

I recall in my roughly four decades of adult life hearing radio and television advertisements for banks and investment firms. The services that were being offered to the listener, over all those years, were roughly the same. But the terminology used to describe those services has undergone a notable change. Until rather recently, the ads would have said that these firms would help me plan for my retirement or invest my *savings*. There was, in general, a strictly middle-class, Franklinesque ring to what was offered. Within the past decade (as best as I can recall), I am now being offered services for *wealth management*. The word "wealth," which would have been unseemly from a middle-class point of view in earlier years, has now become acceptable to say out loud. I can now state publicly that I plan to be wealthy, that middle-class prosperity is no longer enough for me–that I want Donald Trump to move over. I believe that this is one small bit of evidence for a shift in American popular culture that supports the changes I am describing.

The Two Gilded Ages

The moderate idea that those who enjoy material wealth in their earthly life may have been especially favored by God seems gradually to have morphed into the extreme idea that God wishes us to bestow on the super-rich our adulation and unquestioning allegiance. The transition, however, has not been smooth or consistent. At certain times, Americans have seemed ready to withdraw into their own private lives and allow the special interests and the lobbyists to run the country, letting the wealthiest class get away with anything they wished. At other times, Americans supported major reforms to limit the excesses of wealth and power in the hands of the few, and to demand protections and support for those at the bottom and middle of the social ladder.

Historian Stephanie Coontz suggests that we've had two Gilded Ages in our history, the first roughly 1870-1890 and the second more or less a century afterwards (though I would suggest that we have not yet emerged from the second). She lists the major parallels: "In both periods . . . there was an orgy of wealth-seeking among the rich, an intensification of economic distress among the poor, and a retreat of the middle class from previous involvement in social reform."[29]

The parallel between the two Gilded Ages is even more striking, however, because during each the same religious and moral arguments were trotted out in defense of the common prejudices of the day. Seeing these further parallels reinforces the claim that today's economism-related beliefs have origins that go well back in our religious history.

For example, Reverend Russell Conwell's lecture called "Acres of Diamonds" proved so popular after he first wrote it in 1870 that he was called upon to give it six thousand times over the next quarter century. He preached: "I say you ought to get rich, and it is your duty to get rich." The possibility that anyone among his audience might have difficulty in carrying out this injunction appears not to have bothered him much: "There is not a poor person in the United States who was not made so by his own shortcomings, or by the shortcomings of some one else. It is all wrong to be poor, anyhow."[30] Bishop William Lawrence of Massachusetts chimed in, "Godliness is in league with riches . . . [Wealth is] a reward and honor which God delights to bestow upon an upright people."[31]

Alongside the notion that God favors the wealthy (and so must super-favor the super-wealthy) re-emerged the evangelical tendency to decry any efforts to offer assistance to the poor out of fear of worsening their lot in this world, if not in the next. Andrew Carnegie, the steel magnate who was probably the richest man in the world at the start of the 20th century, recommended in his essay, "The Gospel of Wealth," that his fellow millionaires live modestly and give back the majority of their wealth to the community by supporting such institutions as libraries, museums, and schools. But Carnegie also believed firmly in what conservative economists in the late 1970s would term moral hazard, as we'll explore at length in Chapter 6. Here Carnegie waxes eloquent about how a friend of his nearly destroyed Western civilization through a single ill-considered act of so-called charity:

> A well-known writer of philosophic books admitted the other day that he had given a quarter of a dollar to a man who approached him as he was coming to visit the house of his friend. He knew nothing of

the habits of this beggar; knew not the use that would be made of this money, although he had every reason to suspect that it would be spent improperly. ...[T]he quarter-dollar given that night will probably work more injury than all the money which its thoughtless donor will ever be able to give in true charity will do good. He only gratified his own feelings, saved himself from annoyance,—and this was probably one of the most selfish and very worst actions of his life, for in all respects he is most worthy.[32]

It seems clear that Carnegie bought thoroughly into the old evangelical distinction between the deserving and the undeserving poor—though, if he had listened to preachers like Conwell and Lawrence, he might well have concluded that no poor people actually fell into the deserving class, as their very poverty sufficed to condemn them morally. However, if there was anything that distinguished the first Gilded Age from the second, it was the view that moral hazard was equal-opportunity, threatening the rich and middle-class as well as the poor. A would-be social reformer declared in 1887 that the gift of a single cord of wood could "ruin the best family in Boston."[33]

By contrast, during the second Gilded Age--in the decade of the 1990s when the Internet boom was riding high, just before the dot-com bubble burst-- Thomas Frank was astounded by the degree to which American culture granted privileged status to the new super-rich. People became ecstatic over the news that billionaire executives went to work in jeans, that Bill Gates and Warren Buffett loved to wolf down hamburgers just like common folk. The super-rich were extolled for working extremely hard and long hours—"The none too subtle implication, of course, was that these men deserved their riches. They were rich because they had somehow done the labor of a million other men, created all manner of good things in direct proportion to their reward."[34]

Frank saw here a huge inversion of American popular cultural values within one generation. During the 1950s and 1960s, he noted, it was simply taken for granted that what made America great was the relative equality in wealth and opportunity. Yet by 1999, Lester Thurow, an economist ecstatic over the rise of the dot-com economy, could proclaim that Americans were "comfortable with inequalities" and that one could not find "anyone of importance to suggest that Americans ought to change the system" that promoted an increasingly unequal distribution of wealth.[35] *Wired* magazine, similarly glorying in all the new Internet start-up companies that would soon cause a major crash in the stock market, even went so far as to claim that the middle and upper classes had traded places—the poor CEOs were overworked while the obviously less productive middle class had become the new leisure class.[36]

Wealth and Culture Codes

How does all this look to a person who is not originally a member of our American society? Clotaire Rapaille, a psychoanalyst turned business consultant, emigrated from France to the U.S. Puzzled by the differences in the cultures of these two nations, he developed methods for studying and eliciting what he came to call the "culture codes," which he described in a popular book of that title.[37]

Among the concepts that Rapaille looked into was *luxury*, and he concluded that in the American culture, the "code" for luxury was "military stripes." As he explained it:

[T]his Code is an extension of the Code for money. Military stripes are a form of proof, something you wear on your sleeve for all to respect. These Codes are very closely linked, not only because one needs money to buy luxury items but because when Americans attain the 'proof" of money, they use luxury items to show it off.[38]

And just what is money and luxury goods "proof" of?

What is the purpose of these [military] stripes? Largely, it is recognition; not recognition of how much money you have, though, but of your goodness. At an unconscious level, Americans believe that good people succeed, that success is bestowed upon you by God. Your success demonstrates that God loves you.[39]

Rapaille studied psychoanalysis but not cultural anthropology. Had he looked into the latter, he might have found some criticisms of his approach–in particular, his assumption that culture is largely a static thing, and is not constantly evolving as different cultures constantly rub up against each other. With those criticisms in mind, he might have asked–just for how long has the

American culture seen luxury as "encoded" by military stripes? Had he asked, he might have decided that this shift was of fairly recent origin. Until recently, the more traditional version of the Puritan ethic might have held sway, and with it the idea that luxury was unacceptable ostentation, ultimately a sign of wastefulness and idleness. Only in a nation and culture in which economism has come to dominate public policy discussion, might it seem routine to imagine that luxury acquisitions could function as "military stripes" in this sense.

Believing in Bubbles

Now that the fully updated Protestant ethic is in place in our culture, let's explore its possible implications with just one more recent example. Consider one of the economic debacles of the 21st century: Enron. Defenders of the market, and of supply-side economics, will immediately object that it's unfair to focus on this example. The Enron executives that got into that mess engaged in illegal behavior. We should not blame the entire business community because a few crooks go over the top.

The point to which I want to call attention here, however, is not how typical or atypical Enron might be, or what its behavior says about other companies. I simply want to make note of the fact that (so far as I can tell), right up to the time when the bubble burst, the architects of Enron *were thought of very widely in the U.S. as financial geniuses* and were vastly admired.

To an economics neophyte such as me, Enron looked like a classic bubble. I think we all know what a financial bubble is—we'll talk more about bubbles (and about Enron in particular) in Chapter 9. Enron, to the uninitiated at any rate, appeared to stop producing anything of value early on; after that it merely made a lot of deals and spun off subsidiaries. The subprime mortgage market seemed like a novel fiscal invention until one made note of the fact that it was based on the hope that housing prices would always rise. In hindsight, both of these phenomena appeared clearly to be bubbles. So the question is–if they looked like bubbles, walked like bubbles, and quacked like bubbles, what led apparently smart people to conclude that they were works of financial genius?

One fairly straightforward answer presents itself. Through history, bubbles have followed one another at varying intervals, and whenever the next one arises, people forget whatever lessons they learned the last time. We humans, offered apparently easy money, get greedy, and greed clouds our judgment. Each time something new appears on the scene, offering us fast riches for no effort but looking on close inspection like a classic bubble, we find all sorts of reasons why *this time* it must not be a bubble, but some totally new financial invention never seen before. Surely, in the past, everything that looked like this turned out to be a bubble; but *this time* very smart people are in charge and they have figured out a new, magic formula to make sure that it really is a sound, risk-free investment. And so we continue to prove (as P.T. Barnum apparently never actually said) that suckers are born with considerable frequency.

But a second answer is now available to us that can keep company with the first answer. Certainly our own greed and wish-fulfillment play a role. But suppose, in addition, we have been conditioned to believe that wealth is an infallible sign of God's favor. The Enron executives all became extremely rich. If so, then what could possibly be wrong with their schemes? God had clearly smiled on their efforts; in effect, they were doing God's work. To doubt their financial acumen would seem almost sacrilegious.

The Enron example illustrates how deeply into the basic American cultural consciousness the evolved Protestant ethic may have wormed its way. We imagine that the rich are especially worthy people, because their wealth is a sign of God's favor. We may add, if we think about it, that they must be wealthy *because* they worked very industriously to get that way; we dismiss any thought that they could be wealthy because of luck. But this reasoning is really circular. We assume they worked hard because they have been favored by God, and we assume God would only favor the industrious; and we know that they are industrious because God favored them, and we know that God favored them because they are rich. So, when the rich are involved, we seem willing to suspend our judgment to a considerable degree. Behavior that would seem frankly slimy if folks like us did it–such as creating a speculative bubble as a get-rich-quick scheme–somehow becomes commendable when the rich engage in it.

Economism: Religion, Ideology, or Opportunism?

Before we leave Puritanism and evangelicalism, I should address a final question. I have, up till now, been referring to economism as *religion*. But there are at least three alternative ways to view it.[40]

- *Economism as religion*: I prefer this alternative for two main reasons. First, I have tried to show that in terms of its internal logic, economism functions more like religion than like science. Second, I have tried to trace economism's historical roots to religious sources.

- *Economism as ideology*: Economism, as it functions today, seems much more like an ideology than a true religion.[41] Moreover, calling it a religion might hint at an underlying anti-religious attitude, which is not at all what I wish to convey.

- *Economism as opportunism*: As we will see in the next chapter, economism seems to be shot through and through with stealth, hardly ever showing its true colors. So why do we not simply acknowledge this? Why glorify it as either religion or ideology, as if it is a truly coherent and comprehensive system of beliefs? Why not just say that a set of wealthy and greedy people have captured the reins of power in our society, and that economism is simply their propaganda campaign to get the rest of us to accept and even celebrate their victory—regardless of whether it makes any sense for us or for the public good?

I am sympathetic to the claims of ideology as an alternative label. Regarding internal logic, there is little difference between a religious and an ideological belief system, at least for our purposes here. And viewing economism as ideology would follow sensibly from Weber's comment about "ghosts of dead religions"—how a set of beliefs that at one time was at home within a religious framework have morphed subsequently into an ideology relatively divorced from those religious origins.

I do, however, believe that we give up something of importance if we too quickly adopt the label "ideology." One of the most important questions we have to answer about economism is: why have we, the American public, been so eager to drink its brand of Kool-aid? If it is as little supported by any facts, and its consequences have been so deleterious, as I have described, why do we swallow it so readily? I believe that an important part of the answer (as we'll also explore more in the next chapter) is how comfortably its thinking seems to live alongside some of our core value commitments as Americans—our dedication to freedom and democracy, individualism, individual responsibility, and an ethic of hard work. Economists Richard Kozul-Wright and Paul Rayment describe the thinking of 19th-century political economists this way:

> [T]he combination of private property right with competition, with the associated elements of personal initiative and voluntary contract, not only underpinned the market economy but also reinforced the private virtues of hard work, honest dealing, self-reliance and personal responsibility, virtues also sanctioned by religion and seen as underpinning family life and the moral fabric of society at large.[42]

"Given the coalescence of an economic model with private virtue and public religion," Kozul-Wright and Rayment add, those 19th-century thinkers were certain that their economic truths would be spread around the world "by impersonal missionaries more powerful than those of Christianity and Islam."[43]

I suggest that the label "religion" captures that a bit better, especially in light of economism's historical roots, than does "ideology."

In the end, though, I completely agree with Duncan Foley: "Whether we call this ideology or theology or just plain opportunism is of less importance than recognizing it when it is happening and resisting it."[44]

We have now traced the religious thinking that undergirds today's economism back to its two sources, in evangelical and Puritan thought. Next we will explore further what shape economism takes today and how it manifests this religious heritage while disguising itself as hardheaded, mathematically precise science.

Notes

1. Hilton B. *The age of atonement: the influence of evangelicalism on social and economic thought, 1785-1865*. Oxford, UK: Clarendon Press, 1986, especially pp. 102-134

2. Weber M. *The protestant ethic and the spirit of capitalism*, trans. T. Parsons. Mineola, NY: Dover Publications, 2003.

3. Weber, *Protestant ethic:* 74-5.

4. Tawney RH. Foreward. In Weber, *Protestant ethic:* 8.

5. Ryken L. *Worldly saints: the Puritans as they really were*. Grand Rapids, MI: Zondervan, 1986. I am grateful to Dr. John H. Carrier for recommending this book.

6. Ryken, *Worldly saints*: 57.

7. Ryken, *Worldly saints*: 14-16.

8. I am grateful to Rabbi James Kessler of Galveston for pointing out that these respective images of God from the Old and New Testaments are stereotypes and omit important nuances.

9. Ryken, *Worldly saints*: 58.

10. Weber, *Protestant ethic:* 110-12.

11. Ryken, *Worldly saints*: 14-16. I am grateful to Dr. John H. Carrier for comments on the general continuities of Protestant thought from the time of the Reformation to the present day.

12. Weber, *Protestant ethic:* 160.

13. Ryken, *Worldly saints*: 29.

14. Ryken, *Worldly saints*: 32.

15. Ryken, *Worldly saints*: 31.

16. Ryken, *Worldly saints*: 67.

17. Ryken, *Worldly saints*: 60-62.

18. I have constructed the fictional tale of Josiah Benson from facts provided in a number of articles in Wikipedia, about the Puritans in England and in New England, and the histories of the towns alluded to; www.wikipedia.org.

19. Quoted by Ryken, *Worldly saints*: 63.

20. Ryken, *Worldly saints*: 29-32.

21. Weber, *Protestant ethic:* 163.

22. Weber, *Protestant ethic:* 164.

23. Weber, *Protestant ethic:* 53.

24. Weber, *Protestant ethic:* 53.

25. Weber, *Protestant ethic:* 182. Ryken, for his part, sees Franklin's beliefs as quite different from true Puritan thinking, for the reasons we discussed above; Ryken, *Worldly saints:* 29-30.

26. Weber, *Protestant ethic:* 171.

27. Weber, *Protestant ethic:* 176.

28. Weber, *Protestant ethic:* 177.

29. Coontz S. *The way we never were: American families and the nostalgia trap.* New York: Basic Books, 2000:104. The "previous" involvement in social reform among the middle class included the antislavery movement and active engagement in a variety of civic, religious, and political organizations prior to the Civil War. On the second Gilded Age, see also Bartels LM. *Unequal democracy: the political economy of the new Gilded Age.* New York: Russell Sage Foundation/Princeton University Press, 2008.

30. Coontz, *Way we never were:* 103.

31. Coontz, *Way we never were:* 106.

32. Carnegie A. The gospel of wealth. In: *The 'gospel of wealth' essays and other writings.* New York: Penguin, 2006: 1-12, quote p. 11.

33. Quoted in Coontz, *Way we never were:* 104.

34. Frank T. *One market under God: Extreme capitalism, market populism, and the end of economic democracy.* New York: Anchor, 2001:10.

35. Thurow L. *Building WEALTH,* New York: HarperCollins, 1999:199; quoted in Frank, *One market under God:* 12-14.

36. Frank, *One market under God:* 12-14.

37. Rapaille C. *The culture code: an ingenious way to understand why people around the world live and buy as they do.* New York: Broadway Books, 2007.

38. Rapaille, *Culture code:* 166.

39. Rapaille, *Culture code:* 166.

40. I am grateful to Jan Heller for this suggestion.

41. Margaret Somers, discussing market fundamentalism, which I argued is a synonym for economism, describes it throughout as an ideology; Somers

MR. *Genealogies of citizenship: markets, statelessness, and the right to have rights*. New York: Cambridge University Press, 2008; see especially pp. 73-74.

42. Kozul-Wright R, Rayment P. *The resistable rise of market fundamentalism: rethinking development policy in an unbalanced world*. New York: Zed Books, 2007: 21.

43. Kozul-Wright and Rayment, *Resistable rise*: 21. They in turn quote (in part) Hobsbawm EJ. *The age of capital*. London: Weidenfeld and Nicolson, 1977.

44. Foley DK. *Adam's fallacy: A guide to economic theology*. Cambridge, MA: Harvard University Press, 2006: 226.

Chapter 6.
The Reverse Robin Hood Rule: Economism as Stealth Policy

The Triumph of Supply-Side Economics

Jonathan Chait, senior editor of *The New Republic*, has written a highly partisan but still informative and entertaining book about supply-side economics, the most extreme form that economism has taken in the U.S. in the last thirty years. Supply-side economics adheres in many ways to neoclassical economics, but differs in attributing economic growth almost exclusively to tax rates. The message is: cut taxes (especially for the rich) and we will all be wealthy; increase taxes and we will experience economic disaster. Just what Chait thinks of supply-side thinking can easily be deduced from the title of his book--*The Big Con: The True Story of How Washington Got Hoodwinked and Hijacked by Crackpot Economics*.

Since "crackpot economics" is a serious charge, Chait goes to considerable lengths to back it up. First, as we briefly discussed in Chapter 3, Chait argues that it is almost impossible to find a legitimate professor of economics in a university department who believes wholeheartedly in supply-side theory. The originators of supply-side theory were for the most part not economists, but commentators like George Gilder who had few if any credentials in the field. Second, since supply-side economics became a central feature of American policy in the early 1980s, we have now had three decades to see how it works. Chait believes that the answer is clearly in–it does not work. The U.S. middle and lower classes are still waiting for the "trickle-down" prosperity that was promised as a result of the rich getting big tax cuts and investing that money in ways that create new jobs and expand the economy. The "rising tide that lifts all boats" has gone up and down since the Reagan years, but hardly ever in the way that supply-siders predicted. As we have noted, the yachts of the wealthiest are indeed riding high, but the dinghies of the middle class have gone up scarcely at all. Getting rid of burdensome government regulation, as supply-side theory demanded, yielded first the savings-and-loan debacle, and more recently the subprime mortgage bubble and the near-total collapse of the global financial system. Lionizing the leaders of industry who appeared to be acting in the ways most compatible with supply-side promises made the architects of Enron into national heroes, just before they were carted off to jail for their crimes.

Supply-side economics is a brand of economism because, as Chait shows, none of these actual experiences in the real world altered the faith of the true believers. The right wing of the Republican Party has responded to each proof of supply-side's failure by claiming that the problem is that people did not believe in it devoutly enough. Every policy that failed did so not because it was supply-side inspired; it failed because it did not go far enough in the supply-side direction. George W. Bush started out his presidency as a supply-side hero and ended as a widely reviled villain. The theory as to his downfall is not that supply-side policies did not work. Instead Bush was seen as not sufficiently like Reagan. Reagan, as Chait is careful to show, was himself not sufficiently like Reagan, and in his second term, some of the true supply-side faithful had doubts about him. To worship Reagan as they do now, the Republican right has had to reinvent Reagan, conveniently forgetting about some actions he took as president that did not hew to the supply-side creed.

Chait does not hold the rank and file of the Republican Party responsible for these developments:

> The anti-tax movement's triumph does not represent a bubbling up of grassroots sentiment within the Republican Party. It is a top-down takeover by an elite ideological vanguard that has successfully redefined Republicanism as conservatism, conservatism as Reaganism, and Reaganism as a relentless and uncompromising opposition to taxes, especially those paid by the rich. . . . the Republican agenda has increasingly become synonymous with the accumulated desires of its funding base.[1]

The phenomenon that Chait is describing here is what we most want to investigate in this chapter–how an economic policy that actually has widespread bad consequences could somehow be sold to us as the best ticket to success.

If the Calvinist-Puritan-Protestant ethic has the power over American popular thinking that I suggested in the previous chapter, then we are all susceptible to arguments that something is good for everyone because it is good for the wealthy. Chait observes:

> [Conservatives] believe very earnestly that what is good for the rich is good for the country. Some do so from their adherence to tenets of supply-side economics. Probably a greater number simply believe it in their gut. . . . Phil Gramm, the conservative former senator, used to say: "No poor man ever gave me a job."[2] This is a very old conservative sentiment–less Adam Smith than Edmund Burke, and one often verging on outright plutocracy. It has less to do with the Laffer Curve than an almost mystical faith in the centrality and virtue of the upper class.[3]

Chait uses the phrase "almost mystical faith" in a tone of wonderment, as if he cannot believe that what seems to be religious faith is, in fact, religiously based. After our history lessons, we should not be surprised to find a frankly religious sort of belief walking about the countryside dressed up as economic doctrine.

So how are we to explain the triumph of supply-side theory? Do we all, in fact, in our gut, believe that the rich deserve to be on top and that we should be happy with whatever crumbs they leave for us? Or is there a greater element of deception at work here–that those who call for supply-side policies have not described them accurately? This chapter will explore the latter possibility in more detail.

Economism: Deception at Its Core

While it may seem that I've been beating up on economism pretty severely thus far, I've actually been holding my fire. Let's stop for while to take stock of this idea: *Economism, at its very core, is a tissue of self-contradictions, inconsistencies, and falsehoods.* This sounds like an extreme condemnation, so let's take it step by step.

Let's start with economism's basic nature, which as we have said is to glorify and worship *the market.* Just what is "the market"? As we saw in Chapter 3, most people, when asked what the word "market" conjures up in their minds, would most likely describe something down-home and comfortable like a village market or a farmer's market. Unless you happen to be a stock trader or a speculator, the impersonal, global, financial monster we deal with today is unlikely to first come to mind. The comfortable, homey view of the market embodies very well what Adam Smith appears actually to have had in mind when he discussed markets in 1776. He was thinking of an institution that would be influenced and regulated by the social structures and moral values of the community. He had in mind a system where there was a rough equality of economic power, and where the actors knew each other as neighbors— whatever happened in the marketplace was something they had to live with in their community afterward. It's doubtful that Adam Smith had in mind a system where I could walk into a big-box store and buy a cheap shirt made halfway around the world, and never have laid eyes on the people who made the shirt, let alone become informed as to their lives and working conditions, or what the factory was doing to their local environment. To take the term "market" and then apply it, without modification or qualification, to the latter situation marked by such a high degree of impersonality, ignorance, and power disparity, is at its best a sort of bait-and-switch subterfuge.

Now of course economism is not only interested in glorifying "the market." Almost always, we are told, it is not just any old sort of market, it is the *free* market. So we might next ask what exactly is added to the concept of "market" by putting the word "free" in front of it. (It turns out that if you look carefully at the long text of *The Wealth of Nations,* Adam Smith talked about "market" all the time, but in only one place did he actually use the phrase "*free* market," and that was in the context of criticizing regulations legislated at the behest of woolen manufacturers to secure monopoly advantages.[4])

As we have also noted previously, when we try to find anywhere in the real world an example of an unregulated, unrestrained "free" market, we come up empty. Margaret Somers notes that there is no such thing as a market that does not function within a set of rules laid down by laws, tax codes, and so forth.[5] Economists Richard Kozul-Wright and Paul Rayment insist that:

> ...the economy is not an entity *sui generis* but a component of a larger political and social reality, a reality from which the market economy draws its legitimacy rather than the reverse. ... The idea that free markets are self-regulating provided that a few clear and well-enforced rules of the game are in place is a chimera; regulated markets are the norm.[6]

Duncan Foley adds:

> Contrary to the exaggerated claims of [those who distort Adam Smith], market capitalism is not a stable, self-regulating system. Just as it requires conscious political effort to foster the institutions necessary to make it function at all, it requires continuing political and regulatory intervention to keep the pursuit of self-interest from running off the rails.[7]

If no truly free markets exist, and markets by their very nature could not function if they were free, then why do advocates of economism insist on repeating the mantra "free market"? Margaret Somers offers an answer, that the "ideology of absolute market freedom is almost totally at odds with actually existing successful market societies, which rely heavily on social institutions (e.g. laws and tax codes) to protect the rich from the full market exposure while forcing market 'freedoms' on the rest of us."[8] In other words, the true way that real-world markets function is captured by the Golden Rule that does not appear in the Bible—that he who has the gold makes the rules. The rules that make the market unfree are virtually always designed so as to make the wealthy wealthier, and to give them ever more control over the strings of the economy so as to better pursue their own interests. But this is one of those dirty little secrets economism cannot say out loud; so its devotees hope that if they keep repeating the invocation "free market" enough times, we'll start to believe it and simply not notice for whose advantage the rules are actually working.

The phrase "free market" plays yet a further role in the economism agenda. As both Somers and Thomas Frank point out, one of the things economism hopes to convince us of is the legitimacy of the market, and of all "decisions" that can be attributed to it, and the corresponding illegitimacy of the actual democratic institutions in our nation, particularly government.[9] This shell game serves two purposes. When government sets out to regulate the market in a way that threatens the interests of the wealthy, distrust of government, and the supposed superiority of the market as a democratic institution, can be used to fight off the threat. But when the wealthy, as usually happens, manage to capture government, and bend its laws and tax codes to their own advantage, talk about the "free market" again serves to conceal what has occurred. According to health economist Robert Evans, who we'll spend more time with in the next section, talk of this sort "serve[s] to draw a veil over the activities of those who do in fact exercise power, and to screen them from public accountability for its use: 'nobody here but us competitors, all obeying the laws of the market.'"[10]

At this level, Somers summarizes the inherently stealth nature of economism as follows:

The state is the critical instrument for appropriating power. Under [economism] government institutions once dedicated to social, regulative, and redistributive policies have been steadily conquered and reorganized to support marketization and contractualization. So while public ... narratives still rail against "the problem of big government," what [economism] regimes *actually* do is use big government as the solution for their marketizing ambitions.[11]

Economism is against one form of big government and for a different form—the form that it can bend to its own advantage. But it cannot say so. In short, the Golden Calf that economism would have us worship is a doubly false god. It is not even gold, but perchance brass or tin.

I have now laid out a case that economism, at least in theory, is shot through with inconsistencies, and cannot state its true nature without exposing these inconsistencies. But what form does this stealth campaign actually take in our society?

The Reverse Robin Hood Rule

Robert G. Evans, a professor of economics at the University of British Columbia, is an unabashed supporter of the Canadian government-run health care system, and compared to most American economists would be seen as quite far to the political left. Nonetheless his credentials as a health economist are, I believe, beyond challenge.

A little more than a decade ago, Evans set out to explore the same problems that Dan Callahan and Angela Wasunna addressed in their more recent book, *Medicine and the Market*.[12] Evans surveyed the data available back then and concluded what Callahan and Wasunna observed some years later–there was hardly any compelling evidence to show that the marketplace was effective or efficient in providing health care to everyone who needed it. Yet, as he looked at the developed countries of the world, Evans observed influential lobbies in nearly all of them calling for increased privatization of health care. If the record was so clear that private enterprise did not work for health, why the popularity of privatization as a solution for any perceived ills of different nations' health systems? Keep in mind that in the other nations that Evans was talking about, health care cost much less than in the U.S., the system covered all citizens, and indices of population health such as life expectancy were as good or better than in the U.S. So the supposed "ills" of these other systems, that caused these influential interests to demand more privatization as a fix, were actually hardly anything compared to the ills of the American system, which was already the most privatized of any. Evans was struck by the irony of countries that had escaped most of the health care problems that America then faced (and now faces in spades) being instructed that the only way to solve their own problems was to become more like America.

Evans then compared the reassuring language with which these special interest groups described their schemes with what he considered the realities of privatization. We must be clear here that he had in mind a particular sort of privatization. One common form of privatization is the replacement of government workers with private-contract workers, such as happened to a massive degree in the U.S. Iraq war. In the old days, the U.S. Army used to cook for itself, leading to the popular comic-strip images of the private on K.P. duty peeling potatoes. In Iraq, the Army simply cut those positions from its own ranks, and the Pentagon paid private contractors to come in and feed the troops. This form of privatization eliminates government jobs and replaces them with private-sector jobs. Whether that is a good thing or a bad thing, on balance, need not concern us here. What is important is that the Army's meals were paid for out of tax dollars under the old system, and still are under the new system. This sort of privatization is *not* what Evans was talking about.

Evans instead meant to address the form of privatization that occurs when we stop supporting, say, state parks with as many tax dollars, and instead charge higher entrance fees for anyone who wants to use the parks. Replacing public tax dollars with private user fees, as a way to fund services, *is* the form of privatization that we here want to analyze.

Evans then looked carefully at various proposals to change government-run health care systems so that they depended less on tax dollars and more on private user fees. Being an economist, he relied a lot on tables and numbers and graphs. When he was done, he announced his basic conclusion–that *any privatization of the sort we are talking about here amounts to a net transfer of resources from the poor to the rich.*[13]

Evans never gave a specific name to his key concept. When I started to use Evans's work with students in the classroom, I decided that it needed a catchy title, and so I took to calling it the *Reverse Robin Hood Rule*. That is, privatization of previously-tax-supported services amounts to robbing the poor to give to the rich. In 2008, Paul Krugman, in one of his *New York Times* economics columns, used a similar phrase ("Robin-Hood-in-reverse") to describe supply-side economic thinking generally.[14]

An Example: The City Bus System

One reason that I took to calling Evans's insight the Reverse Robin Hood Rule was because on studying it, I became convinced that it went well beyond Evans's own argument. Evans never tried to extend the principle beyond health care financing. I thought, however, that it described the effects of privatization generally in just about any sector of life–health, education, transportation, or what have you. Because health care financing is so complex, it will be easier to explain how the Reverse Robin Hood Rule works if we take a non-health example to begin with.

Imagine that there is a city bus system that charges low fares to riders and is mostly supported by a progressive tax (a tax where those with higher incomes pay proportionately more, like the U.S. income tax). Let's consider the rich fellow and the poor fellow both trying to get to work—we can call them for convenience Richie and Needy. Richie pays taxes that support the city bus system, and he could ride the bus and take advantage of the low fares if he chooses to. The convenience of driving his own car wherever he wants and not having to wait at a bus stop probably dictates that he'll own a car and drive it to work. (Let's further imagine that this is a medium-sized city, and not one of the major metropolitan areas where traffic is so bad that no one drives who can possibly avoid it.) The amount of taxes Richie pays to support the bus system is more than what Needy pays, but is still so low a sum that it does not dictate Richie's behavior. Given his total income, the costs of owning, operating, and parking a car, and also paying the taxes that he owes, still leaves Richie with a lot of discretionary income for other purposes. Richie suffers no true hardship as a result of supporting both the bus system and his own private vehicle. Besides, the bus system is always there as a backup, in case his car breaks down or some other emergency arises.

Needy pays a lot less in taxes–maybe none at all–to support the bus system. But owning a car, keeping it in repair, and buying gas might easily be much more than Needy can afford. Since the bus fares are low, it makes more sense to ride the bus to work, even if it means walking an extra distance and maybe changing buses several times. Needy relies much more on the bus system for his basic daily needs than Richie does.

Now suppose that city government is reformed in the way that supply-siders would favor. The bus system is a real problem because it is subsidized so heavily by tax dollars. This is obviously bad policy, so we must reduce the tax subsidy or maybe eliminate it entirely. The fairest way to pay for buses, according to this line of thought, is private user fees–why make somebody pay for the bus who doesn't ride the bus? So fares have to be raised to meet the actual costs of running the bus system.

In practice, raising the fares as much as would be needed to cover costs of operation might well mean that ridership would be greatly reduced. If that happened, then the bus system could no longer operate and would shut down. That would be the desirable result from the supply-side viewpoint. After all, the bus system could not compete successfully in the open market, so it was obviously inefficient. Propping up an inefficient system with tax dollars is hardly the best way to govern. When we think about the consequences of the new privatized plan, we have to imagine both possibilities–that the system keeps operating but with greatly increased fares; or that it has to close.

What is the impact of this change on Richie? He benefits to the tune of saving the tax dollars that previously went to supporting the bus system. As he is in an upper income and high-tax bracket, that savings might be somewhat substantial, even if not huge. What about the bus being more expensive, or perhaps not being there at all? That probably makes no difference to Richie. He will, after all, keep driving his car where he wants to go. If his car breaks down, he can rent a car for a few days, or take cabs, and those options are easily affordable for him. In sum, he has given up nothing of real value to himself, and he has saved some tax dollars.

The impact on Needy is quite different. If the cost of a bus ticket doubles or triples, the daily ride to work will become a much bigger burden, as a higher percentage of his total wage (compared to Richie's) is spent on transportation. If the bus system goes under completely, that might be the end of Needy's employment; he may not be able to get to work, and there may be no jobs for people of his skill level within walking distance. So the increased cost of a bus ticket means either a greater economic burden or even total economic ruin.

But doesn't Needy's tax savings make up for this? If Needy is in the lowest possible tax bracket, he may pay no tax at all, so his tax savings is zero. If he pays some tax, the amount that he will save from the bus system's closure as part of his own tax bill probably amounts to only a few dollars, much less than Richie's share. With those few extra dollars, if they exist at all, Needy is completely unable to go out and buy a car, or take a taxi more than a few times.

Let's add up the totals. The change from a well-subsidized to a poorly-subsidized bus system has made Richie a little better off and Needy considerably worse off. If we add up each person's total resources, including both actual cash income and opportunities (like the option to get to work every day within a price range one can easily afford), we see that the total resources available to Richie have slightly increased, and the total resources available to Needy have been drastically reduced. *In short, the privatization of the bus system, replacing tax subsidy with user fees, has produced a net flow of resources away from the poor of the community and into the pockets of the rich.*

Extending the Rule–by Stealth

We have seen how the Reverse Robin Hood Rule works for the hypothetical city bus system. Is that a special case? I believe that you'll soon see, if you do the same sort of reasoning for each example, that the Rule works generally across the board. Try it out on an example of replacing taxpayer-supported schools with private schools charging tuition. Or do it with the state park example we mentioned previously.

The same general characteristics will crop up each time. The rich person has many options open besides the tax-supported option, and if there's a tax refund or rebate, he will get the most money back of anyone–which he can then use further to expand his other options. The poor person is least likely to have any realistic options outside of the tax-supported program. However, if the tax supported program goes under, the poor person gets back only pennies in tax savings, compared to the dollars received by the rich person. However you look at it, these various privatization schemes make the rich better off and the poor worse off.

Evans, we recall, made no effort to extend the Reverse Robin Hood Rule beyond health care. As he analyzed it, the Rule had one additional implication in that setting. There was, as in all the other examples, a net transfer of resources from the poor to the rich. There was also a net transfer of resources from the sick to the healthy. The people who would benefit the most from privatizing the health care system are the healthy and wealthy. Fortunately for the rich, that is a common state of affairs; poor health is most often concentrated disproportionately among lower-income people.

Since we have now seen reasons to imagine that the Rule has general applicability, we are in a position to go back to another of Evans's main points. Why the popularity of privatization schemes?

Evans showed that the healthy and wealthy stand to gain the most from privatizing health care, so he was not surprised when he surveyed the world scene and found that it was mostly the healthy and wealthy who formed the special interest groups lobbying for privatization. Among them he found large segments of the medical profession, who figured that under privatized schemes they could rake off more income than was often available in a government-run system. If Evans, writing in 1997, had had access to a crystal ball, he would not have been surprised to contemplate the rise of the Tea Party in the U.S. elections of 2010, and to learn that while the Tea Party portrayed itself as a populist uprising, its candidates strongly supported the principles of economism, and the movement was funded disproportionately by a few wealthy magnates known for their strong opposition to government regulation of corporations.[15]

Nevertheless, Evans found hardly a single country where it would work as a political strategy to announce, "Vote for our plan! It will take money from the poor and give it to the rich!" So all these special interest groups had to engage in some form of deception about the real consequences of their proposals. In most cases the deceptions were drawn from the language of economism.

Dean Baker, an economist with the Center for Economic and Policy Research, provided a specific example of such deception related to the health reform debate in the U.S. He first showed that to level a charge of "rationing" against the proposed health reform bill was bogus on several counts. First, the U.S. already rations health care in an especially cruel way, based on ability to pay and by whom one is employed. Second, those opposing health reform most strongly were the same who previously complained that Medicare was costing too much—as if the cost of Medicare could not be contained without some sort of "rationing" of care.

Baker went on:

> The underlying issue here is very simple. The insurance industry, the pharmaceutical industry, the medical supply industry and the A.M.A. are very worried about the threat that health reform presents to their future income. It would look unseemly for millionaires to get out in front of the public and say that we don't want health reform because it will jeopardize our income. So instead, they go into a nonsense rant about rationing.[16]

Baker observes that the deception here is effectively doubled. First, the opponents of reform manage to conceal from us that they are really out primarily to maximize their own income. Second, by invoking "rationing" as something that all of us presumably fear (and leaving unexamined the implication that their favored plans, by contrast, would not ration care at all), they send a strong message that they are *really on our side and looking out for our interests*, when in fact the opposite is the case.

So much for health reform; what about when the Reverse Robin Hood Rule is being applied to other public policies? How can its advocates conceal its true implications? The simple word "privatization" works as a political statement in the U.S. because we have now been conditioned for decades to view government as bad and private enterprise as good. If it needs supplementation, we can always add that privatization is a way to take advantage of the "efficiency of the marketplace."[7] "Shrinking big government" also works most of the time today in the U.S. Even the Democratic administration of Bill Clinton was so cowed by the forces of economism that they felt that they had to promise to continue to reduce the size of government. George W. Bush felt that he needed yet an additional variation, so early in his first term he came up with the "ownership society" to describe the forms of privatization that allowed more tax cuts for the wealthy.

Now, as the Reverse Robin Hood Rule shows, "privatization," "shrinking big government," "the efficiency of the free market," and the "ownership society" all are the equivalent of "robbing the poor to give to the rich." But even in America, where economism has conditioned us to believe that the poor are undeserving and the rich are God's chosen, that harsh phrase, "robbing the poor to give to the rich," sounds awkward and unpleasant. It sounds, in fact, just a bit too much like allowing a million Irish to starve in the name of reforming their backward agricultural system. So it is very important that this implication of privatization be kept quiet.

In one way, all this talk of the poor and the rich ignores a basic American political reality. Most of us do not consider ourselves poor or rich. We consider ourselves middle-class. So where do we fit into the equation? The supply-side stealth campaign has relied on creating the impression that the "rising tide that lifts all boats" applies equally to the rich and the middle-class. If only the poor are left out, we can tolerate that problem, after all, because the poor are seen as (morally) undeserving.

So among the facts that cannot be disclosed to the larger public are, as summarized by Jacob S. Hacker, "The spoils of our system are now so unevenly divided that we must reach back to the Robber Barons of the 1890s and Gatsbys of the 1920s for a similar comparison to today's gap between middle-income Americans and the super-rich."[18] Hacker, in short, appears to agree with historian Stehanie Coontz (Chapter 5) that we are presently in a second Gilded Age. Hacker goes on to quote *The Economist*, hardly a left-wing publication, that "a growing body of evidence suggests that the meritocratic ideal is in trouble in America. Income inequality is growing to levels not seen since the Gilded Age, around the 1880s. But social mobility is not increasing at anything like the same pace: would-be Horatio Algers are finding it no easier to climb from rags to riches, while the children of the privileged have a greater chance of staying at the top of the social heap."[19]

The fact that has to be concealed is that under the sway of supply-side economics, real middle-class income in the U.S. has hardly budged since the end of the 1970s. To the extent that middle-class families today are wealthier than they were then, the difference (or at least three-quarters of it) can be attributed solely to one factor–the increasing number of hours worked by women outside the home. Moreover, in recent years, it has gotten worse–the middle class, like Shelly and Darin Graham, has to work more hours just to stay at the same level. The rising costs of basic household expenses such as housing, health care, transportation, and education have considerably outstripped the average hourly earning power.

If, therefore, the middle class in the U.S. actually looked at the statistics, we would have considerable reason to doubt the wisdom of supply-side economics. The economism stealth campaign tries to assure that we don't look at those figures. Instead we are to be lulled to sleep by repeating comforting phrases: privatization, shrinking big government, and (as we'll see in a moment) taking personal responsibility. Above all else, economism must repeat the mantra that we dare not interfere with the workings of the free market, because God might get angry.

Extreme Stealth: The Shock Doctrine

The extent to which economism relies on a strategy of stealth in order to succeed as public policy is illustrated best by what Canadian investigative journalist Naomi Klein calls "the shock doctrine." She focuses on one especially potent version of economism–the form of neoclassical economics called the Chicago School, led by the University of Chicago's Nobel-Prize-winning economist, the late Milton Friedman. The Chicago School promotes the "policy trinity" of "the elimination of the public sphere, total liberation of corporations, and skeletal social spending."[20]

Friedman and the Chicago School set themselves in opposition to the Keynesian economics that formed the theoretical basis for the New Deal, according to which the state had a legitimate role in regulating markets for the public good. Friedman and his disciples early on discovered a serious problem. If you attempted to impose their system on a nation by democratic means, as occurred in Britain with the election of Margaret Thatcher and in the U.S. with Reagan, you had to deal with the messy social reality that many Keynesian institutions and policies were already in place, and dismantling them, even if it were possible, might take decades. Friedman, in the early 1970s, suggested that the ideal way to implement his agenda was via "shock treatment."[21] You needed, in short, a war or a natural disaster–something that would be so disruptive and disorienting that the public would tolerate wiping the slate clean, dismantling the old institutions and laws wholesale and allowing the "Chicago Boys" (as Friedman's armies of young trainees were called) to build their new system unopposed from the ground up.

Friedman preached "freedom" as the essence of his economic system. Typical of economism, his idea of freedom included only the narrow right to buy and sell freely in the marketplace. (This individual "freedom" existed alongside the implicit freedom of the wealthy and the corporations to manipulate the market to their own ends, thereby constraining the conditions under which everyone else was "free" to buy and sell.) The political freedoms of speech, conscience, and the right to vote democratically to guide your nation's future policies, along with the material freedoms to have a roof over your head and to be protected from starvation, figured not at all in Friedman's "freedom" catalog.

It was no great surprise, then, that the "Chicago Boys" found themselves closely allied with profoundly undemocratic forces–first, the military juntas that took over the governments of the large South American nations in the 1970s, and later Boris Yeltsin's Russia and the Chinese government that suppressed the popular uprising in Tiananmen Square. The Chicago-style "free market" that was imposed on each of these countries made multinational corporations and an elite cadre of well-connected local politicians extremely rich, while shredding the social safety net and causing massive unemployment and poverty among the great majority of the population.

Domingo Cavallo was a strong advocate of Chicago School policies in Argentina, first during the rule of the military junta, and then later during that nation's hyperinflation crisis. He explained how runaway inflation creates the perfect setting for Friedman-style "shock therapy." As the people see their earnings being eaten up by inflation, they demand that the government do something. This gives the policymakers the authority to step in to stabilize the currency. The opportunity is then created to sneak in other so-called reforms such as deregulation, privatization, and slashing government spending. If the truth were known, the people would see that these "reforms" really have nothing at all to do with currency stabilization. But the truth is not known because the policymakers proceed by stealth, insisting that it must be the entire "reform" package or nothing at all.[22] (In the spring of 2011 we witnessed similar efforts to apply the shock doctrine within the U.S.—first, the efforts of Wisconsin governor Scott Walker to use the budget crisis in his state as an excuse to dismantle public-sector unions; and then attempts by the Republicans in Congress to use the urgency of deficit reduction as an excuse to privatize major public programs such as Medicare.)

The Chicago Boys also managed to take over most of the important posts in the World Bank and International Monetary Fund, thereby influencing the way those institutions treated economic development in the Third World. Dani Rodrik, a Columbia University economist who worked extensively with the World Bank, admitted in a 1994 presentation to a group of experts that the free trade policies that the Bank routinely forced on countries seeking aid really had nothing to do with stabilizing their currencies and getting them out of their immediate financial crises. Rather, it was essential to slip these demands in during the "shock" phase of the crisis, else the nation would never allow its arms to be twisted to adopt these policies that so favored the large Western corporations and other interests dear to Washington's heart.[23] Klein comments:

It was a staggering admission. At this point in history, the bank and the fund were publicly insisting that governments the world over had seen the light and realized that the Washington Consensus policies were the only recipe for stability, and therefore democracy. Yet here was an acknowledgment, made inside the Washington establishment, that developing countries were submitting to them only through a combination of false pretenses and bald extortion.[24]

The efforts of the Chicago School to guide policy both in the U.S. and internationally illustrate economism's need for stealth at several levels. We have already noted how the only way to implement these policies fully was to do an end run around democratic choice of the people, either by riding on the back of a war or other disaster, or by using an economic crisis as an excuse for a powerful agency like the World Bank to force unwanted policies on developing nations. The governments that worked hand in glove with the Chicago Boys to realize this vision of the ideal economic blank slate, on which to create the Eden of privatization and unregulated capitalism, were universally prone to political killing, torture and other serious abuses of human rights. Yet the Chicago School managed to escape the appropriate accountability for hanging out with such undesirable characters. The various truth commissions and human rights bodies that investigated and exposed the abuses of these governments bent over backwards so as not to seem ideologically motivated. They generally adopted a narrow, legalistic account of "human rights" and simply listed the abuses that had been perpetrated by Augusto Pinochet in Chile and other Chicago Boys patrons. They seldom inquired deeply into the economic motivations, the *why* of these massive assaults on human rights and democratic processes. Thus, the essential tie between economism and dictatorship was further concealed by stealth; Friedman and his followers could express regrets over the human rights abuses as a minor side issue and never openly accept the fact that these abuses were *required* in order to advance their policies. One exception to the stealth campaign on this score was the Brazilian truth commission report, *Brasil: Nunca Mais*, which was produced independently of both local government and foreign foundation support. The report called it like it was and gave as the key reason for the abuses: "Since the economic policy was extremely unpopular among the most numerous sectors of the population, it had to be implemented by force."25

Economism further invites a stealth strategy simply as a result of its inherent doublethink and doublespeak tendencies. The Bush Administration's attempt to remake Iraq as a model Middle Eastern "democracy" and capitalist economy, in a manner certain to enrich large U.S. corporations, was only one of the most recent examples of Friedman's "shock therapy." Richard Perle, a prominent neoconservative within the U.S. defense establishment, was picked by Secretary of Defense Donald Rumsfeld to head the Pentagon's Defense Policy Board, at the same time that Perle headed a corporation that stood to profit immensely from the Iraq war. CNN's Wolf Blitzer confronted Perle with journalist Seymour Hersh's charge that Perle was engaged in a massive conflict of interest. Perle responded with indignation. He called the award-winning Hersh "the closest thing American journalism has to a terrorist" and insisted, "I don't believe that a company would gain from a war...The suggestion that my views are somehow related for the potential of investments in homeland defense is complete nonsense."26

The important point here is that we have every reason to regard Perle's indignation as genuine. A conflict of interest requires, as you would expect, a *conflict* of interests. Usually such a conflict occurs between a public interest (such as giving the Department of Defense the best possible advice to serve the interests of the American people) and a private interest (like making Richard Perle wealthy). If you believe in economism, however, you believe that there is no such distinction among interests. The real public interest consists in adhering to immutable natural laws laid down by God. One's private interest similarly consists in adhering to those laws. God created the market as his central means of assuring his laws on earth; his market works via self-interest (greed); greed is divinely sanctioned; so there can be no possible conflict of interest if one enriches oneself while serving in a public government capacity (so long as one enriches oneself through the correct sort of corporate activity). The stealth campaign is greatly eased when someone like Perle can *genuinely* express moral outrage and claim the moral high ground, while advancing the economism agenda all the way to the bank.

The Privatization of Middle-Class Risk

Jacob Hacker, a professor of political science at Yale, wrote about the statistics that supply-siders don't want us to dwell on in *The Great Risk Shift: The New Economic Insecurity and the Decline of the American Dream.*[27] The growing income gap between the middle-class and the very rich is not, as it turns out, the main theme he wishes to stress. Rather, he wants to talk about a different sort of privatization and its consequences–the privatization of risk.

Hacker believes that the statistics about the income gap, as scary as they are for defenders of supply-side thinking, actually conceal even worse statistics about the current state of the American middle class. The figures we have reviewed so far assume that the rich, the middle class, and the poor are more or less the same people year after year. This is in fact not so. As *The Economist* said, we can be pretty sure that it is true for the rich. But at the borderline between the middle class and the poor, there is much more churning than these figures would indicate, as we saw in Chapter 2.

What Hacker is describing, in broad terms, is the shredding of the safety net that was designed mainly for the poor (when the New Dealers first constructed it during the Depression) but which greatly buttressed the lives of the middle class too, as Stan and Carol Wyzansky discovered. Many different events (as Shelly and Darin well know) can quickly turn a middle class person or family into a poor one–a layoff, a cutback in work hours, a serious illness, kids needing to go to college, retirement, divorce. The programs that might have been there to cushion these often predictable shocks of modern life have gradually been stripped away in the name of privatization. The result, says Hacker, is a deep-seated insecurity that is taking a far greater toll on American productivity and well-being than any income numbers could capture.

Here, from our vantage point, Hacker's analysis falls short. Like Chait, he believes that a very moderate and reasonable brand of conservative Republican thinking, prominent during the Eisenhower and Nixon years for example, has been displaced by a much more radical and extreme viewpoint. According to that older conservatism, the best way to maintain the social safety net that was the legacy of the New Deal was an active partnership between government and the business community. This moderate view was replaced with the rabidly pro-business, anti-government attitude of supply-side. But what Hacker fails to see fully is that this has taken the form more of a religious conversion than of a shift in political and policy ideas. Like Chait, Hacker uses terms that show here and there that he senses what is actually going on. He quotes anthropologist Katherine Newman, that for the middle class, the psychological toll from loss of income is experienced as a "falling from grace."[28] He speaks approvingly of the concept of social insurance as embodied in Social Security during the New Deal: "Insurance was an affirmation of free will over fate. If not an effort to stay the hand of God, it was an attempt to soften his blow."[29] He refers to Health Savings Accounts as a "near-theological aspiration of the Right,"[30] and of the 2003 Medicare drug benefit as arising from "faith-based reliance on the private sector."[31] But in the end he regards this use of language as purely metaphorical, and does not consider that it may be quite literally true.

Hacker calls "the great risk shift" that has created this epidemic of middle-class insecurity the Personal Responsibility Crusade.[32] Once again, this is the way ideas have to be prettied up to get the voters to accept something as radical as pulling the rug of economic security out from under the middle class. Hacker traces the original assault on the New Deal concept of social insurance to a cadre of neoclassical economists and right-wing political operatives in the 1970s. The tool they used to attack social insurance was *moral hazard*. This was same idea that Andrew Carnegie and his associates worried about, during the first Gilded Age, that any aid or gift to anyone would destroy individual initiative. But the notion that had first been restricted to a concept of personal morality was now enshrined as an economic principle.

Moral hazard, within limits, is a perfectly sound and reasonable economic model. If you insure a person against the loss that accompanies a certain behavior, in at least some circumstances, you make that behavior relatively more attractive–which could have undesirable social consequences and high social costs. For example, one might wonder–is there a level of low premiums and generous payouts for home fire insurance, that would cause the average homeowner to neglect basic precautions like smoke alarms? We'd guess that the payouts would have to be very large to overcome the fact that most of us do not want our houses to burn down, for reasons that have relatively little to do with money. Yet, in fact, some people do burn down their houses to collect the insurance. Or to take another example, family historian Stephanie Coontz generally marshals a good deal of evidence to dispute claims that most welfare programs produce an ongoing "culture of poverty" and simply encourage the poor to remain unemployed and dependent on handouts. But she acknowledges an exception--the idea of a negative income tax when applied to young people less than 21 years of age. There, she admits, the programs have shown a negative impact on work-force participation.[33] This sort of selected and targeted argument based on evidence is far different from the indiscriminate use of moral hazard as all-purpose ideology.

According to Hacker, the Personal Responsibility Crusaders went way beyond any useful economic construct and turned moral hazard into a sweeping condemnation of any social insurance program, regardless of the actual facts.[34] He notes, "In the early 1980s, conservative scholar Charles Murray coined a simple syllogism to explain why good-intentioned programs inevitably went bad: 'Any social transfer increases the net value of being in the condition that prompted the transfer.' In other words, helping people just creates more people who need help–moral hazard with a vengeance."[35]

The leaders of the anti-moral-hazard crusade insisted that they were engaged in nothing but sober economic modeling. Hacker quotes neoclassical economist Mark Pauly that moral hazard is not a sign of "moral perfidy" but rather represents "rational economic behavior."[36] He continues:

> But in the rhetoric of the Personal Responsibility Crusade, morality was never far beneath the surface. "What moral hazard means," according to James K. Glassman, a resident fellow of the conservative American Enterprise Institute (and a leading advocate of Social Security privatization), "is that, if you cushion the consequences of bad behavior, then you encourage that bad behavior."

> Statements like these might suggest that the language of moral hazard resonated only on the fringes of conservative thought. Yet nothing could be further from the truth. The concept was powerful precisely because its core message–personal responsibility, self-reliance, individual discipline, private probity–resonated so strongly with so many Americans at a time when concern about the cost and economic impact of existing programs was rising. And yet, while millions of

Americans happily repeated the mantra of responsibility, the message of moral hazard was, underneath it all, fundamentally in conflict with many Americans' strongest beliefs about fate, security, and justice.[37]

Hacker notes accurately that the late 1970s was a time of economic insecurity for the country as a whole, with stagflation leading to out-of-sight interest rates. What he fails to add is that the reason these ideas "resonated" so well with the average American is their extended historical *and religious* pedigree (as we discussed in Chapter 5). Personal responsibility, after all, is exactly what Stan and Carol, and Henry and Carolyn in the next generation, tried to teach their children—without ever dreaming that the New Deal and the social safety net would ever be repealed in the name of these ideals. Armed with our historical survey, we can see in "moral hazard" an almost exact replication of the attitude toward the poor in 19th-century English evangelicalism. If we try to help the poor, instead of atoning for their sins and maybe achieving salvation in the next world through their suffering in this one, they will become even worse sinners and lose any chance of eternal grace. We can even hear in the background the dread predictions of Malthus, that if we feed the poor, they will simply reproduce faster, outstrip the food supply, and starve in even greater numbers. "Moral hazard" is called *moral* (otherwise a very odd term to occur in an economic model) for a very good reason. Moral hazard is the opposite of taking personal responsibility. Personal responsibility means living in accord with divine law and its commandments.

Around 1850, evangelical thought lost its grip on British public policy when writers like Dickens convinced the general public that when bad economic things happened to people, *they often happened for reasons outside that individual's personal control.* A vengeful God who condemned you to Hell for eternity, for things that were actually out of your control, no longer seemed the image of God to whom Christians felt allegiance. During the Depression, it was quite clear that the massive economic dislocations were happening for reasons over which most individuals had no power. In that time, it made perfect sense to call for social insurance programs. By the late 1970s, apparently enough people had forgotten the lessons of the Depression to make "personal responsibility" once again an attractive slogan. By the first decade of the 21st century, many seemed oblivious to the fact that once again, the Great Recession that caused Shelly to lose her job, or Darin's developing Crohn's disease, were actually well outside of most people's personal control.

Finally, we must ask: how does 'moral hazard' fit in with economism's stealth campaign? Do economism's advocates in fact believe that *whenever* you reduce the risks associated with bad behavior, people will then behave badly? Or do they believe that this is true of other people, but not of themselves? Steve Keen, in advancing his argument that neoclassical economics is internally inconsistent, cited a remark by John Kenneth Galbraith, "that the poor don't work hard enough because they're paid too much, and the rich don't work hard enough because they're not paid enough."[38] Unless one believes that the rich and the poor follow quite different psychological rules, it is hard to see how economism could justify (for example) paying corporate CEOs huge bonuses, or generous severance packages after they have nearly destroyed their companies.

Personal Responsibility and God's Design for the World

How well public policy arguments about "personal responsibility" resonate with the religious heritage we have surveyed was well illustrated by a series of letters in the *Atlanta Journal-Constitution* in 2007.[39]

Apparently anxious to put a human face on PeachCare for Kids, Georgia's State Children's Health Insurance Program, the newspaper ran an article profiling Connie and Michael Post. Michael had left a $42,000-a-year job as a full-time pastor to work as a free-lance minister, and supplemented his income with house painting and other odd jobs. Connie, who had a college English degree, worked at a horseshoeing school for $25,000 annually. With basic expenses (including high-deductible health insurance for Connie and Mike) running $2883 per month, they lived from paycheck to paycheck.

At the time of the interview, the Posts were expecting their fourth child. Connie and Mike's middle child, Cadence, had autism. She was, however, doing well with the support of two weekly therapy sessions costing $135 each. Their oldest child had a sensory deficit and had previously needed one $135 therapy session each week, but now no longer required them. PeachCare paid for these sessions that would otherwise have simply been unaffordable for the Posts.

"You can imagine how grateful we are for PeachCare," the newspaper quoted Connie.

If we can accuse the *Journal-Constitution* (whose editorial page favored the expansion of PeachCare) of doing a little editorializing in this news article, we can see how the Posts might seem well suited to carry the banner for the cause. Michael was a minister; both parents were employed and Michael took on extra part time work to make ends meet; two of their children had significant disabilities. There seemed little doubt that readers would identify and sympathize with them.

If this was what the editors had assumed, they must have been shocked to receive a series of letters saying things like:

- "[The Posts] have deliberately chosen to limit their income by giving up a high paying job–yet they continue to have children and shift the responsibility for medical care to the taxpayers."
- "While reading this story, my blood pressure spiked. . . . Whenever you reward bad behavior, that behavior will continue. This is why we need to cut these programs for all but the truly needy. These people aren't needy, they are lazy. PeachCare simply encourages said laziness."
- "Unfortunately, it appears that the Posts do not themselves believe in being responsible. [P]erhaps without multiple children they could not afford to provide for, they would be doing just fine."
- "The responsible thing for this couple to do would be to practice some sort of birth control."

Had Michael Post asked my advice at this juncture, I would have suggested that his personal and family life was none of the business of these newspaper readers, who seemed to wish nothing but to twist any truth that they were told. But Michael Post instead wrote a column defending himself. He told the world that he and Connie had used an apparently reliable method of birth control, and were shocked to find that she was pregnant again. He explained that his previous pastoral job had not provided any health benefits, so his decision to leave that job did not impose any additional burden on the taxpayer. He noted that to be able to afford all the services needed for Cadence's care on their own, they'd need to gross at least $125,000 a year. He concluded, "We are not looking for a hand-out but rather affordable health care."

Michael's laying his personal life out for public viewing seemed only to further inflame the angry letter-writers. One wrote back to object to the Posts' "appalling sense of entitlement." Another wrote to instruct them on which methods of birth control were more reliable. Attacks on their "personal responsibility" continued unabated.

With what we have surveyed so far, we can see some familiar patterns in the letters. Clearly the notion of "responsibility" resonates deeply with this segment of the public. The writers have also internalized the message of "moral hazard" and are quite sure that if you come to people's aid, it will just encourage them to behave even more irresponsibly. The comment about restricting PeachCare only to the "truly needy" makes one wonder who, according to that writer, would fit that description, if anyone.

Yet what remains unexplained in all this is how the writers of these angry letters so quickly managed to label the Posts as *different*. The newspaper imagined that they had chosen a hard-working, middle-class couple to profile. The readers were having none of it. The Posts, they had decided, were not *people like them. They* were responsible, while the Posts clearly were not.

Charity Scott, a law professor at Georgia State University, writing about this incident in the *Hastings Center Report* (a bioethics publication), offered a further theory about where these letter-writers were coming from.[40] She cited survey research showing that many Americans believe very strongly in a just world. A just world is one that works according to God's plan. The good are rewarded and the bad are punished. This is, in short, the world view of evangelicalism as it existed in 19th century England.

Presented with a story like that of the Post family, people have two choices. They could decide that the Posts are people like them, and that their limited income and the plight of their children are due to factors mostly beyond their control (like the generally high cost of health care in American society, and which jobs in America carry generous health insurance benefits). If they decided that, however, they would come uncomfortably close to believing that the world is not just. The Posts were decent, hard-working, religious, and so forth; and yet bad things seemed to be happening to them.

Since this first possibility was so uncomfortable, Scott suggested, people are forced to the second choice. They can continue to believe in a just world, which in turn requires that they find a way in which the Posts did something bad that they deserved to be punished for. The Posts, to allow the just-world belief to persist, have to be shown that they brought all their troubles down on their own heads. And so the letter-writers dutifully constructed such a scenario. They had to pretty severely mangle many facts in order to do so. But most of us will play pretty fast and loose with the facts, when a pet theory that lies near the very core of our lives is threatened. The letter writers acted like Job's so-called friends in the Bible, insisting that since God has punished Job, Job must have been guilty of some sin, even though Job knows better. (Perhaps that explains why the Book of Job was such a favorite with both the evangelicals and the Puritans of old.)

Let me be clear on what I am saying in bringing up the example of the Posts. Do the letter-writers have the right to make negative judgments about them, based on the writers' religious beliefs? Absolutely. If the *Journal-Constitution* ran a story about a gay couple trying to get married, and your religious views cause you to hate gay marriage, then you have every right to hate the people in the story, as much as I might find that personally repugnant. Do the letter-writers also have the right to vote for political candidates who mirror their own religious views? Absolutely, again.

My concern is rather for the political stealth campaign that occurs when supposedly neutral and objective economics gets mixed up with religious faith. The ease with which our political discourse in the U.S. goes back and forth among "personal responsibility," moral hazard, belief in a just world, and the perceived need to dismantle social safety-net programs like health care for the poor, illustrates how intertwined religion, economics, and politics have become during the era of economism.[41]

A further analogy may be helpful. What happens when people get enraged about the science of biology because it seems to be saying something contrary to their own religious beliefs? What happens when those enraged people design a "biology" of their own that conforms to their religious creed–but that hardly meets the standards of *science*? What if, when challenged as to the unscientific nature of their alternative "biology," they change its name and try to hide the religious content even deeper, while still proclaiming that what they have produced is a science and ought to be taught in science classrooms in public schools? The next chapter will explore how that example compares with economism.

Notes

1. Chait J. *The big con: the true story of how Washington got hoodwinked and hijacked by crackpot economics.* Boston: Houghton Mifflin, 2007: 102.

2. Since ex-Sen. Gramm is remembered as one of the prime architects of Reaganomics and as an enemy of government handouts, historian Stephanie Coontz found it interesting to explore his life story. She reports that Gramm's father lived on a federal veterans disability pension, that he himself attended a publicly-funded university with a grant from the federal War Orphans Act, that his graduate work was financed by a National Defense Education Act fellowship, and that he got his first job at another publicly funded university, Texas A&M. Coontz S. *The way we never were: American families and the nostalgia trap.* New York: Basic books, 2000: 69.

3. Chait, *The big con*: 126.

4. Smith A. *The wealth of nations.* Blacksburg, VA: Thrifty Books, 2009: 465 (Book IV, Chap. 8, par. 26)

5. Somers MR. *Genealogies of citizenship: markets, statelessness, and the right to have rights.* New York: Cambridge University Press, 2008: 4.

6. Kozul-Wright R, Rayment P. *The resistable rise of market fundamentalism: Rethinking development policy in an unbalanced world.* New York: Zed Books, 2007: 22.

7. Foley DK. *Adam's fallacy: A guide to economic theology.* Cambridge, MA: Harvard University Press, 2006: 224.

8. Somers, *Genealogies of citizenship*: 4.

9. Somers, *Genealogies of citizenship*; Frank T. *One market under God: Extreme capitalism, market populism, and the end of economic democracy.* New York: Anchor, 2001.

10. Evans RG. Going for the gold: the redistributive agenda behind market-based health care reform. *Journal of Health Politics, Policy and Law* 22(2):427-465, 1997; quote p. 432.

11. Somers, *Genealogies of citizenship*: 94.

12. Callahan D, Wasunna AA. *Medicine and the market: equity v. choice.* Baltimore: Johns Hopkins University Press, 2006.

13. Evans RG. Going for the gold: the redistributive agenda behind market-based health care reform. *Journal of Health Politics, Policy and Law* 22:427-65, 1997.

14. Krugman P. From hype to fear. *New York Times*, Jan.7, 2008; http://www.nytimes.com/2008/01/07/opinion/07krugman.html?scp=1&sq=paul%20krugman%20from%20hype%20to%20fear&st=cse (accessed Nov. 21, 2010). Apparently Krugman had used this phrase earlier in a speech in 2004; http://www.independent.co.uk/opinion/commentators/paul-krugman-bushs-economic-policies-are-robin-hood-in-reverse-732557.html (accessed Nov. 21, 2010). A more recent use is by Alan S. Blinder, former vice chair of the Federal Reserve: Blinder AS. Paul Ryan's reverse Robin Hood budget. *Wall Street Journal*, April 19, 2011: A17.

15. Stan AM. Tea Party Inc.: the big money and powerful elites behind the right wing's latest uprising. State-Journal.com, October 26, 2010, http://www.state-journal.com/news/simple_article/4919566?page=0 (accessed December 27, 2010).

16. Baker D. It's not rationing, stupid! Truth-out Perspective, July 13, 2009; http://www.truth-out.org/071309H (accessed Nov. 21, 2010).

17. As our old friend from Chapter 3, the "scrupulous" economist, Uwe Reinhardt, put it, "When you hear us economists wax eloquent on the virtue of greater efficiency—beware!" He used this as a prime example of how some economists disguise moral/value judgments as hard economic science. Reinhardt U. When value judgments masquerade as science. *New York Times* economics blog, August 27, 2010; http://economix.blogs.nytimes.com/2010/08/27/when-value-judgments-masquerade-as-science/ (accessed December 27, 2010).

18. Hacker JS. *The great risk shift: the new economic insecurity and the decline of the American dream*. Revised and expanded edition. New York: Oxford University Press, 2008: 21.

19. Hacker, *Great risk shift*: 24.

20. Klein N. *The shock doctrine: the rise of disaster capitalism*. New York: Picador, 2007: 18.

21. Klein, *Shock doctrine*: 8.

22. Klein, *Shock doctrine*: 209-10.

23. Klein, *Shock doctrine*: 205-6.

24. Klein, *Shock doctrine*: 206.

25. Klein, *Shock doctrine*: 155.

26. Klein, *Shock doctrine*: 406.

27. Hacker, *Great risk shift.*

28. Hacker, *Great risk shift:* 30.

29. Hacker, *Great risk shift:* 41.

30. Hacker, *Great risk shift:* 152.

31. Hacker, *Great risk shift:* 157.

32. Hacker, *Great risk shift:* 52.

33. Coontz, *Way we never were*: 84.

34. Hacker, *Great risk shift:* 47.

35. Hacker, *Great risk shift:* 52.

36. Hacker, *Great risk shift:* 48.

37. Hacker, *Great risk shift:* 53.

38. Keene S. *Debunking economics: the naked emperor of the social sciences.* New York: Zed Books, 2001: 76. Keene cites Galbraith JK. *The socially concerned today: the first honorary Keith Davey Lecture.* Toronto: University of Toronto Press, 1997.

39. The entire episode is summarized in Scott C. Belief in a just world: a case study in public health ethics. *Hastings Center Report* 38(1):16-19, 2008.

40. Scott, Belief in a just world.

41. Duncan Foley, as we saw in Chapter 3, would see this intertwining as inevitable, since in his view all of economics is ultimately about value judgments; Foley DK. *Adam's fallacy: A guide to economic theology.* Cambridge, MA: Harvard University Press, 2006.

Chapter 7.

Economism and Intelligent Design: Religion Masquerading as Science

Introduction

Gordon Bigelow, describing the basic principles of neoclassical economics and their roots in 19th century evangelicalism, summarizes, "Predicated on the belief that markets operate in a scientifically knowable fashion, [neoclassical economics] sees them as self-regulating mathematical miracles, as delicate ecosystems best left alone." He then adds, "If there is a whiff of creationism around this idea, it is no accident."[1] Just what is Bigelow up to by invoking creationism in an essay about the history of economics? Is this just a form of liberal piling-on? Does Bigelow invoke creationism here because it suggests an extreme fundamentalism, making neoclassical economics guilty by association?

In this chapter I want to suggest that there is a useful and pertinent analogy between economism and the creationist doctrine of intelligent design. There is much more to it than the personal coincidence we noted in Chapter 3–that George Gilder, one of the original prophets of supply-side economics, having lost both his own fortune and his reputation in the dot-com bubble, was last heard from touting intelligent design. The current intelligent design "movement" typifies two features that we have seen to be central to economism. First, the line between religion and science is deliberately blurred. Second, in order to sell the resulting doctrine, its proponents engage in a stealth campaign. Comparing economism and intelligent design, I suggest, helps us understand more clearly what is going on in both cases.

Judge John Jones and the Dover School Board

As my central exhibit on intelligent design, I will rely heavily on the opinion issued by Judge John E. Jones III of the U.S. District Court, Middle District of Pennsylvania, on December 20, 2005 in the case of the Dover, Pennsylvania school board.[2] In October, 2004, the Dover school board approved a resolution to inform their ninth-grade biology students that there were gaps in Darwin's theory of evolution and that other alternative theories, especially one called intelligent design, existed. The Board then developed a statement to be read in all biology classes, specifically recommending an alternative textbook called *Of Pandas and People*, written from a creationist perspective. The science teachers refused to read this statement, claiming that it unconstitutionally inserted religion into the classroom of public schools, and so administrators were sent to the classrooms to read the statement. Eventually this led to a lawsuit, which came before Judge Jones.

I have no idea whether the defendants in this case engaged in any venue-shopping, but they ought to have been pleased with the choice of judge. Jones had been involved in Republican politics in the state, and was known to be an advocate of privatization. He was appointed to the Federal bench by George W. Bush.[3] But, if the defendants were looking forward to a friendly ruling from the bench, they were disappointed. Jones's 139-page ruling against the school board earned him death threats from several fundamentalist groups.

Jones's ruling is of special use to us for several reasons. It is a basic feature of law that when there are several reasons to find for one side in a case, all the judge has to do is to show that one of the reasons holds, and she can then say nothing at all about the remainder. The law is basically a conservative institution and judges often prefer to make rulings based on the narrowest possible grounds.

Now, whatever "intelligent design" may apply to, it certainly did not refer to how the majority of the Dover school board went about their business. For several years, the leaders of the faction on the school board that pushed the proposal had loudly proclaimed their religious agenda all around town. They had proclaimed that the Constitutional principle of separation of church and state was a myth, and that they planned first to implement the teaching of creationism, and then to move on to instituting school prayer. At one point, when there was a delay in getting the official funds to purchase the *Pandas and People* textbook, a board member took up a collection in his church for the purpose.

Then, when they found themselves embroiled in a lawsuit, the board members belatedly discovered that their only legal defense was to show that "intelligent design" was science and not religion–since previous efforts to teach creationism in public schools, under the label of "creation science," had already been ruled unconstitutional by the federal courts. (The attorney for the school district had pointed all this out to the board several years earlier, but no one had paid any attention.) Apparently chastened, the board members then came into Judge Jones's court and, in the judge's own words, simply lied about all of their previous claims that their support for intelligent design (if they even knew what it was, and how it supposedly differed from creationism) was based on their religious faith. The extent to which these board members stretched the truth when testifying, in a way that totally trashed their own credibility, led to a later debate about why these (now former) board members were not prosecuted for perjury.

The judge therefore had a ready-made reason to declare the board policy unconstitutional. A public school is not supposed to endorse the teaching of a particular religious creed. The past record of the public statements of the school board majority showed that clearly this is what they had intended. The judge could have documented the past record of public statements, noted the utter lack of credibility of the statements to the contrary at the trial, and called it a day.

Judge Jones, however, had sat through many days of testimony from national experts on the debate over creationism and intelligent design. He suspected, from the nationally funded pro-creationist, religious groups that had come to the defense of the school board, that he was not going to be the last judge to hear such a case. So he said that he felt duty-bound to place on record his analysis of the core philosophical question before his court–was "intelligent design" science or religion? Because he went ahead to address that question, and did so with considerable logic and insight, his opinion stands as a very helpful review of this controversy in all its aspects–scientific, religious, legal, and philosophical.

What Is a Theory?

Before we get into the meat of Judge Jones's opinion, I want to address a question that he took up only briefly, because it seems to be a recurring source of confusion regarding the scientific standing of evolution. Just what do we mean when we say something in science is a "theory"?

Opponents of Darwinian evolution get a lot of mileage out of the fact that textbooks commonly refer to the *theory* of evolution. They do not then proceed actually to investigate the role that evolutionary thinking plays in biological science as a whole. They instead run to the dictionary, look up 'theory,' and find that it can mean something skin to an unproven hunch. So they then insist that nothing about evolution is a *fact* but rather is only a *theory*.

All of this represents a serious misunderstanding about how science works, and the fact that ordinary citizens could be fooled by this semantic flim-flam shows what a poor job our schools do today in teaching non-scientists about the nature of science. To be brief, whether something in science is called a "theory" or a "law" or whatever is usually an accident of history. There is no international scientific ruling board, like the International Olympic Committee in sports, that sets clear standards for when a Theory has become so well supported by evidence that it ought to be changed to a Law, or anything of the sort. We can only tell the true role that an idea plays in the active enterprise we call science by looking at how science is carried out.

Normally what we would call a "theory" according to the usual dictionary definition would, if we compare science to a tree, be a single branch of the tree. The basic idea is that, if for whatever reason we decide that this branch is unsound, we can saw it off, and the rest of the tree will continue to thrive.

Any careful evaluation of biological science today will show that evolution does not function at all like this branch. If anything, evolution is part of the trunk of the tree. It has become so basic a part of so many aspects of biology, from our understanding of molecules and cells all the way up to organisms and ecosystems, that we cannot really imagine modern biology without evolution.

Some years ago the Kansas Board of Education went off on a creationist tear and seemed poised, for a while, to impose that doctrine upon all schools in the state—presumably including the medical school.[4] As a career medical educator,

I wondered just exactly how you could design a medical school curriculum, if you were under orders not to include any ideas grounded in evolution. My own best guess is that it is simply not possible to teach modern medicine without bringing in evolution in a number of ways. I do not see how a medical school could responsibly admit a student who had never studied evolutionary biology. I say this not by way of attacking people's religious beliefs, but simply to demonstrate how central to all biological science (including human medicine) the "theory" of evolution has become.

Even the most well-accepted scientific ideas have some ragged edges. So one will always be able to find parts of evolutionary theory that are now not well understood or not well supported by available evidence. What will happen in the future with regard to these aspects of evolutionary thinking is anyone's guess. Further research could fill in most of the gaps–Judge Jones listed in his opinion a number of areas in which new discoveries within the past decade or so have strengthened evolution. Alternatively, sometimes it is among these ragged edges of well-established theories that scientific revolutions originate. In the 1890s the areas of physics that were in dispute, and that eventually led to the new quantum mechanics and relativity, seemed to be of only minor importance. We cannot exclude the possibility that in the future, evolution will be replaced by a new scientific theoretical system, and that new system may get its start from its ability to fill in the present gaps in Darwinian theory. Nevertheless, as Judge Jones also was at pains to emphasize, to talk about Darwinian evolution as *uniquely* plagued with gaps and flaws, instead of having just about as many unanswered questions as any scientific account would be expected to have, is disingenuous. If you compare the current gaps in evolution with its undeniably central role in biological thinking, there are a great many more reasons to adhere to the theory than to reject it. This is especially true as there is no real *scientific* alternative to Darwinian evolution–as Judge Jones next proceeded to explain.

Is Intelligent Design Science?

Judge Jones started by reviewing the legal history of the debate over teaching Darwin in the public schools. He observed that the previous effort to insert creationism into the school curriculum came with the development of so-called "creation science." This was a flop. The courts uniformly held that "creation science" was bogus and that it was religion and not science. Only after that failed effort did creationists then come up with the label "intelligent design."

Intelligent design has a long and distinguished pedigree–but not in science. A theologian, John Haught, who testified against the school board, argued that today's intelligent design was born as one of the syllogisms to prove the existence of God, offered by Thomas Aquinas in the 13th century. The syllogism goes: "Wherever complex design exists, there must have been a designer; nature is complex; therefore nature must have had an intelligent designer."[5] Judge Jones further noted among the exhibits presented to the court a "Wedge Document" from the Center for Renewal of Science and Culture of the Discovery Institute, one of the main creationist bodies that provided for the school board's legal defense. The Wedge Document gave as a major goal "to replace science as currently practiced with 'theistic and Christian science,'" and "to change the ground rules of science to make room for religion, specifically, beliefs consonant with a particular version of Christianity."[6]

What, exactly, is wrong with a "theistic science"? Simply the fact that it is not science, at least as we have understood that term for the past several centuries. Judge Jones quoted a statement of the National Academy of Sciences:

> Creationism, intelligent design, and other claims of supernatural intervention in the origin of life or of species are not science because they are not testable by the methods of science. These claims subordinate observed data to statements based on authority, revelation, or religious belief. [Proponents] do not offer hypotheses subject to change in light of new data, new interpretations, or demonstrations of error. This contrasts with science, where any hypothesis or theory always remains subject to the possibility of rejection or modification in the light of new knowledge.[7]

Modern science as we understand it could be defined as the attempt to explain the natural world as far as we can without invoking divine or supernatural intervention. This was a decision based on the difference between methodological rigor and methodological laziness. Over millenia, we have learned that humans get very lazy in their thinking when anything puzzling can be explained by a supernatural being. By contrast, we started to make real progress when we forced ourselves to leave out the supernatural and to insist whenever possible on natural explanations for events. For example, if we were still inclined to argue that epidemics occurred because God was angry with us for our sinful ways, we probably never would have discovered germs, and with them the actual, practical means to fight epidemics. And during the centuries that science has thought in this fashion, we have generally understood that science may be *apart from* religion but is not *against* religion.

I expressed the sort of attitude that the National Academy of Sciences here calls "scientific," when I said previously that for all we know, someday biology will develop a successor theory to Darwinian evolution. That stresses the tentative and temporary nature of any scientific "facts" (and incidentally, shows why people who keep repeating the term "scientific facts" often fail really to understand what science is about). One test of whether intelligent design could be a science is to ask its advocates if they can envision a more refined and developed theory replacing it someday. They will, of course, deny the very possibility of that occurring. They must, because to them, intelligent design is divinely inspired truth. But if it is that, then it cannot be science.

Judge Jones looked for other evidence that intelligent design might be a part of science. Had any recognized scientific bodies been willing to endorse it, or at least grant it some credence? Had any publications written by intelligent-design backers appeared in peer-reviewed scientific journals? Is there any evidence that intelligent design has been offered to respond to any serious scientific quandaries or concerns, instead of simply representing the religious beliefs of non-scientists? Jones could find no evidence of any of these factors that could go toward locating intelligent design within the realm of science. So he concluded that intelligent design had no proper home there.

Judge Jones had to pay attention to legal precedent as well as to a logical analysis of what counts as science and what does not. If previous courts had ruled that creationism or creation science was actually religion, then he was bound by those precedents. In that regard, the advocates for intelligent design made his job easy. Judge Jones was presented with ample evidence that as soon as the courts had ruled that requiring the teaching of "creation science" was unconstitutional, writers of documents (including the *Pandas* textbook) simply went through and crossed out every place where "creation" appeared and replaced it with "intelligent design"; and everywhere that "God" had been mentioned, that word was crossed out and replaced with "designer." The words and labels changed, but the logical structure of the ideas did not. So Judge Jones had no hesitation deciding that if "creation science" had run afoul of the constitution, then "intelligent design" must also, for the same reasons.

Judge Jones concluded,

[W]e express no opinion on the ultimate veracity of [intelligent design] as a supernatural explanation. However, we commend to the attention of those who are inclined to superficially consider [it] to be a true 'scientific' alternative to evolution without a true understanding of the concept the forgoing detailed analysis. It is our view that a reasonable, objective observer would, after reviewing both the voluminous record in the case, and our narrative, reach the inescapable conclusions that [intelligent design] is an interesting theological argument, but that it is not science.[8]

The judge here was very careful in his choice of words. If intelligent design is actually religion and not science, it would be in its own way as wrong for a judge on the bench to instruct its believers about their religious doctrines, as it was for the Dover school board to foist it off on school children as part of their high school biology class. So Judge Jones made clear that he was not passing any judgment on intelligent design *as religion*. It only came under his purview when its advocates tried to claim it was something it was not, in order to dodge the constitutional prohibition against a governmental body "establishing" a religion.

Levitation Science: A Fanciful Example

Judge Jones for the most part was careful not to step over the line of trying to argue religion with the intelligent-design advocates. In one way, however, he walked right up to that line; and we will have to see whether his argument is defensible. He asserted:

Both Defendants and many of the leading proponents of [intelligent design] make a bedrock assumption which is utterly false. Their presupposition is that evolutionary theory is antithetical to a belief in the existence of a supreme being and to religion in general. Repeatedly in this trial, Plaintiff's scientific experts testified that the theory of evolution represents good science, is overwhelmingly accepted by the scientific community, and that it in no way conflicts with, nor does it deny, the existence of a divine creator.[9]

Just what sort of argument is Judge Jones offering us here? If he is making a religious argument, then we could accuse him of stepping over the line. He seems to suggest that he is making a scientific argument, because he cites the testimony of "scientific experts." But this scientific argument seems to be about a belief in God, which appears to contradict what we have been saying up till now. So what is going on here?

A fanciful example may help clarify this point. Let's suppose that I have a revelation and declare a new religion. I decide that the most spiritually exalted state for a human being is that of floating freely in the air. The notion that one should somehow be tied down to the earth seems, by contrast, crassly materialistic. I therefore declare that in my religion, it is necessary as a show of faith to deny the reality of the law of gravitation. I study all the physics textbooks carefully and discover here and there that questions have been raised about some aspects of gravitation. I carefully collect all these concerns and declare that there are "gaps" in the law of gravitation, and that these "gaps" show that the law is "controversial" and so should not be crammed down our throats as if it were "fact."[10]

So far, from the point of view of religious thinking, I am well within my rights. This new religious belief may well seem silly to the average person, and I may attract very few converts. But it does fine so far as its purely logical structure is concerned–it claims to be a religion, and that is the logical form that it takes. It is also clear at this point that the discussion is *solely* about religion and is not, in any real sense, a *scientific* discussion. This might seem a strange statement because what we are talking about is, after all, a law of science; so how could the discussion not be scientific? But observe that our discussion of the law of gravitation remains purely within a religious context. To dispute my account of my religion, you would have to make religious arguments, not scientific ones. I have made no scientific objection to the law. I have not done any experiments that have caused one to have scientific doubts about gravitation. I have, it is true, mentioned some scientific facts that I looked up in a textbook, but I am tossing these facts into a discussion that remains all about religion. My reasons to object to the law of gravitation are purely religious. The reasons have to do with how I view the ideal relationship between the material and the spiritual realms–reasons that the science of physics, which restricts itself to the material world, cannot address.

Now, suppose that I go one step further. Suppose that I now declare that there is such a thing as "Levitation Science." Levitation Science teaches us that the law of gravitation is false–that is, it teaches what my religion wants us to believe. I demand that the public schools include units on Levitation Science in their science classes as a counter to teaching only about gravitation. The students, I declare, should be able to study the controversies about gravitation and make up their own minds.

Did a discussion that used to be solely a religious one, now suddenly turn into a scientific discussion? The correct answer is no. The invocation of "Levitation *Science*" appears to be a transparent device to give a pseudo-scientific veneer to religion. Just calling it a science did not alter the fundamental issues, that I have discovered no new facts nor done any new experiments nor done any work that is recognizably scientific in its method or nature. I have invoked a so-called "controversy" that I have created in my own mind and that is not shared by any recognized body of competent scientists. If a fair-minded court were to judge my assertion that Levitation Science should be taught in public schools, the court would conclude that I am proposing to insert religion into the schools under the guise of science.

The point that my Levitation Science example and the creationist debate have in common is that *when religion talks about science, religion does not itself turn into science*. There can be a robust religious debate over the claims of creationism, that being a good Christian *requires* that you reject Darwin's account of evolution and all evolutionary science that has followed. Many devout Christians, including many biological scientists I have known, completely reject this assertion. Many fundamentalists may accept this assertion. This is a religious dispute about what it means to be a good Christian. It is not, logically speaking, a scientific debate at all. The people opposing evolutionary theory are opposing it because they do not like its implications for their religious faith–not because they have discovered any new scientific facts that call the theory seriously into question. Whatever debate exists in our society about creationism is going on within religious institutions, and not within any scientific institutions, or on the pages of any scientific journals or textbooks. Religious people have every right to engage in this debate. All that I object to is when they mislabel it and say that it is a scientific debate.

In the Renaissance, the first astronomers who declared that the earth revolved around the sun were attacked for religious heresy. Today, creationists attack Darwinian evolution as somehow being un-Christian. If my proposed new religion, despite all odds, gains millions of adherents, someday people may be demonstrating against the teaching of the law of gravitation. Whether any of this is good or bad or indifferent religion I leave to others to decide. I merely point out that none of it is really a debate *within* any sort of science, even if it is a religious debate *about* some form of science. In each case the objection to the offending science is a religious and not truly a scientific objection, however it might be dressed up.

So let's go back to Judge Jones's statement. If I am right in my analysis, then the debate about whether being a good Christian requires you to reject Darwinian evolution is a religious and not a scientific debate. Therefore, it was misleading of Judge Jones to suggest that "scientific experts" were competent to address that matter. One sort of scientific statement that would be pertinent here (but I don't think that was part of the evidence presented to the court) would be social-science evidence, in which American Christians were surveyed to find out what beliefs they actually held. Survey and other social-science data would say nothing, however, of which among the conflicting views of Christianity was the *correct* one.

I think there is a way to understand what Judge Jones might have been trying to say–and to rescue it from the charge that he had overstepped and was instructing people from the judicial bench about religion:

> I have heard many witnesses testify in the courtroom. Some of them claimed that their understanding of Christianity required that they reject the teachings of evolution. Those people could, apparently, not understand Christianity in any other way. But I also heard many witnesses testify that they themselves, and their colleagues, considered

themselves to be practicing Christians and had no problem at all accepting the truth of Darwin's theories. They stated that they believed devoutly in God and saw no conflict between that belief and evolutionary science.

I am therefore forced to the conclusion that the advocates of intelligent design believe that they are speaking on behalf of all good Christians when they insist upon their doctrine, but that they are rather speaking only on behalf of one point of view within Christianity. If we were to base the curriculum of the Dover school system on teaching Christianity to all students, that would violate the constitutional guarantee of separation of church and state. It would be an equally severe constitutional violation if we based the Dover school curriculum on the beliefs of one faction within Christianity, while ignoring the earnestly held beliefs of other Christians. I cannot speak to the rightness or wrongness of either faction's views, but I can speak to the existence of the difference of opinion within the religious realm.

My own view is that if Judge Jones had said this, he would not be taking sides in a religious argument, while at the same time he would have made clear that he was talking about religion and not about science.

A Scientific Disproof of Intelligent Design?

Let me now proceed *apparently* to pull the rug out from under what I have been saying so far. I have been at pains to keep religion and science in separate silos, as the vernacular has it. That would seem to say that it is simply not possible that *intelligent design could be disproved on scientific grounds*. I have just been arguing that many good Christians, including many biologists, believe in both God and evolution and see no problem. If science cannot be a threat to religious belief, and intelligent design (as we have argued all through this chapter) is a religious belief, then how could science *disprove* that religious perspective?

The quick and dirty answer is that it cannot; "disprove" is too strong a word (which we should consign to the same trash heap where we put "scientific facts"). But religious beliefs differ. Some are about the supernatural or spiritual realm only and clearly make no contact of any kind with the findings of science. Other religious beliefs, however, make claims about the real world we live in that sound a good deal like the "facts" the science puts to the test every day.

We did not go into any details about what the religion that we called "levitation science" might teach. Supposing that one of its teachings is that if you lie on the ground and clap your hands three times, your body will rise up into the air and assume a floating position about four feet off the ground. And, for whatever reason, advocates of the religion "levitation science" absolutely insist that this is a true statement about the world. I think we could agree that any scientific investigation of this "fact" would cast very great doubts on its being factual in any sense of the word. That in turn would seem to make "levitation science," at the very least, highly implausible. That particular scientific finding would create great problems for "levitation science" as a religion. That does not mean that in general, science is at war with religion. It simply means that there are times when religious doctrines assume a form that does bring them more or less directly into conflict with scientific findings, and so in those special situations, there could be a clash between science and religion. True believers could still choose to go with religion and reject science.

Intelligent design seems to me to rely very heavily on one of those claims that looks suspiciously like a scientific "fact" about the world. It is taken as truth by intelligent design advocates that *very complex and elegant beings simply could not have come into existence as a result of a purely random process.* (This is simply a restatement of theologian Haught's testimony before Judge Jones, about Aquinas's syllogism regarding the existence of God.) If you could conduct a scientific experiment, and show that a random process could yield very elegant and complicated structures, then it appears to me that you will have made intelligent design a pretty implausible proposition. Note that the claim it makes is very sweeping and so it would take very little evidence to overturn it. When you claim flat-out that something cannot happen no matter what, you can "disprove" that assertion simply by showing that it could happen once. You do not have to show that it could happen easily, or that it happens often. The mere possibility will do as "disproof."

For obvious reasons scientists cannot go into the laboratory and cook up a primordial stew, out of which fish develop and then grow legs and crawl up on land. So actual evolution of animal species is probably something we could not expect to demonstrate. Some scientists have used bacteria such as the common *E.coli* as the species to study to test out various hypotheses regarding mutation and natural selection. Even when one can produce a new generation of bacteria in only half an hour or so, experiments can still take months or years.

Suppose, on the other hand, that you could design a computer program to produce "organisms" of a sort that functionally resemble living species. If you could make these computer organisms mutate and then see what happens to them when they "reproduce" under conditions of natural selection, you might be able to study the dynamics of evolutionary processes in a few days or weeks. There have now been several programs to do just this, and they are becoming sophisticated enough to impress biologists that the results of these computer simulations may be applicable to living species. One program of this type is called Avida and was developed by a team at Michigan State University.[11]

The "organisms" created in the Avida program are something like computer viruses–though fortunately they are designed so that they cannot escape from the experimental computer system. They are essentially strings of commands in computer code. They are able to replicate themselves. The program allows for random variations (mutations) in the strings of commands to occur. The programs then compete for scarce resources within the computer environment–mainly processor time and memory space. The programs that reproduce more quickly and use resources more efficiently end up occupying the majority of the space within the computer environment.

The Avida programmers began by looking for programs that could carry out the equals operation. That means they could scan a series of pairs of digits and determine when the first pair was equal to the second pair. This sounds extremely simple but is not–when the programmers set out to create a program to perform the equals operation, the shortest version they could come up with was one that contained 19 lines of code.

They populated the Avida program with programs that were too elementary to perform the equals function, and set them up to mutate randomly and then to undergo natural selection. They set the program to replicate through 16,000 generations and then ran the experiment 50 times. In 23 of the 50 times, the programs evolved into more complex programs that could perform the equals operation. The experimenters were impressed that the 23 successful programs were all successful in a different way. Many of them performed the equals operation in ways that the experimenters themselves had never anticipated and could not have dreamed up in advance. This helped confirm that the experiment was legitimate–the complexity evolved from a set of random conditions and was not fed into the program in advance.

The experimenters later decided that they had not created Avida so as to mimic evolution in the real world very well, because they found their experiments producing mostly single species and few diverse "ecosystems." They decided they had made a mistake at first by making the resources too plentiful. They reran their experiments with resources being more restricted. When they did that, instead of the equals operation evolving in 23 out of 50 cases, it evolved in all 50 of the experiments.

The equals operation experiment helps to answer one of the common criticisms of evolution. Creationists object that there is no way an organ like the eye could ever have evolved through natural selection. It seems impossible that the eye could emerge all at once in its final form. Yet if it emerged only piece by piece, no portion of the eye, taken by itself, would have worked, so the steps of the evolutionary process would have conferred no advantages on the organism in terms of natural selection.

The Avida programmers note that the chain of commands needed to make a program perform the equals operation presents a functionally similar problem. If any one command is absent from the chain, the operation will not be performed; yet if only some of the commands are present without the others, the operation cannot be performed either. These difficulties did not stop the mutation and random selection process from evolving programs that perform the equals operation, without any instructions for such programs being fed in at the start. And when one looks at the Avida program in action, it seems to resemble what we observe in the fossil record–there are many periods of gradual change punctuated by periods during which massive changes occur very suddenly.

Ever since the first published results of the Avida experiments appeared in 2003, creationists have been notably upset. Charles Ofria, director of the Digital Evolution Laboratory at Michigan State University, told *Discover* magazine that they have made Avida freely available on the Internet, and he is aware of many creationists who have downloaded the program and tried hard to find flaws in it.[12] He's very pleased because the creationists found a few glitches here and there which the Michigan State team has noted and corrected. But the creationists have never discovered a basic flaw in Avida that would disqualify it as what he and his colleagues claim it to be–a functionally adequate simulation of Darwinian evolution, which demonstrates that complex entities can evolve out of simpler entities by random processes.

Creationism and intelligent design seem to be based on a presumed fact about the natural world, that you can look at an outcome, and figure out what sort of process must have created it. Specifically, if you see something simple, you can assume that it might have arisen by a purely random process. If you see something very complicated, however, then it must have come from a nonrandom process–such as having been created by an intelligent designer, whose mind was capable of seeing the thing before it existed. That seems like common sense. We all have had the experience of imagining something, and then going ahead and building it–whether it was a back deck for our house, or a casserole. If we then go around to other people's houses and see casseroles or back decks, it seems only common sense that the same process must have produced those things too. A butterfly or a hummingbird or a coral reef is something that none of us ever could have made by ourselves; so we have to imagine a mind much greater than our own as the designer.

The Avida computer experiments and other similar programs have shown to my own satisfaction that our common sense has simply been misled in the case of the origin of plant and animal species, even though it was right on regarding casseroles and decks. The computer simulations show that random processes can fool us. They can produce much more complex products, and do so faster, than we could have imagined. So, if you want to imagine along with intelligent design advocates that you can look at a complex being and *just know* that an intelligent designer, and not random processes, must have been responsible, you are engaging in an act of faith that seems to have departed from what we know about the natural world that we inhabit. Still, if that is what you want to believe, you are certainly entitled to it.

The Stealth Factor

Judge Jones's final words about the members of the Dover school board majority who testified in his court was, "It is ironic that several of these individuals, who so staunchly and proudly touted their religious convictions in public, would time and again lie to cover their tracks and disguise the real purpose behind the [intelligent design] policy."[13] Had Judge Jones been thinking of an analogy between economism and intelligent design, and had he read the previous chapter about the Reverse Robin Hood Rule, he might have found it predictable rather than ironic.

Here I may appear to be doing a bit of piling on of my own. It seems that the Dover school board members who pushed the intelligent design agenda–and whom the voters had the good sense thereafter to remove–were a particularly bumbling and thoughtless group. Any of us who, involved in a lawsuit, want to go into court and be sure of winning, should hope for opponents like them. So if, in the end, they turned out to be liars as well, how can this be seen as a general commentary on defenders of either economism or intelligent design? Are there not many decent, truthful people who adhere to those doctrines?

I readily admit that there are many honest people who believe in the ideas that I am challenging in this book. But I also admit that in our very brief survey of our topic, we seem to have encountered the problem of deception and stealth rather too often for it to be pure coincidence.

I will offer my suspicion as suspicion only. I am going to hazard a guess as to how the devoutly religious people whom served on the Dover school board could walk into a court of justice and tell lies (which, last I heard, violates one of the Ten Commandments—a document I assume they'd want to see prominently displayed in all school buildings).

The board members clearly thought they were doing God's work in trying to make the local schools more "Christian" according to their own doctrines. They were on a mission. They knew that God wanted them to succeed. To succeed they had to overcome various obstacles. When you are doing God's will you cannot be overly finicky about the means that you use to overcome obstacles. You must employ whatever means are necessary. Clearly that is what God would want of you. Bottom line–if you have to lie to further God's work, then it is a tiny price to pay for a much greater good. (This form of ethical reasoning is called utilitarianism; and it is interesting how often religious devotees who condemn utilitarianism as a Godless form of pseudo-ethics grab for it themselves when in a tight corner.)

My suspicion is that when your political and social choices are actually determined by a deeper religious allegiance, you might be more strongly tempted to lie as a tool of political gamesmanship, because you see yourself as merely a foot soldier following orders in God's army. Ironically, the lie itself turns into God's will. This is not, of course, true of all religious motivation. People whose positions on social policy are motivated by a deeply seated compassion for those less well off, and by a humility regarding their personal frailties, are unlikely to lie to try to advance their cause. But those who view their religion as giving them a power over others, and whose approach to holding that power is arrogance rather than humility (as seemed to be true of the Dover school board), may be the ones tempted to use lies to get their way.

Conclusion: Economism and Intelligent Design

Since I seem, in this chapter, to have strayed rather far from the main theme of the book, I need to go back and retrace the route.

Economism is the belief that the economic sphere of society is the most important, and that it ought to remain free from political interference. It also rises above any ethical judgment because it has its own sort of internal ethic– whatever happens as a result of free market exchanges is the best thing that could have happened.

The economic sphere, when governed by the rules of neoclassical or especially of supply-side economics, appears systematically to favor the rich over the poor. According to economism, this is the working out of a natural process, and to interfere in that process would be to court disaster for rich and poor alike.

Economism claims to have gotten these ideas from an objective, dispassionate, scientific and mathematical inquiry into the way the world is structured. Our history has shown, by contrast, that economism seems to be shot through with religious ideas that it picked up from 18th century American

Puritanism and 19th century English evangelicalism. To thrive as a political force today, economism finds it convenient to conceal those religious elements and to stress instead its supposedly objective and scientific veneer.

If a single religious idea seems to be at the root of economism, it is that *reward and punishment do not happen in this world unless God wants it that way.* Some years ago, a best-selling book by a rabbi offered an explanation of *Why Bad Things Happen to Good People.*[14] That book, however, never made economism's best-seller list; and economism's devotees no doubt regard the title of this book as heresy. Bad things simply cannot happen to good people–as those who wrote angry letters to the *Atlanta Journal-Constitution* about the evil Post family were convinced (Chapter 6). The rich must be good or they would not be rewarded; the poor must be bad or they would not be punished. To say otherwise is blasphemy.

One of the guiding lights of economism is half of Adam Smith–the half that wrote about the marketplace and the invisible hand (Chapter 3). Adam Smith's metaphor of the invisible hand was designed to capture the idea that a great many things could happen, each seemingly at random, each seemingly for a purely individual and private reason, and yet all resulting in an outcome which, viewed as a whole, seemed as carefully coordinated and plotted out as if everyone were performing in a marching band at halftime during a football game. This is the magic of the market, and no matter what you think about how lightly or how heavily the market should be regulated–how well or how poorly you think the market serves the greater social good–you have to admit that the result is truly majestic, every bit as wonderful as the way that an entire flock of birds can turn in midair and fly off in a new direction. Old Adam was surely right on that account.

There are two ways to think about that invisible hand. One is that it is purely a metaphor. The market (an abstraction, not a real thing) acts *as if* guided by an invisible hand. It is mathematically true that events that are individually quite unpredictable will often (but not always) turn out in the large mass to be quite predictable. That mathematical truth is all the "invisible hand" refers to. Things that are random at one level of organization may seem predictable and organized at a higher level of organization. Seen this way, Adam Smith was a version of a Darwinian evolutionary–believing that something elegant could emerge from a whole series of random processes. As a student of the Enlightenment, Smith probably in fact thought this way. He was much more likely to believe in a God that set a mechanism in motion and then let the mechanism work out according to natural laws, than in a God that tinkered with the mechanism and intervened at each step to get the result he wanted.

The other way to think about the invisible hand is the way that the 19th century evangelicals thought of their world–a far cry from the Enlightenment that seemed to them to have gone up in the flames of the French Revolution. In that view of the world the invisible hand is no metaphor, but is simply the very literal and real hand of God. Markets work the way they do because it is God's will and because God directs every aspect of their workings. God makes sure that the good are rewarded and the bad are punished. For us to try to tinker with the laws of the marketplace is to invite disaster in two ways–first, because if we tinker with a delicate, self-regulating system, we are almost sure to make it work badly; and second, if we mess with God's plan, he will get angry with us and want to punish us.

We can now see how economism and intelligent design are both based on very similar views of God's role in the world. That things could *just happen at random*, without God having planned it, seems to be too scary a thought for an advocate of either doctrine to live with comfortably. But neither can exert the necessary power over others, to get all to play along by the same rulebook, if each doctrine is honestly portrayed as fundamentally a religious belief. Therefore, each has to pose as science in order to have its way, forcing its advocates to engage in stealth and deception.

So far the attempt at deception has been generally a failure for intelligent design insofar as the courts and legal precedent is concerned. Judge Jones is given credit for handing intelligent design a defeat from which it has not recovered. In other ways, however, intelligent design has been extremely successful. It has raised doubts in many people's minds about evolutionary theory–doubts that would never exist were the actual science better understood. And very powerful and well-funded organizations like the Discovery Institute have spread the intelligent design and anti-evolution message very widely. A great many school-age children in the U.S. have been brought up thinking that it is a sin to study or to try to understand Darwinian evolution, and that they do not need to, because intelligent design is a credible scientific alternative. A mind, as the old commercial used to intone, is a terrible thing to waste, and in one sense all these young minds are being wasted—certainly there is little chance that they will have a successful career in the sciences. Economism, as we have seen, has been much more successful in posing as a science, and therefore much more successful in having its way in the world of U.S. policy and politics.

In sum, economism and intelligent design resemble each other quite closely in a number of features. They seem grounded in very similar, fundamentalist views of the role of God in the natural world and everyday human life. They are at heart religious and yet claim to be science. They tempt their advocates to stealth and deception as the means to move the agendas forward. Neither is as plausible once the actual religious underpinnings and origins are fully exposed.

We have now devoted a number of chapters to analyzing the logical structure and content of economism. We have also, along the way, studied some of its real-world consequences. In the next chapter, we'll look in more detail at a particularly important and prevalent consequence of economism–layoffs.

Notes

1. Bigelow G. Let there be markets: the evangelical roots of economics. *Harpers Magazine* 310 (no. 1860), May 2005: 33-38, quote p. 34.

2. Tammy Kitzmiller et al. *v.* Dover Area School District et al., 400 F. Supp. 2d 707; 2005 U.S. Dist. LEXIS 33647, Case No. 04cv2688; http://www.pamd. uscourts.gov/kitzmiller/kitzmiller_342.pdf (accessed Nov. 28, 2010).

3. See for example "John E. Jones III," http://en.wikipedia.org/wiki/John_E._ Jones_III (accessed December 27, 2010).

4. See for example: Kansas school boards evolution ruling angers science community. CNN.com, August 12, 1999; http://articles.cnn.com/1999-08-12/us/9908_12_kansas.evolution.flap_1_kansas-decision-kansas-board-evolution?_s=PM:US (accessed December 27, 2010).

5. Kitzmiller *v.* Dover School Board: 718.

6. Kitzmiller *v.* Dover School Board: 720.

7. Kitzmiller *v.* Dover School Board: 737.

8. Kitzmiller *v.* Dover School Board: 745-46.

9. Kitzmiller *v.* Dover School Board: 765.

10. This strategy of creating doubt even when the actual scientific evidence is very strong appears to have begun with the efforts of the tobacco industry to pretend that we did not really *know* that smoking causes cancer. More recently opponents of climate change have used the same strategy to good effect.

11. Zimmer C. Testing Darwin. *Discover Magazine*, February 2005; http:// discovermagazine.com/2005/feb/cover (accessed Nov. 28, 2010). For an excellent overview and critical discussion of creationism generally see Pennock RT. *Tower of Babel: the evidence against the new creationism.* Cambridge, MA: MIT Press, 1999.

12. Zimmer, Testing Darwin.

13. Kitzmiller *v.* Dover School Board: 765.

14. Kushner HS. *Why bad things happen to good people.* New York: Anchor, 2004.

Chapter 8.
Layoffs

Back in the early years of the last century, a peddler sold goods from a wagon drawn by an old horse. The peddler was of course anxious to maximize his profits and to cut expenses to the bone. One of his main costs was the oats that he fed to the horse. He figured that if he suddenly cut back on the oats, the horse would complain and might even get sick. But the peddler reasoned that if he cut back the oats by just a smidgeon each day, the horse would not notice; and that over time he'd save a bundle.

So he carried out his plan, and each day gave the horse just a little less oats than the day before. Over time, the horse grew thinner and thinner, but still managed to pull the wagon. Finally the horse died.

"Doggone that stupid horse!" raged the peddler. "Just when I had trained him to get by on practically no oats at all, he goes and dies on me!"

The attitude of this peddler toward his horse seems to mirror exactly the attitude of corporate America toward its workers. The corporation assumes an absolute right to trim its costs in whatever way it chooses. If it does so by laying off large numbers of workers, the remaining workers are supposed to suck it up and do the same amount of work previously done by the original workforce. If finally the stress of overwork is so huge that the workers cannot handle it any more, America will blame them rather than the corporation.

A great many American workers today have either been laid off, or live in perpetual insecurity in fear of a layoff. Layoffs represent one aspect of an important consequence of economism, the privatization of risk. U.S. policy seems to be that you, personally, are pretty much on your own when facing the ups and downs of life–unless you are wealthy or a large corporation, in which case the government will do a great deal to shield you from the risks associated with your behavior. When the financial markets were tanking in the fall of 2008, we saw how readily Republicans and Democrats agreed that large firms needed an emergency bailout–and how much less willing they were to approve any bailout measures that directly assisted workers about to be laid off or homeowners facing foreclosure.

Then and Now

As a college freshman in 1967, I moved to Michigan. (Recall from our family story in Chapter 2 that this was about the same time that Henry Wyzansky, Stan and Carol's son and Shelly's father, also graduated from high school and started college.) One of the first new concepts that I was introduced to, as part of the local culture, was "30 and out." A young man in Michigan and many of the other Rust Belt states could graduate from high school at age 18, walk a few blocks to the local automobile plant, and get a job. While I was studying in the college classroom, my 18-year-old peer would be learning his trade on the auto assembly line, and earning decent money in the process.

If my peer worked hard he could count on having a job with the giant auto firm until he retired 30 years later. (If he worked for one of the Big Three automakers, General Motors, Ford, or Chrysler, he would have laughed himself silly had you suggested to him that there was a chance that the company might not still be in business after 30 years.) After a year or so he could probably afford a new car. When he was perhaps 25 he could afford to get married and buy a modest house in a working-class neighborhood. He could afford all this on his single income, while his wife remained home to raise the children. (We might today thoroughly reject the sexist discrimination that so severely limited the wife's career options, while still being wistful about the power of a single salary to at least provide the spouse with the option of staying at home to rear the family.) At age 48, the worker could retire from the auto plant with a guaranteed pension. With his pension he could afford to start up a small business or begin a second career. Then, at age 65, he could retire for good, enjoying both his auto plant pension plus his Social Security income. With that level of income he could plan a retirement that included a lot of golf and winters in Florida, or a modest summer home on one of the lakes that dot the landscape of northern Michigan.

Today, we equate the big auto companies of those days with all that is wrong in American manufacturing, so it might seem that here I am extolling a cushy lifestyle that the worker enjoyed only by causing the company to become weak and inefficient. So it is important to recall that the description I just gave of the worker's life came with two very important provisos. First, I am assuming that he was willing to work hard for those 30 years, at a job that was both arduous and boring. Second, I would remind today's readers that the life of leisure and financial security that worker enjoyed upon retirement was partly paid for by considerable scrimping and saving during at least the family's first couple of decades. Dinner for that worker's household much more often consisted of hamburger or chicken, and steak was a rare treat (as was eating out). A vacation was a few days at a beach on Lake Michigan, not a flight to Cancun or to Europe. In short, this was the lifestyle that Stan and Carol Wyzansky were used to in the 1950s and 1960s, while they were raising their three children.

Assuring him of all these benefits of his hard and boring work was the United Auto Workers union. The idea that he should have had the "right" not to join this union when he went to work for the auto company would have been as laughable to that 18-year-old as the idea that his employer firm might not remain in business during his entire lifetime. The union would assure that his working conditions were safe and as decent as possible, and especially that he had excellent health care coverage for himself and his family, as well as to guarantee the pension that served as the central incentive for his entire career. Stan Wyzansky, as an attorney, was not a member of any union, yet he strongly supported the union movement. He recalled vividly the days of the Depression and had seen what happened when workers had no organization and hence no power.

Putting all these pieces together, the auto plant option seemed an excellent career choice for the 18-year-old who lacked a strong motivation or aptitude for college. Given the tenor of the times, I doubt that many of my age peers who chose that career path imagined that their children would repeat this cycle, even as many of them were repeating the careers of their fathers. Rather they imagined as a matter of course that their own children would better themselves by attending college. A level of income that would allow them to put all their children through college was another benefit they simply took for granted.

Then came economism. First, Ronald Reagan, as one of his first acts in office, took on and defeated the air traffic controllers' union. Many at first saw this as a limited attack on union overreaching, and did not realize the extent to which Reagan intended to be a union-busting president. Then the Clinton administration took office and told us that the days of "30 and out" were over. Today's worker should expect to have several careers between ages 18 and 65. The key was education and training. Being laid off might well be a blessing in disguise. It would be the signal that it was time to move forward, and to educate oneself better for new careers that were just appearing. Our government policies should never waste resources by trying to protect dead-end jobs. The role of government was mainly to assist workers to train for other jobs and careers. Workers who took advantage of those programs could anticipate steady advancement in their new lines of work. Those who failed to apply themselves, or who wasted time and energy protesting being laid off, would of course not succeed, but they had only themselves to blame.

Statistics show that American workers are among the most productive in the world and have remained so for many years.[1] This productivity has not led to any corresponding job security in today's corporate world, any more than the peddler's horse got additional oats as his reward for loyally continuing to pull the wagon. Firms during the 1990s needed little provocation to lay off massive numbers of employees. It often seemed that if you wanted to see the value of your company's stock rise on Wall Street, all you had to do was announce huge layoffs to "cut expenses."

Nor have things changed. Journalist Bill Moyers, speaking at Boston University in October, 2010, related to his audience a recent news report, that Harley-Davidson had reported second quarter profits of $71 million, or three times the earnings compared to the previous year. The company made these record profits partly as a result of plans to cut a total of about 3500 jobs over the period 2009-2011. The result: Wall Street is ecstatic about the value of the motorcycle company's stock. Moyers quoted the chief economist at Bank of America Merrill Lynch, Ethan Harris: "There's no question that there is an income shift going on in the economy. Companies are squeezing their labor costs to build profits."[2] (Do you remember the promise of Reagan's supply-side economics—that if we gave the rich enough tax cuts, they'd invest in corporations, and that would allow corporations to expand and hire more people at better wages?)

When corporations in the 1990s were laying off workers in droves, the Clinton Administration said that this was perfectly all right. Why did a Democratic administration do so little to stand up for the average worker? Harold Meyerson, editor-at-large of *American Prospect,* suggested that this was a natural outgrowth of economism. The belief system that easily captured the allegiance of conservative Republicans had, by 1992, become so dominant in America that few Democrats could escape its grip either. "The doctrine of laissez faire has been so dominant, so pervasive over the past three decades that hundreds of Democratic politicians can deliver a paean to the market at the drop of a hat, but not a single Republican pol can plausibly defend government as a check on capitalism run amok...."[3] The Democratic willingness to bend a knee at the altar of economism was especially pronounced among neoliberals like Bill Clinton—and increasingly appears to be characteristic of the Obama Administration as well.

The Consequences of Layoffs

Louis Uchitelle, a journalist with long experience covering economic issues, studied layoffs in depth for his book, *The Disposable American.*[4] Uchitelle's research shows that the comforting Clinton ideology is mostly false. Two things are highly predictable following a layoff. First, even if one works hard to get education and training, the end result will almost always be a lower paying job. It is very rare for a laid-off worker, even a very well-trained one, to advance rather than regress in the job market. Workers who went through the Clinton federal job retaining programs, if they were employed at all 2-3 years following layoff, averaged 14 percent lower pay than in their previous job.[5] With jobs going overseas at a rapid clip, there are simply not enough high-paying American jobs to take up the slack.

The second highly predictable consequence of a layoff is the human psychological toll. Uchitelle catalogues first the short-term fallout, including:
    . . . income loss, downward mobility, a decrease in family cohesion,
  a rise in the divorce rate, the unwinding of communities, the impact on

children, the impact on survivors who dodge a layoff but are left feeling insecure and guilty that they kept their jobs while colleagues did not. Extended periods [without work] bring a cascade of damages, including depression, and these too are documented. One study, for example, found that for every percentage point change in the employment rate, up or down, the national suicide rate rose or fell in tandem, and so did the frequency of strokes, heart attacks, crime, and accidents.[6]

While mental health professionals and scientists are familiar with these consequences of layoffs, Uchitelle adds, "In the damage that results from layoffs, incapacitating emotional illness almost never appears on the lists that economists, politicians, sociologists, union leaders, business school professors, management consultants, and journalists compile."[7]

The emotional devastation produced by layoffs is, once we come to think about it, a natural outgrowth of the widespread adoption of the cultural values that have come to be called the "Protestant Ethic" (Chapter 5). The same cultural beliefs that made the workers of Northern Europe and America the perfect manpower for the Industrial Revolution guaranteed that they would have no emotional or cultural defenses against layoffs. It often helps to think of our lives in terms of the stories that we tell about them. Social scientists have found that most of us have a deep need for our lives to make sense both to ourselves and to others.[8] A measure of our lives making sense is our ability to tell a coherent and connected story about who we are and where we came from. Our careers are usually a major part of our life stories. A sense of aimlessness in our careers, a sense that our careers are not valued by those with power over us, leads to a deep experience of personal inadequacy and loss of meaning in our lives.[9] The society that we live in has taken full advantage of our dedication to our work, our sense that being a valued worker is a big part of what gives our lives meaning (a sense of *calling* as Max Weber phrased it (Chapter 5)). We would like to imagine that the same society would then feel some sense of obligation to us when we are rendered most vulnerable by having this sense of self-worth abruptly jerked away, through no fault of our own.

However, it is not just that the laid-off worker goes through a period of depression or similar emotional problems immediately afterward. The effects occur over a longer term. All future job, and even life decisions are made with timidity and tentativeness because of the overriding fear of being laid off again in the future. Workers who used to be creative risk-takers become meek followers of routine. Uchitelle tells us the story of Tim Dewey, formerly a well-paid worker for a major airline, who some time after being laid off in Indianapolis found a job in Florida operating a tourist boat:

> Here was a skilled and experienced aircraft mechanic who had opted to drive a launch around a bay, the sort of minimally skilled work that students do on summer vacations. He had migrated from industrial importance to the equivalent of roadside kiosk proprietor hawking boat rides to passing tourists. And no one noticed. In a nation that parcels out layoffs so easily, the mindless destruction of skill is an overlooked by-product. Dewey had dropped out to protect himself from the psychological damage and financial uncertainty of still another layoff, and in doing so had deprived the United States of his true value as a skilled worker.[10]

In other words, when layoffs are rampant, the American economy loses two things of great value. First, it loses a group of well-paid workers and replaces them with a group of lower-paid workers. Second, it loses a special type of worker, who is exactly the sort we need most in a rapidly changing world.

Layoffs and the Privatization of Risk

Layoffs are a prime example of what Jacob Hacker calls the privatization of risk.[11] There was a time, back in the "30 and out" era, when keeping productive workers employed at high salaries was seen as a national priority that was protected by a powerful triumvirate. The corporations wanted to maintain the competitive edge that a well-trained and loyal work force could provide. Unions wanted to protect their members, and had sufficient power to bargain as co-equals with the large corporations. Government wanted to keep both corporations and union members happy, and had a tradition of generally supporting the union movement as an antidote to the industrial exploitation of the robber-baron era during the first Gilded Age. Hacker then shows us how, in the 1970s and after, this social support system unraveled. Government and business came to agree that the highest corporate profits could be made in a world where individuals had to assume the greatest burden of financial risk by themselves. Government saw its mission as aiding the wealthy and the large corporations through deregulation and tax cuts, so the programs that used to support workers and cushion the blow of a layoff disappeared. Uchitelle found in his research that in an era when most U.S. citizens have been brainwashed to cringe when they hear the very words "labor union," the remaining unions have been so cowed by the current climate that they no longer stand up for the workers. Union leaders will acquiesce in the layoff of 5000 workers because the corporation threatens them with the later layoff of 10,000 if the union does not cooperate.

Many other distortions of the corporate job climate occurred in this environment. Corporate leaders became convinced that massive layoffs were actually good. Workers, they reasoned, would become more productive and more efficient. Commonly after a layoff, as many as one-fifth of the white-collar workers let go would be hired back on as consultants, so managers could imagine that the idea of a layoff had lost its sting. Since stock values commonly rose when a company laid off workers, pension fund managers became a cheering section favoring more layoffs–ironically, the very people supposedly bringing you old-age financial security were working for your immediate loss of job security.

If, under neoliberal or Republican rule, the Federal government seems indifferent to layoffs, the same is not true of city and county government. The impact on the local economy of hundreds or thousands of layoffs when a large plant closes usually forces governments to take action. In the absence of a coordinated Federal policy, however, this action is often in vain. Local governments became patsies for corporate shakedowns. Large firms have now become adept at threatening to close a plant as a way of extorting local tax breaks. The mayor or county commission is usually willing to grant massive tax breaks to firms that promise to keep the local factory open or to build a new plant in town. In 2004, some $30 billion in tax revenue was lost in this way.[12] This loss of tax revenue is a double waste. In economic hard times, it is often the local government that most quickly suffers from the consequences of unemployment. Moreover, the loss of tax revenue is a complete waste from the national point of view, since a plant that is opened in one community simply means a plant that is lost to another. Having exhorted the maximum tax benefits, the firm is then free to close the plant down anyway a few years later, capping the whole process with the final snub.

Electing a Democratic administration in 1993-2001 did nothing to reverse the privatization of risk represented by layoffs. The entire Clinton message was that if you are laid off, it was your own fault. You obviously did not get the right training or else you positioned yourself badly in a rapidly changing economy. The problem lies with you. It does not lie with a system that rewards corporations for treating loyal, highly skilled workers as if they were paper towels. Uchitelle characterizes the extent to which even Democrats had bought into the world-view of economism as the dominance, during the 1980s and 1990s, of "the largely mythical, nostalgic, and debilitating view that in America, people pulled themselves up by their own endeavors, acting heroically and alone . . . Taxes and regulations only got in the way, as did unions and job security."[13]

The Merger-Layoff Cycle

According to economism, layoffs and their emotional consequences are all a working out of divine will. Uchitelle cites Jack Welch, CEO of General Electric during the 1980s, as one of the main architects of the merger-acquisition pattern of doing business that made layoffs a way of life:

The Welch way... diverted the wages of tens of millions of laid-off workers into corporate cash flow and profits, or into repayment of the loans that were floated to pay for all the maneuvering, or into the bloated incomes of the deal-makers.[14] . . . America's entrepreneurial energy focused not on production but on the financial maneuvering and the chasing of profits through acquisition that Jack Welch had done so much to promote. Raising shareholder value became the great justification for merger and acquisition activity, and out of this breeding ground came a new creature, the corporate raider, who multiplied the acquisitions and reorganizations–and the accompanying layoffs.[15]

According to the dominant view:

The raiders were doing God's work . . . They were forcing complacent managers of overstaffed companies to cut costs through layoffs and to close down or sell off underperforming divisions. True, mayhem often resulted but the alternative was bankruptcy, or so the argument went. Better to save sixty jobs out of a hundred if that could be done by laying off forty employees and thus ensure survival in the new global market.[16]

Whether a corporate takeover attempt succeeded or was warded off, the result was indebtedness that required cost cutting and hence layoffs. Most important, companies increasingly found that when they resorted to layoffs, there were no adverse reactions from either the stock market or from consumers. For the corporate world, layoffs were safe.

The layoff culture is, in other words, economism's dream. The super-rich get richer because stock values rise and corporate deal-makers earn huge salaries and bonuses. The workers who are laid off overwhelmingly blame themselves, and never question whether something is wrong with the system. Worker solidarity is destroyed–everyone fears that if she makes waves her job is the next to go–so the cohesion that led to the formation of the early labor unions in the past has disappeared, and corporations need not fear the unions. As Uchitelle explains it, "At some operations the bottom 2 or 3 percent were laid off annually, and those ranked just above them became the bottom 2 or 3 percent, vulnerable in the next layoff."[17] The personal and social costs of layoffs conveniently fail to show up on any economist's balance sheet. (Going back to Bill Moyers quoting the economist Ethan Harris, when companies make record profits as a result of layoffs, no actual flesh-and-blood people are involved; they are simply "squeezing their labor costs." Apparently no people were harmed in the making of this film.[18])

Karl Rove, the political mastermind behind George W. Bush's successful campaign for the Presidency, was quoted as pining for the days of William McKinley as the golden era of the American nation.[19] With the merger-layoff cycle, it seems that the contemporary workplace environment has now come to resemble the typical labor practices during the first Gilded Age. But there is a difference–in the late 1800s no one knew any better. Uchitelle suggests, "What has happened since the late 1970s, on the other hand, is a long and dismaying fall back toward the days of the early twentieth century, and the tragedy is that people know what they are losing and that the loss damages them."[20] Even if we tend to blame ourselves and not the system when we are laid off, somewhere deep in our bones we realize that it does not have to be this way. The fact that it *is* this way nonetheless is a measure of what we have lost as a people and as a community.

The Disappearing Union Movement

When, with the aid of the Chicago Boys, economism-driven right-wing dictatorships were installed in South American nations like Chile, Brazil and Argentina (Chapter 6), the first target of the new junta and its forces was labor unions. Among all the purported enemies of new regime, the union leaders were rounded up most quickly, often on the very first day the junta was in power (long before anyone had any time to commit any actual "crimes" against the new government). The large U.S. corporations operating in those countries often aided the juntas to break the unions within their own plants.[21]

The Bush Administration's response to Hurricane Katrina was arguably as much an exercise in economism-as-policy as those South American juntas. Naomi Klein writes that the Bush forces, goaded by Milton Friedman, lost no time in using the hurricane as an excuse to privatize the New Orleans school system: "In sharp contrast to the glacial pace with which the levees were repaired and the electricity grid was brought back online, the auctioning off of New Orleans' school system took place with military speed and precision."[22] One clear target of the privatization campaign was the city's teacher's union– all 4700 union teachers were fired, and only a few got jobs in the new system of charter schools, generally at lower pay. Now, we must admit that inefficiency and official corruption were rampant in New Orleans prior to the hurricane. It is not hard to imagine that the teacher's union participated in that unfortunate system to some degree. But does it make sense to imagine that *every single member* of the union was a bad teacher?

Union-busting as general strategy raises this question across the board. In a balanced system where unions are strong enough to go toe to toe with large corporations, unions have power. Anyone who has power can abuse it. There are many cases on record from the middle years of the 20th century where unions abused their power. Admittedly, by the 1960s and 1970s, the old-style unions had serious problems with corruption and featherbedding. Creating labor unions is no public-policy panacea. But the current system, where unions have virtually no power, is effectively a throwback to the first Gilded Age, when large corporations held all the cards. From the workers' standpoint that system is obviously worse than taking a chance with unions. Yet it seems that the very concept of a labor union has disappeared from the average American's consciousness. In 2010, *Newsweek* magazine published an article, "Are Fed-Up American Workers Getting Their Gumption Back?" with the subtitle, "Surveys show employees are tired and disillusioned with their employers." Yet the word 'union' did not even appear within the article.[23]

Thomas Frank, describing American popular culture during the 1990s, gave a number of examples of how anti-union sentiments have worked their way into our everyday thinking. Commenting on reactions to union demonstrations against the World Trade Organization in Seattle in 1999, Frank counted how many defenders of U.S. corporations' rights to use sweatshop labor in the developing world portrayed the union members, and the college students who joined them, as mindless automatons. "This is why," he explained, "in the culture of the nineties, [corporate] CEOs were 'leaders' and union chiefs were 'bosses,' regardless of the fact that unions are often democracies while corporations are almost always dictatorships."[24]

Why have we allowed labor unions to become the outcasts of our society? Can we look at the behavior of today's corporations, whether in using layoffs as the preferred way to generate cash or in risking workers' health to make a few extra cents profit, and argue that allowing government policy to systematically weaken the labor union movement was actually a good idea? To allow union excesses to tarnish the entire record of the labor movement throughout the 20th century seems excessive and short-sighted.

Harold Meyerson of the *American Prospect* commented on how, in early 2009, China and the U.S. effectively shared the unemployment caused by the global financial meltdown. The U.S., with reported unemployment at 7.6 percent, appeared to be doing considerably better than it had during the economic crises of the 1980s when unemployment was above 10 percent. The reason for that was that so many American jobs had been outsourced to China, where it was estimated that 20 million migrant factory workers had lost their jobs.

Meyerson went on to describe the relationship between the U.S. and China as "misshapen economic codependency." When the U.S. export market dried up, China suddenly found that it had no domestic market capable of buying the goods its factories produced, since wages in China were so low. America is in trouble because we replaced well-paying manufacturing jobs with low-paying service jobs, but maintained our middle-class lifestyle largely through rising debt, which we expected the Chinese to finance for us.

What do the U.S. and China have in common that helped create this unhealthy codependency? Meyerson adds, "They are the only two major economic powers that are resolutely hostile to unions." Ironically, had each country been more friendly to the union movement, it would now be in a better position to weather the economic shocks it is faced with.[25]

Given all the publicity given to the problem of multinational corporations outsourcing American jobs overseas, Bill Moyers found irony in what happened when a new BMW plant recently opened in South Carolina and advertised for 1000 workers. With the terrible economy, the plant was swamped with over-qualified applicants, who had been laid off from executive positions and who held advanced degrees. The applicants were all standing in line for jobs that paid $15 an hour. The irony was that this is about half what similar BMW workers are paid in (unionized) Germany. It is scary to think that under the policies of economism, the United States of America has become the sort of third-world nation to which more advanced countries can outsource their routine jobs to save on costs.

Beyond Economism?

What if economism was no longer allowed to dictate the agenda? What solutions would then be proposed for the layoff mania? Uchitelle favors a federal wage insurance program, which was briefly considered and then abandoned by the Clinton administration.[26] Such a program would help to insure that workers who were laid off and who did any retraining that was required did not lose wages as a result. I had not even heard of such a program before I read Uchitelle's book–suggesting how far off the public radar screen such proposals remain in a world in which economism gets to control the political agenda.

Several other measures also seem pertinent as possible solutions. If there are serious social costs to layoffs, why should corporations who engage in layoffs not pay some of those costs? Is there a way to structure corporate taxes so as to reward a company that treats its workforce as a valuable resource, over one that treats its workers as disposable? The increased taxes paid by the bad actors could fund the federal wage insurance–since if all companies acted like the most responsible ones, the need for such insurance would be minimized.

In the end, Uchitelle suggests, "Shrinking the number [of layoffs] is possible, but before we can make it happen, we have to address a philosophical issue: Are we going to once again be a community of people who feel obligated to take care of one another, or are we going to continue as a collection of individuals, each one increasingly concerned only with his or her well-being?"[27] Economism's answer to this question is clear. The basis for all of human life, and the rules that ought to govern us, is the marketplace idea of each of us trying to maximize our own self-interest. There is simply no room for community or caring in that marketplace, unless you can purchase it at the going rate.

A resurgence, not a further withering away, of unions seems called for to counter the excessive power of the large corporations. The idea that workers can have appropriate rights and security, without having to pay for these through some reasonable level of union dues, must be exposed as a myth promulgated by economism's defenders. I have a hard time imagining that most laid-off workers, if they could be convinced that being a union member would have saved their jobs, would in hindsight have refused to pay reasonable union dues in exchange for that advocacy.

Against Economism and Layoffs: A Glimpse of Hope?

Paul Bremer, who later became President Bush's point man for the U.S. occupation and reconstruction of Iraq in 2003, tried to cash in on the September 11 attacks as a private counterterrorism consultant. He wrote a report for his corporate clients in November 2001, admitting that a system of free trade "requires laying off workers. And opening markets to foreign trade puts enormous pressure on traditional retailers and trade monopolies, [leading to]...growing income gaps and social tensions."[28] Bremer warned that this could lead to anti-Western backlash, including terrorist attacks. In this way he exactly predicted the outcome in Iraq, after he took over implementation of Bush's Iraq strategy, since he did precisely what he had earlier warned against.

Iraq policy aside, what seems most striking about Bremer's statement is the bald acceptance that economism and layoffs are joined at the hip. You can do the math. If a corporation is to maximize its profit it must cut its costs. Cutting costs entails doing whatever is necessary to get fewer workers to do more work for lower pay, and to make them too fearful of losing their jobs to complain. In short, lay off as many workers as you can, both to cut costs directly but also to terrorize the workforce that remains. And especially be sure that no union remains with the spine to do anything about it.

In the last chapter we'll learn about the work of British epidemiologists and policy analysts Richard Wilkinson and Kate Pickett.[29] They are interested in the many social problems that all have income inequality as a common origin. Here we can take a look at just one of their suggestions to create a better future—democratic employee-ownership of corporations.

Wilkinson and Pickett note that a number of companies in their native Britain have moved toward employee share-ownership schemes. But in many cases, employee ownership of small pieces of the company does not change the way the company is run. The result instead is to try to make workers even more compliant under the thumb of management. The worst abuse of employee share-ownership occurs when no regulations preclude the employees simply selling their shares back to external shareholders, negating the entire system.

Wilkinson and Pickett note that real change occurs when share ownership is linked with active employee participation in the management of the company. When both happen at the same time, an increasing number of research studies show that multiple benefits result.

One factor that makes today's layoff culture so toxic is the sense among employees that they have no control over their workplace. This sense of loss of control is magnified when shareholders of large corporations can buy and sell companies at will. Since a great deal of the value of any corporation is its workforce, that system really amounts to investors being able to buy and sell people. If you are one of the people being bought and sold, you can easily imagine the negative mental-health (and even physical health) consequences of being in that demeaning position.

By contrast, when employees own a substantial share of the company and have a proportionate role in management, a corporation is on the way to becoming a true working community.[30] The workers gain the benefits of having a real say in the way their work environment is structured and managed. The company gains the benefit of a more dedicated and engaged workforce, ready to give the sort of management advice that can only come from an intimate knowledge of all facets of the company's work. This combination can lead to impressive commercial success. Wilkinson and Pickett mention the Mondragon Corporation in Spain, an employee cooperative system that has grown over about 50 years to include 120 employee-owned companies with a total workforce of 40,000. Its companies are twice as profitable as the average Spanish firm, and boast the highest labor productivity in the nation.

Michael Moore, in his film "Capitalism—A Love Story," adds the example of a cooperative bread factory in California, which is financially robust and is governed by a democratic vote among all the workers. The assembly line workers make about $65,000 annually, which is three times the starting pay of commuter airline pilots (a group, as Moore explains, that is represented by a union, but that has been beaten down by continued corporate layoffs and cost-cutting salary reductions).[31]

Other research has shown that the more workers in a given city that are involved in employee ownership, the lower the crime rates and the better statistics for education and health that city boasts. This research suggests that even greater general social benefits could accrue to the U.S. if employee ownership and participation were to account for an increasing share of the total market.[32]

If we wished to, we could create government policies that encouraged employee ownership and shared management of firms. Economism would oppose any government policies of that sort, and would insist instead on preserving today's dysfunctional culture of layoffs and the fear of layoffs. That's just one more reason to rid ourselves of the mental shackles of economism.

In the next chapter we'll examine the role that economism played in another massive form of social dysfunction—in this case, one that nearly destroyed the global financial markets and produced misery for millions of people across the world, as well as driving up unemployment and adding to the layoff frenzy.

Notes

1. A United Nations report in 2007 showed American workers producing more wealth per worker than any other country, and outperforming all other countries except Norway in the amount produced per worker per hour; U.S. workers world's most productive: United Nations report says longer hours worked, more achieved per hour. CBS News, September 3, 2007; http://www.cbsnews.com/stories/2007/09/03/business/main3228735.shtml (accessed December 27, 2010).

2. Moyers B. Bill Moyers: "Welcome to the plutocracy!" Truthout, http://www.truth-out.org/bill-moyers-money-fights-hard-and-it-fights-dirty64766 (accessed Nov. 28, 2010).

3. Meyerson H. It's time for an obituary on unregulated capitalism: its failure spells huge loss for economic conservatives. *Houston Chronicle*, October 19, 2008:E6.

4. Uchitelle L. *The disposable American: layoffs and their consequences*. New York: Vintage, 2007. Uchitelle's account is largely vouched for by Stein HF. *Nothing personal, just business: a guided journey into organizational darkness*. New York: Praeger, 2001.

5. Uchitelle, *Disposable American:* 199.

6. Uchitelle, *Disposable American:* 179-80.

7. Uchitelle, *Disposable American:* 179.

8. One such investigation is Linde C. *Life stories: the creation of coherence*. New York: Oxford University Press, 1993. I have written about the role of stories in making sense of illness in people's lives; Brody H. *Stories of sickness*, 2nd ed. New York: Oxford University Press, 2003.

9. Uchitelle, *Disposable American:* 190-91. Uchitelle here quotes from Sennett R. *The corrosion of character: the personal consequences of work in the new capitalism*. New York: W.W. Norton, 1998.

10. Uchitelle, *Disposable American:* 87.

11. Hacker JS. *The great risk shift: the new economic insecurity and the decline of the American dream*. Revised and expanded edition. New York: Oxford University Press, 2008.

12. Uchitelle, *Disposable American:* 75-76.

13. Uchitelle, *Disposable American:* 128-29.

14. Uchitelle, Disposable American: 134.

15. Uchitelle, *Disposable American:* 139. Thomas Frank observed that Jack Welch as CEO of General Electric was paid 1400 times what the average American worker in that company made, and 9571 times what the average GE worker in Mexico made, after the company outsourced many U.S. jobs south of the border; Frank T. *One market under God: Extreme capitalism, market populism, and the end of economic democracy.* New York: Anchor, 2001: 7.

16. Uchitelle, *Disposable American:* 140.

17. Uchitelle, *Disposable American:* 143.

18. Moyers, Welcome to the plutocracy.

19. Von Drehle D. Republicans admire Bill...McKinley, that is. *Washington Post,* July 24, 1999, http://www.washingtonpost.com/wp-srv/politics/campaigns/wh2000/stories/campaign072499.htm (accessed November 28, 2010).

20. Uchitelle, *Disposable American:* 35. Uchitelle here cites Cappelli P. *The New Deal at work: managing the market-driven work force.* Cambridge, MA: Harvard Business Press, 1999.

21. Klein N. *The shock doctrine: the rise of disaster capitalism.* New York: Picador, 2007.

22. Klein, *Shock doctrine:* 6.

23. Cook N. Are fed-up American workers getting their gumption back? *Newsweek,* August 6, 2010; http://www.newsweek.com/2010/08/06/are-fed-up-american-workers-getting-their-gumption-back.html (accessed November 28, 2010).

24. Frank, *One market under God*: xiv.

25. Meyerson H. The dysfunctional duo. *Washington Post,* February 18, 2009:A13.

26. Uchitelle, *Disposable American:* 200.

27. Uchitelle, *Disposable American:* 205.

28. Klein, *Shock doctrine:* 457.

29. Wilkinson R, Pickett K. *The spirit level: why greater equality makes societies stronger.* New York: Bloomsbury Press, 2009.

30. Wilkinson and Pickett, *Spirit level*: 250. Here they quote from Oakeshott R. *Jobs and fairness: the logic and experience of employee ownership*. Norwich, UK: Michael Russell, 2000: 104.

31. Moore M. Capitalism—a love story. Overture Films/Paramount Vantage, 2009.

32. Wilkinson and Pickett, *Spirit level*: 252-3 (citing an unpublished PhD thesis by David Erdal).

Chapter 9.

Economism and the Great Recession of 2008

One of the best places to hunt elk is on the shores of a remote backwoods lake accessible only by air. A pilot landed his pontoon plane on the lake and unloaded three hunters and all their gear. He instructed them: "There are only two rules. First, be back at this clearing at noon on Sunday and I'll be here to pick you up. Second, this is a small plane, so be sure to have no more than one elk to take back."

The pilot duly returned on Sunday, to find in the clearing the three hunters with three dead elk.

"Look," he exclaimed, exasperated, "I told you the rules. The plane cannot possibly carry this much weight."

The first hunter winked and nudged him with his elbow. "Listen, we heard this speech before. You flew us in last year and said the same thing. Last year we showed up back here with two elk. You grumbled and groused and finally we offered to pay you double and you then agreed to take us out with the two elk. So this year we'll pay you triple for the three elk."

The pilot argued for a while but finally agreed. They loaded the plane with the three elk and the hunters and all the camping gear. The pilot took off. The plane struggled to gain altitude over the lake, and finally crashed into the woods at the far end.

One hunter regained consciousness after a while and staggered over to where his two companions were trying to revive the pilot. He demanded, "Does anyone know where we are?"

The more alert of the other two looked around and offered, "I think we're about fifty yards from where we crashed last year."[1]

Most Americans, I would guess, were surprised when the financial markets collapsed in the fall of 2008, following directly upon the subprime mortgage meltdown over the previous year. Our surprise ought to have been tempered by an awareness of how many times that same plane had crashed in the same place.

If we are willing to go back a ways into history, we can talk about economic bubbles (or financial bubbles or speculative bubbles) generally. I had thought that the first such bubble was the South Sea Company bubble in England in 1720, but Wikipedia helpfully informs us that the first bubble in modern history was the Dutch tulip bulb mania of 1637. Wikipedia goes on to say that economists are divided on bubbles.[2] Some say the behavior that leads to a bubble is not necessarily irrational; that bubbles can occur even in tightly regulated settings where no speculation is possible; and that you can, in fact, tell that it was a bubble only in hindsight. At risk of going beyond my depth, I would suggest that there is some behavior that has recurred historically and that ought to warn us that a huge run-up in prices, leading a great many people to make lots and lots of money without doing anything obvious to earn it, counts as a bubble about to burst. In particular, when people admit that what is happening seems to violate all sorts of rules of the marketplace and even of common sense, and then proceed to tell you not to worry, because for some reason the rules don't apply *this time around*, we are probably headed for trouble.

If we think all that history is too ancient, we can fast forward to the savings-and-loan debacle of the late 1980s. That was a forerunner of the financial market collapse of 2008–supposedly reliable financial institutions failed and the U.S. taxpayer had to step in with a very expensive bailout package to prevent collateral damage. In hindsight we could see that the problem was that the savings and loan companies had evaded regulations intended to stabilize banks, and that because they were sufficiently like banks in the ways that ended up causing trouble, they needed to be regulated like banks too. They had not been, in part because the powerful owners of the largest savings and loan companies had lobbied the government to keep these regulations off their backs while they made handsome short-term profits.

Then we had the dot-com bubble of the early 2000s. That was more like the traditional historical (or hysterical) bubble, with stock in Internet startups fetching outrageous prices despite the fact that the companies had yet to earn a dime. It seemed to represent three elements of the famous bubbles of the past–average investors fearful that they had to act right away to get in on the profits; people's good sense being overwhelmed by herd behavior; and the magical belief that just because a company had the wondrous name "Internet" attached to it, its stock could only rise in value and never fall. (Just a few years later we'd transfer our allegiance to the magical terms "housing" and "real estate," with similar results.)

Next came the Enron scandal of 2001, followed by similar accounting scandals at other large U.S. firms. Enron had originally been a company selling energy, mainly via its extensive network of natural gas pipelines. As such it made legitimate profits by providing legitimate products and services. Over a number of years Enron more or less got out of the energy business and started dealing in pieces of paper--futures and derivatives. It inflated its profits by counting future earnings as full profits, and it hid its losses by bookkeeping scams that attributed the losses to mysterious offshore subsidiaries.[3] Ultimately the corporate leaders of Enron went to prison because they lied to investors, insisting that the stock would rebound even when they knew that it was worthless and even when they were feverishly unloading their own stock. Their policy of lying greatly increased others' losses when the company finally sank into bankruptcy.

The lesson of Enron has been widely misrepresented by those smitten by economism. It's not fair, they complain, to use Enron as evidence of the alleged excesses of free-market capitalism in today's world. The Enron leaders were not capitalists, but criminals, and they were punished as they deserved. One should not generalize to the corporate world as a whole.

This objection misses the entire point. It is not just that Enron collapsed amidst scandal and that its leaders were found guilty of fraud. The main issue (as we saw in Chapter 5) is how Enron was praised and lionized by those who were supposed to be the experts in free-market capitalism, nearly up to the very moment of bankruptcy. *Fortune* magazine named Enron "America's Most Innovative Company" for six years running. George Bush, both father and son, sang the praises of the company and its executives loudly and consistently. One would think that these supposed experts would have noticed that Enron was actually producing nothing of value any more, and instead was pushing around pieces of paper while engaging in accounting practices which were surely "creative" but hardly acceptable. It is hard to explain this worshiping at the Enron altar without (as we noted in Chapter 5) invoking the tradition of American Puritanism–that somehow we became convinced that the Enron executives were divinely favored because they were rich and because the value of their stock had climbed so high. To question any of this would be to question God himself.

Yes, the executives committed fraud to hide what they were doing. The scandal is how relatively easy the fraud was to pull off for so long, in the faces of a bunch of people who prided themselves on knowing better. As to the purported uniqueness of Enron as a criminal enterprise, Kate Murphy, a journalist who covered the Enron collapse, has noted that several of the flaky accounting practices used by Enron executives also featured in the 2008 collapse of the giant financial firms AIG, Bear Stearns, and Lehman Brothers.[4]

The 2008 Meltdown

And so finally, because we insisted on flying the plane out with just one more elk just one more time, we had the financial crisis of 2008, which was set off by the crisis in subprime mortgage derivatives. The eventual toll included the demise of three major investment banks, the near-destruction of the U.S. auto industry along with many commercial banks and numerous other businesses, a loss of more than $13 trillion in U.S. household wealth by the end of 2008 alone ($50 trillion globally), and the fall of the stock market's Dow Jones Average from 14,000 to around 6500.[5] We were also left with a huge burden of unemployment that approached 10 percent and showed little sign of easing three years later.

In hindsight, we realized two things. The first was that a lot of people whose credit was insufficient to afford to pay for the house that they had bought were granted mortgages, based solely on the bubble theory that since the value of the house would keep climbing indefinitely, there was no risk because they could always sell the house at a profit and pay off the mortgage. Among these buyers, no doubt, were a number of shameful speculators "flipping" their fourth or fifth house. But also mixed up in this mess were a lot of honest and decent home-buyers who simply wanted a nice home for their family, as they believed the age-old American dream promised them. They bought these flaky mortgages and invested in more home than they could really afford because the lenders persuaded them that this was simply the way it was done today, and that everything would be all right. When both the real estate broker and the lender tell us that a certain piece of paper means a certain thing, or that a certain figure is simply the normal amount for that transaction, how many of us think we have the knowledge to question it?

The second thing we came to realize is that these subprime mortgage loans became toxic not simply because they were offered to people who could not afford to pay them back. They affected the financial markets and ultimately threatened to bring down the worldwide banking system because financial wizards decided that profits could be made by bundling and reselling these mortgage debts several times over, until the bad assets were so mixed up with good assets that even the smartest financier could no longer tell what anything was truly worth anymore. They were allowed to do this because of an ideology that said that government regulation was bad and was stifling innovation in the financial industry, and because once again (as with savings and loans) new forms of institutions had been created and regulations had not kept up. They were allowed to do this by a White House and Congress that believed that government regulation is always bad, and that markets always self-regulate much better than any outside force could regulate them.

Fareed Zakaria in *Newsweek* attempted to list the factors at work in producing this financial meltdown.[6] Individually, Americans bought beyond their means and borrowed: "The average household owns 13 credit cards, and 40 percent of them carry a balance, up from 6 percent in 1970."[7] (Unfortunately, here Zakaria seemed to forget that as a result of the massive privatization of risk, many middle-class households find themselves forced to use their credit cards for basic necessities and not for luxuries.[8]) Collectively, we have maintained spending while cutting taxes and running up huge deficits. "The whole country has been complicit in a great fraud," said Zakaria. "As economist Jeffrey Sachs points out, 'We've wanted lots of government, but we haven't wanted to pay for it.'"[9] He reminded us that the national debt, which had been $3 trillion in 1990, now stood at $10.2 trillion. "If there is a lesson to be taken from this crisis, it's a simple and old rule of economics: there is no free lunch. If you want something, you have to pay for it. Debt is not a bad thing. Used responsibly, it is at the heart of modern capitalism. But hiding mountains of debt in complex instruments is a way to disguise costs, an invitation to irresponsible behavior."[10]

Yet another contributing factor was the sort of person in charge of the financial institutions. Here Zakaria quotes Boykin Curry, the managing director of Eagle Capital:

> For 20 years, the DNA of every financial institution had morphed dangerously. Each time someone at the table pressed for more leverage and more risk, the next few years proved them 'right.' These people were emboldened, they were promoted and they gained control of ever more capital. Meanwhile, anyone in power who hesitated, who argued for caution, was proved 'wrong.' The cautious types were increasingly intimidated, passed over for promotion. They lost their hold on capital. This happened every day in almost every financial institution over and over, until we ended up with a very specific kind of person running things.[11]

In other words, at first the true believers in economism were balanced by more cautions and sober colleagues. As time went on, the cautious and sober were gradually eliminated from positions of leadership, leaving only the zealots. (In a minute we'll see how the Citigroup story illustrates this point.)

The combined effect of these two factors–imagining that they had revoked the rules and so a free lunch was not only possible but there for the taking, and putting the wrong sort of people in charge of financial institutions–was summarized by prominent Houston businessman Paul W. Hobby:

> [T]he monetary new math said that $2.5 trillion in excess leverage (comparing the traditional relationship of bank debt to GDP) was OK because the risk had been securitized through asset-lite Enronomics, where the markets parse derivative and speculative risk intelligently, and create wealth for the most efficient market participants–in the absence of any fundamental value creation in the underlying economy. It isn't OK, and a lot of people are getting hurt who never bargained for the risks they now face.[12]

If that all now sounds like gibberish, that's part of what went wrong. Because it sounds so intelligent to be talking about "derivatives" and "efficient market participants" (or embarrassing to have to admit that you don't know what those words mean), it ended up seeming smart to take a bunch of financial debt, repackage it, sell it on the market, then take the resulting debt, repackage that, and sell that, in one grand shell game, all the while forgetting to ask the old-fashioned question—was any of this moving of paper around the board actually adding any value to anything real? It was the same question that Enron (or its auditors and stock analysts) forgot to ask when the company stopped selling gas pipeline services, which provided real value for money, and started to specialize in derivatives and futures, which did not. At some point, the observation that the supposed "market value" of all of these pieces of paper had topped $2.5 trillion, far more than the total GDP of most nations, should have been a tip-off that all was not well.

Here's how lawyer and former banker Charles Morris, author of *The Trillion Dollar Meltdown*, characterized the role of economism in driving the run-up to the 2008 debacle:

> For years now, even Democrats have been drinking the free-market Kool-Aid that the best economy is whatever markets decree it should be. So for most of the past two decades, the U.S. economy has been driven by whatever Wall Street is best at financing — mostly bigger houses, fancier cars and more electronic toys from Asia. We have become a nation where people struggle to make payments on four-bedroom houses with faux-marble bathrooms and two SUVs in the driveway even as they worry about their lousy health insurance, evaporating pensions, shaky Social Security benefits and tapped-out 401(k)s.

> Wall Street, meanwhile, prospered mightily. Financial-sector profits, which typically average about 10 to 15 percent of corporate profits, had leapt to 40 percent by 2007. Total corporate profits also soared, nearly doubling as a share of national income. But instead of triggering an investment boom, the gains were mostly distributed to shareholders. Exxon brags that it has invested $90 billion in exploration and new plants since 2003, but it has distributed even more — nearly $120 billion — to shareholders. The cash incomes of the top 1 percent hit an all-time

high in 2006, just a tad higher than the previous record in 1929. That's the cash that fed the hedge funds, private-equity funds and the other yield-chasers that inflated the decade's asset bubble.[13]

The Citigroup Story

How all this came about—prestigious investment banks turning into gambling casinos whose exploits eventually threatened the global financial system—is illustrated by the story of Citigroup, as told by *New York Times* investigative business reporters Eric Dash and Julie Creswell.[14] At the time Dash and Creswell wrote, Citigroup had suffered $65 billion in losses, its stock value had plummeted from $244 billion two years previously to $20.5 billion, and the company was seeking a Federal bailout. Journalist Charles Gasparino, in his book, *The Sellout,* describes the origins of the 2008 crisis in considerable detail, both confirming the account of Citigroup offered by Dash and Creswell, and also showing that what happened at Citigroup was really a microcosm of what was happening all across Wall Street.[15]

In the early 1980s, Wall Street firms became addicted to two risky ways of doing business—mortgage-backed derivatives and leverage. Derivatives are bonds that are made up of debt, then sold to investors. These bonds were initially portrayed as a win-win. Local banks granted mortgages, then sold the mortgages to an investment bank. The big bank repackaged the mortgage debt as derivative bonds and sold the bonds to investors. The investors, over the years, were gradually paid back, with interest, as the mortgage holders paid off their mortgages. Because the banks were compensated for the mortgages and moved the mortgage loans off their own books, they quickly had more money to lend to new borrowers. Consumers benefited because credit was easier to get. The investment banks benefited because they could charge high fees for these new bonds. Investors liked the derivatives because they paid higher interest than lower-risk bonds.

Charles Ferguson, in *Inside Job*, his documentary film about the market collapse, tells the story of Brooksley Born, who in 1998 was head of an obscure Federal agency called the Commodity Futures Trading Commission. Born and her staff became aware of increasing problems in the derivatives markets, and were about to issue a report calling for increased regulation. The Wall Street bankers panicked and called their friends, Treasury secretary Larry Summers and Federal Reserve chairman Alan Greenspan. Summers and Greenspan chewed out Born mercilessly and forced her agency to drop the recommendations. The next year the bankers got their friend, Sen. Phil Gramm, to pass a new law prohibiting any such regulations.

The establishment reacted similarly in 2005 when Raghuram G. Rajan, the chief economist at the International Monetary Fund, gave a paper before the leaders of the financial community at the exclusive Jackson Hole, Wyoming conference. Rajan warned explicitly of a looming disaster, almost exactly predicting what actually happened two and three years later. Larry Summers got up and denounced Rajan's paper in terms that would usually be reserved for that of an undergraduate student who had somehow wandered into a meeting of senior professors.[16] So the financial gurus had multiple warnings of what was about to happen, and systematically ignored them in the frenzy for easy profits.

"Leverage" refers to the increasing habit of the investment banks to borrow money to float these bonds. Toward the end of the housing bubble, firms commonly borrowed $35 to $40 for every dollar of their own money that financed an offering. Debt-based securities and high ratios of leverage came to seem low-risk to Wall Street because, for most of the era 1983-2008, the Federal Reserve system kept interest rates low, an environment that especially favors riskier bonds and makes borrowing money easy and cheap. Investment banks also developed sophisticated computer systems to predict and manage risk.

Three times, in 1987, 1994, and 1998, the Fed abruptly raised interest rates. This led to three mini-crises, during which investors quickly dumped mortgage-backed securities in favor of safer Treasury bonds, companies lost millions, and fund managers who had been the darling of Wall Street the previous week were fired. The fancy computer programs predicted none of these crises. Each time, the Wall Street gurus took a deep breath, and as soon as interest rates dropped, started dealing again in risky derivatives at higher rates of leverage, and tweaking the computer programs so that *next* time they'd be *sure* to warn them in time. In 1994, Congressional hearings were held and there was talk of the need for sterner regulation of the financial markets. This talk quickly fizzled as profits soared once again.[17]

Citigroup was the brainchild of Sanford "Sandy" Weill, who engineered a series of mergers that eventually brought together Citicorp and the Travelers Group in 1998 to form the world's largest bank. His goal was a one-stop-shopping megabank, that could meet all the needs of its customers under a single roof.

Citigroup was initially hamstrung by a depression-era law, the Glass-Steagall Act, that prevented the merger of a commercial bank with an investment bank. This seemingly antiquated regulation became the target of Weill and his newest ally, Robert Rubin, formerly a partner at Goldman Sachs and then Bill Clinton's Secretary of the Treasury. Rubin negotiated a job with Weill that most of us would envy. He held the title, "chairman of the executive committee," that seemed to have no specific responsibilities attached to it, and no employee reported to him. Essentially Citigroup paid him $15 million a year to travel around the world and talk to his cronies. But Rubin initially earned his keep by using his insiders' knowledge of Washington. In 1999, the Republican congress and the Clinton Administration passed the Gramm-Leach-Bliley Financial Services Modernization Act. Besides preventing Federal regulation of derivatives, as we saw above, the law gave Citigroup a green light to merge its investment and commercial banking functions. This had the impact of bringing investment bank funds under the protective umbrella of the Federal Deposit Insurance Corporation that protects your savings in a commercial bank. As Gasparino commented, "In effect, the federal government, and hence taxpayers, was subsidizing the risk-taking activities of the big banks such as Citigroup."

In 2002, Charles O. Prince III took over as CEO of Citigroup's corporate and investment bank. Prince was an attorney who had been Weill's longtime legal counsel and reportedly had helped Weill out of several jams. Prince had no real expertise in banking and so was unable to address the core problem at Citigroup—which was, according to Gasparino, that the merger had been a flop. To serve as an effective megabank, the different segments of the corporation all had to work in a coordinated fashion, and neither Weill nor anyone else had yet figured out how to make them do that. So Prince naturally turned to the one area of Citigroup that was actually generating impressive profits—its bond trading division. And his orders to the bond traders mirrored the advice that Rubin consistently gave, in between international flights—take more risks. A former Citigroup executive told *Times* reporters Dash and Creswell, "Chuck [Prince] didn't know a CDO [collateralized debt obligation] from a grocery list." He did know, however, that the firms that created the CDOs charged between 0.4 percent and 2.5 percent of the sale value as fees, so that in 2005, Citigroup made $500 million from that product line.

By this time, several factors had merged to make the latest generation of derivatives like CDOs much riskier than their predecessors. One was sheer magnitude—Gasparino notes that between 1989 and the early 1990s, the derivatives market grew by an estimated 371 percent. As more and more wealth (at least paper wealth) became tied up in these bonds, the derivatives market became more intricately interconnected with all different sorts of financial institutions and their assets.[18]

Another factor was the type of mortgage that was being packed into the newest mortgage-backed derivatives. Wall Street was running out of mortgages to sell and resell, and demanded more and more "product" from mortgage brokers. They, in turn, started digging deeper and then deeper yet into the subprime pool. From the highest level of subprime borrowers, solid workers who had one or two bad marks on their credit ratings but essentially could be depended to pay back their loans, brokers turned to worse and worse risks, eventually giving mortgages to the unemployed to buy half-million-dollar McMansions. It was at this point that the derivatives market and its accompanying risk-taking met the housing bubble. In the mid-2000's the conventional wisdom stated that housing prices would only go up and never down, so no mortgage loan was too risky; you could always sell your house for more than you paid for it.

Finally, the reason CDOs were now the most popular form of mortgage-backed derivative was that the Wall Street gurus again insisted that they had found a way to take all the risk out of risk. CDOs combined mortgage debt with various other forms of consumer debt such as car loans and credit card debt. In theory, even if one of these markets tanked completely, the others would remain strong and effectively hedge the bets you had taken. Bond salesmen essentially convinced investors they could have it both ways—they could earn the hefty interest rates paid by derivatives, that supposedly was due to the fact that these are higher-risk investments so that buyers ought to be rewarded with higher returns; and yet the true risk was said to be so low that these bonds were almost as safe as Treasury notes. I am reminded of a friend who firmly believes that if you break cookies into small enough pieces, there are no calories left and you can eat as many as you want without gaining weight.

The low-risk mantra spread to the extent that whenever the bond market temporarily slowed, investment banks simply held onto the bonds to earn the higher interest rates for themselves. When the crash came, the big Wall Street firms found themselves stuck with billions of dollars in suddenly nearly-worthless paper—only *how* near to worthless no one knew, because the instruments had become so complex by then that no one knew their actual market value. The inability to say what the assets of many banks were actually worth explained two features of the crash that eventually resulted—its reaching out into all corners of the global financial market, and the eerie slow-motion way in which institutions were affected, as weeks and months passed with no way to be sure that the bleeding had yet stopped.

There were two possible ways the executives at Citigroup could have been warned that they were taking on more risk than they could ultimately afford. One would have been to have its own in-house ratings experts. Citigroup elected instead to rely on external ratings firms. Gasparino notes that rating agencies underwent a basic change in business model in the 1990s. They began to be paid on quantity, not quality, of assessments. This allowed banks to play raters off against each other as they competed for business. Predictably, raters started to affix AAA ratings to CDOs that eventually came to be worth 20 cents on the dollar. (Gasparino can today see nothing to do with these ratings firms except abolishing them.)[19]

The other responsible entity within Citigroup was its risk management department, overseen by David C. Bushnell. He was supposed to keep a watchful eye on the activities of Thomas G. Maheras, the executive who oversaw trading, and Maheras' deputy, Randolph H. Barker. But Barker, Maheras and Bushnell were all very good friends, frequently socializing together. It was generally known at Citigroup that if you wanted to close a risky but profitable deal, all you needed to do was talk with Barker, and he would persuade Bushnell that the deal was all right.

In summer 2007, as the subprime mortgage market was causing the collapse of major firms like Bear Stearns and credit was starting to tighten, Citigroup's executives met to review their holdings. Believing the assessment of the ratings agencies that the risk of default of their mortgage-backed securities was less than one-hundredth of one percent, Maheras assured his colleagues that the company "would never lose a penny." In October 2007, Citigroup told investors it would have to write off $1.3 billion in subprime-mortgage-linked securities. By November, the write-down had gone to $11 billion, Maheras and Barker had been fired, and Prince resigned. Rubin was named to Obama's presidential transition team, though he was passed over for the top financial posts in the new administration. (Rubin, according to the *Times* inquiry, refused to accept any personal responsibility for Citigroup's downfall, saying that he had never advised on any specific deals.)[20]

Economism's First Reaction--Blame Greed

The numbers had hardly started to drop on the stock tickers in the fall of 2008 when advocates of economism rushed to defend their religious faith. One commonly heard excuse was that the problem was the age-old story of human greed. There was no reason to think that the underlying system–the blind reliance on an unregulated market, for instance–was in any way flawed. It was simply that people got greedy, and we all know what happens when people fall prey to that vice.

Almost as if by illustration, at the same time as the financial markets were tumbling throughout the world, Colombia's government was shutting down a widespread, popular pyramid scheme in that nation. The populace, instead of praising the government for stopping the fraud, idolized the crooks who had launched the scheme, casting them as Robin Hood wannabes, and lambasted the government for interfering with the pyramid. While everyone above the age of ten or so is supposed to understand what a pyramid scheme is, we also know that if you get in first, you can make a lot of money at it. That money is scammed from those who come in at the bottom of the pyramid, but if you're the one at the top making money, you may easily miss that fine point. So, if simple human greed led to such an illogical result in Colombia, why not in the U.S.?

The first point to note about the greed rebuttal is that it is yet one more example of what Jacob Hacker called the privatization of risk–always blame the individual, never the system.[21] The next point is a deeper development of the first one. We would expect average Americans, just like average Colombians, to act irrationally when in the throes of greed. But we do not expect our leaders–whether in business or in government–to act similarly. Their supposed immunity to such emotions and vices is precisely what we expect in leaders.

What has to be explained in America is not greed and the excesses it produces. What has to be explained is a system, and the supposed leaders of that system, who since 1980 have enshrined unrestrained greed as a national virtue, as the economic engine that will guarantee prosperity for all through the free, unregulated market.

Let's take as an example someone who seems at first glance to be a poster child for greed. We are told, for instance, of the Bakersfield, California strawberry picker who made $14,000 a year, spoke no English, and was able to get a mortgage from Long Beach Financial to buy a $720,000 house with no down payment.[22] Presumably the subprime meltdown was all his fault. He bought a house much bigger than what he could afford, at payments he could never keep up.

We conveniently forget in this account that he was preached to for years that he could some day afford that house, because the rising tide of supply-side economics would lift his boat along with all others. And he could be forgiven if he thought that he could afford a nice house because he worked hard, as the American dream promised. He probably toiled far more mightily picking strawberries, than did the geniuses at Enron and Citigroup who made their millions not through hard work but by creating clever new varieties of paper securities lacking real value. When apparently responsible and smart business people came to him and offered a new home and a mortgage, and assured him that all would be well because the price of the house could never fall in the future, how was he supposed to know any better?

The advocates of economism held back one important bit of information from this (presumably Hispanic) strawberry picker. Had they been completely honest, they would have told him, "When we said that if you voted for our candidates and our policies, we'd make people wealthy, we did not mean the great majority of people like you. We meant the small minority of folks like us." Of course, concealing that crucial bit of truth-in-advertising was an essential ingredient of economism's stealth campaign.

Economism's Second Reaction—Blame Democrats

By mid-2009, the Republican rank and file had gotten its marching orders. Whenever the policies of the Reagan-Bush years, especially financial market deregulation, were held responsible for the current recession, blame the Democrats instead. According to Republican revisionist history, the core of the problem lay with big government and its creations, Fannie Mae and Freddie Mac—the government-sponsored enterprises (GSEs) that act partly like government utilities and partly like private firms. Years of Democratic congressional leadership had led to laws forcing first the GSEs, then other mortgage brokerage firms, to make ever-riskier loans, in the name of extending home ownership to poor and minority groups. This led to the housing bubble, the subprime mess, and all the subsequent ills.

Our best source on the truth of this assertion is Charles Gasparino, who agrees that the Democrats in Congress—he singles out especially Rep. Barney Frank and Sen. Christopher Dodd—share some responsibility for the eventual disaster. Gasparino (who depicts himself as a free-market economic libertarian who nevertheless believes that financial markets need regulation to function well) then dismisses as too simplistic the notion that somehow the Democrats and the GSEs made this mess all by themselves.

Gasparino notes the policies that Congress, led by Frank and Dodd from their powerful committee chair positions, and the Clinton Administration pushed onto Fannie and Freddie were ultimately self-defeating. By forcing mortgage lenders to commit a larger percentage of funds to lower-income borrowers, the policies eventually led to housing prices inflated beyond what lower-income people could afford, unless they resorted to government subsidies or the adjustable-rate mortgages that led to so many foreclosures in 2008-2009.[23]

But while some Republican congresspeople objected to these policies, others, in the thrall of Wall Street lobbyists, saw only huge profits for investment firms. President George W. Bush gave a speech touting liberalized home ownership for the poor at the height of the housing bubble, and many Republicans saw that position as a way to ingratiate themselves simultaneously with Wall Street and with minority voters.[24]

It's also important to recall what the policies called for and what they degenerated into. Angelo Mozilo founded Countrywide Financial, a California mortgage lender that led the foray into the subprime market, out of a sense of outrage at how the real estate market discriminated against the poor and minorities. But he pioneered a method of assessing mortgage lending risk very carefully and loaning only to the best risks within the large subprime pool.[25] Mozilo's initial success inspired Democratic politicians to call for more of the same—especially after some key Democrats received mortgages and loans from Mozilo's firm at highly discounted rates.[26]

By contrast, mortgage firms in 2004-2006 were heavily peddling what jaded old-line brokers called "liar's loans," in which only outright fraud could create the appearance that the lender could possibly pay back a mortgage of that size. The FBI issued warnings about an epidemic of mortgage fraud in the subprime market as early as 2004, but of course no one wanted to listen.[27] The poor were not lining up outside the brokers' doors to sign up for these loans; the brokers had to go out aggressively into the community and twist the arms of lower-income people to get them to apply. The Wall Street firms, desperate for "product" to package into CDOs, repaid the brokers with expensive gifts, fancy dinners, and other incentives.[28]

In 2006, there were early reports of a possible "correction" in the housing market, the first sign that the subprime mortgage bubble was about to burst. A financial reporter wondered what the bond traders at Citigroup thought of this development, and walking over to chat with a group of them, found them completely blasé. One finally shrugged, "What's the worst that can happen? We make $200 million and then we get fired."[29] According to Charles Gasparino, this attitude was the root cause of the financial collapse of 2008—the idea that one could get rich quickly by taking big risks with other peoples' money. That was not a policy that some cabal of Democrats forced onto the U.S. banking industry.

Have We Learned Our Lesson?

The next way to dismiss the lessons about economism and its failings is to admit the truth of all that I have said–but as yesterday's news. Why waste ink and paper on this book when, as soon as the bottom fell out of the financial markets, the lessons were obvious to all? Given that economism has run into the 2008 version of the Irish potato famine, and been exposed in all its flaws, what more is there to say?

One suggestion that at least some political conservatives may have seen the light comes from David Brooks, *New York Times* columnist. He begins:

> Once, classical economics dominated policy thinking. The classical models presumed a certain sort of orderly human makeup. Inside each person, reason rides the passions the way a rider sits atop a horse. Sometimes people do stupid things, but generally the rider makes deliberative decisions, and the market rewards rational behavior.

> Markets tend toward efficiency. People respond in pretty straightforward ways to incentives. The invisible hand forms a spontaneous, dynamic order. Economic behavior can be accurately predicted through elegant models.[30]

Sound familiar? That seems to be the neoclassical economics which is prone to deteriorate, when pushed beyond its limits, into economism. But Brooks continues:

> This view explains a lot, but not the current financial crisis -- how so many people could be so stupid, incompetent and self-destructive all at once. The crisis has delivered a blow to classical economics and taken a body of psychological work that was at the edge of public policy thought and brought it front and center.[31]

Just what is the new psychology that is finally getting some attention? Brooks explains:

- In human decisions, "Context...matters a lot."
- "[W]e don't perceive circumstances objectively."
- "Biases abound."
- "Most important, people seek relationships more than money."

- In conclusion, "This crisis represents the flaw in the classical economic model and its belief in efficient markets. Republicans haven't begun to grapple with the consequences."[32]

In short, Brooks has belatedly come to join the Paris economics graduate students (Chapter 4), who protested their neoclassical professors' obsession with mathematical theories that had nothing to do any more with real human social behavior. If we were to believe Brooks, then perhaps the lessons have finally been learned and we can all go home. But any such hope would prove premature.

Harold Meyerson, editor-at-large of *American Prospect*, suggested both why economism deserved to be buried, and how difficult it was going to be to keep it in its grave. First he recalled a 1949 book by a group of famous writers explaining why they had originally been attracted by communism, but had later abandoned it. They called their book *The God That Failed*. Meyerson suggested: "Today, conservative intellectuals might want to consider writing a tome on the failure of their own beloved deity, unregulated capitalism. ... the nation can't afford to worship at the altar of these failed gods." Meyerson went on to explain how these failed gods nevertheless remained extraordinarily influential: "The doctrine of laissez faire has been so dominant, so pervasive over the past three decades that hundreds of Democratic politicians can deliver a paean to the market at the drop of a hat, but not a single Republican pol can plausibly defend government as a check on capitalism run amok, even at the drop of thousands of points in the Dow."[33]

Paul Krugman (as we saw in Chapter 1) kept up a drumbeat of criticism in his *New York Times* economics column from late 2008 all through 2010, warning of inadequate regulatory responses to the crisis. He commented on December 14, 2009 of a vote in the House of Representatives the previous week on what he called a "quite modest effort to rein in Wall Street excesses," in which 27 Democrats and every Republican voted "no." He reviewed the entire history of deregulation from the Reagan years to 2008: "Given this history, you might have expected the emergence of a national consensus in favor of restoring more-effective financial regulation, so as to avoid a repeat performance [of the Great Recession]. But you would have been wrong." He then reviewed the

Republican party denials that deregulation had been to blame, and showed why this version of history left out too many facts. He wondered whether the centrist Democrats who held the swing votes in the Senate had the intelligence and the gumption to approve the measure that the House had just passed.[34]

Other writers addressed the question of whether the regulators who stood in line to assume greater responsibility for overseeing the financial markets were in fact up to the task. Binyamin Appelbaum and David Cho of the *Washington Post* recounted a speech by Federal Reserve Chairman Ben Bernanke in May 2007, when he reassured his audience that despite growing rates of mortgage foreclosures, there was no threat to the general prosperity (wrong) because the largest banks had not exposed themselves to risky subprime loans (wrong) and there was no spillover from the subprime market into the larger financial system (wrong). While Bernanke was widely credited for many of the steps taken to stimulate the economy to right the ship after the collapse of 2008—he had, after all, made his academic career as an economist on the study of the Great Depression—he did not get equally high marks for his ability to see the train wreck coming and to take appropriate preventive action.[35]

Dean Baker, of the Center for Economic and Policy Research in Washington, DC, goes farther and blames the quality of media coverage: "The media relied almost exclusively on the folks who got it wrong,"[36] and who having gotten it wrong, were more concerned about making themselves look good in hindsight than in reporting the facts. For example, the media (according to Baker) let former Federal Reserve chairman Alan Greenspan, who even more than Bernanke had administered the policies at the Fed that led to the market collapse, get away with self-serving excuses that branded him as either hopelessly negligent or hopelessly uninformed:

> The public should demand a real accounting. Why does the Fed grow hysterical over a 2.5 percent inflation rate but think that $10 trillion financial bubbles can be ignored? Where was the Treasury Department during the Clinton and Bush administrations? What about Congressional oversight? Did no one in Congress think that massive bubbles might pose a problem? Why do economists worry so much more about small tariffs on steel and shirts than about gigantic financial bubbles? What exactly do the people who get paid millions of dollars by Wall Street

financial firms do for their money? And finally, why don't the business and economic reporters ask any of these questions?[37]

In sum, after nearly three years had passed since the worst part of the 2008 financial meltdown, it was not yet clear that an adequate response to prevent future calamities of the same sort was forthcoming from those in power. Ferguson, in his documentary film *Inside Job*, emphasizes how many of the principal actors in the market collapse ended up with important jobs in the Obama Administration.[38] There was no guarantee that next time, the plane would not try to take off with four elk. The belief system of economism appeared deeply enough entrenched in the right places, with all of its defenses against learning from the facts firmly in place, even in the face of renewed calls for regulatory reform.

Economism Triumphant?

If there had been any hopes of lessons learned following the 2008 debacle, those hopes were dashed by the results of the 2010 mid-term elections. These elections were a triumph for the forces of economism in two ways. First, the effectiveness of economism as a belief system and as a stealth campaign was proven again. The after-effects of the 2008 financial crisis, especially the massive and persistent unemployment, made many among the public angry; and angry voters proceeded to vent their anger by electing precisely those people who most supported the policies that would perpetuate and repeat what they were angry at. Economism's ideas had such a strong grip on the public mind that somehow the illogical election of so many members of the political wing that had mostly engineered the market collapse—and whose opposition to government stimulus spending was now worsening the unemployment crisis—seemed logical after all, at least to enough people to decisively sway the election.

Economism's second triumph was the means by which the far-right wing of the Republican party enjoyed such a victory at the polls. One key ingredient was the U.S. Supreme Court ruling in the *Citizens United* case, eliminating most controls over corporate contributions to political campaigns, and based on the same legal fiction that played a powerful role in ushering in the first

Gilded Age—that corporations are legally persons, and so deserve the same rights that persons have, including First Amendment speech rights. Unfettered flows of corporate cash into campaign funds predominantly controlled by a few people like Karl Rove ultimately had a huge effect on the election. The second key ingredient was the increasing power of one corner of the U.S. media market, controlled by Rupert Murdoch, an avowed foe of any government interference with his right to make as much money and to accumulate as much power as he can.[39]

Through these right-wing-controlled media sources and through corporate-sponsored advertising, the U.S. public was systematically misinformed about the nature of the problems we face and the options we may choose from. To take just one example in my own field, health care, I still shake my head that a health care reform law basically taken lock, stock and barrel from Republican Mitt Romney's Massachusetts plan, and then stripped of anything (like a public insurance option) that might offend the private health insurance industry, could somehow be called "socialistic." Adam Smith, back in the 1770s, warned us that the greatest risk to global human rights arose when large corporations became so powerful that they effectively captured the machinery of civil government and bent it to their own profit-making interests.[40]

So as I write this, as the nation prepares for the 2012 elections, there seems little hope that the forces of economism in America can be effectively countered. In the next and final chapter I will take up the question of what can be done.

Notes

1. I heard this story told by J. Mark Gibson, Center for Evidence-Based Policy, Oregon Health and Science University, at the Michigan State Medical Society Annual Bioethics Conference, Traverse City, MI, October 2008.

2. Economic bubble; http://en.wikipedia.org/wiki/Economic_bubble (accessed December 28, 2010).

3. Baker D. *Plunder and blunder: the rise and fall of the bubble economy.* Sausalito, CA: PoliPointPress, 2008: 48-52.

4. Murphy K. Bottom line: Enron debacle didn't teach us a thing. *Houston Chronicle*, Jan. 3, 2009:E1, E5.

5. Gasparino C. *The sell-out: how three decades of Wall Street greed and government mismanagement destroyed the global financial system.* New York: HarperCollins, 2009: 491-92. For an excellent documentary film covering the same period, see Ferguson C. *Inside job.* Sony Pictures Classics, 2010.

6. Zakaria F. There is a silver lining. *Newsweek*, October 20, 2008: 27-29; http://www.newsweek.com/2008/10/10/there-is-a-silver-lining.html (accessed Nov. 28, 2010); quote p. 28.

7. Zakaria, Silver lining: 28.

8. Hacker JS. *The great risk shift: the new economic insecurity and the decline of the American dream.* Revised and expanded edition. New York: Oxford University Press, 2008.

9. Zakaria, Silver lining: 28.

10. Zakaria, Silver lining: 28-9. Zakaria's concern with excess deficits indicates how even the supposedly liberal news media can become caught up in the frame of reference that typifies economism and conservative thinking; his comments here presage the deficit hawks in the Republican party.

11. Zakaria, Silver lining: 29.

12. Hobby PW. America's math problem yields no simple solutions. *Houston Chronicle*, November 22, 2008: B9.

13. Morris C. The upside to a serious downturn. *Houston Chronicle*, November 23, 2008: E1.

14. Dash E, Creswell J. Citigroup saw no red flags even as it made bolder bets. *New York Times*, Nov. 23, 2008.

15. Gasparino, *Sell-out.*

16. Ferguson, *Inside job.* On the Rajan incident see also Cassidy J. *How markets fail: the logic of economic calamities.* New York: Farrar, Straus and Giroux, 2009: 20-23.

17. Gasparino, *Sell-out:* 29-116.

18. Gasparino, *Sell-out:* 97.

19. Gasparino, *Sell-out:* 495-98.

20. Dash and Creswell, Citigroup.

21. Hacker, *Risk shift.*

22. Lewis M. The end. www.portfolio.com, December 2008 issue, http://www.portfolio.com/news-markets/national-news/portfolio/2008/11/11/The-End-of-Wall-Streets-Boom (accessed Nov. 28, 2010).

23. Gasparino, *Sell-out:* 111-12.

24. Gasparino, *Sell-out:* 234.

25. Gasparino, *Sell-out:* 162.

26. Golden D. Countrywide's many 'friends': Senators Dodd and Conrad are among the government officials who scored V.I.P. loans from C.E.O. Angelo Mozilo. An exclusive Portfolio investigation. Portfolio.com, June 12, 2008; http://www.portfolio.com/news-markets/top-5/2008/06/12/Countrywide-Loan-Scandal/index.html (accessed December 28, 2010).

27. Ferguson, *Inside Job.*

28. Gasparino, *Sell-out:* 156-61.

29. Gasparino, *Sell-out:* 195.

30. Brooks D. An economy of faith and trust. *New York Times*, January 16, 2009: A29.

31. Brooks, Economy of faith.

32. Brooks, Economy of faith.

33. Meyerson H. It's time for an obituary on unregulated capitalism: its failure spells huge loss for economic conservatives. *Houston Chronicle*, October 19, 2008: E6.

34. Krugman P. Disaster and denial. *New York Times*, December 14, 2009.

35. Appelbaum B, Cho D. Fed leader's prediction fell far short. *Houston Chronicle*, Dec. 21, 2009.

36. Baker, *Plunder and blunder:* 143.

37. Baker, *Plunder and blunder:* 144-45. Baker notes in passing that the *New York Times* was a notable exception to the media's general failure to cover the growing bubbles.

38. Ferguson, *Inside Job.*

39. Moyers B. Bill Moyers: "Welcome to the plutocracy!" Truthout, http://www.truth-out.org/bill-moyers-money-fights-hard-and-it-fights-dirty64766 (accessed Nov. 28, 2010).

40. Muthu S. Adam Smith's critique of international trading companies: theorizing "globalization" in the Age of Enlightenment. *Political Theory* 36:185-212, 2008.

Chapter 10.
Conclusion: What Next for America?

We've covered a lot of material since we introduced the Carol Benson-Stan Wyzansky family in Chapter 2. We've looked at the definition of *economism* and seen how it differs from "scrupulous" economics and from social science generally. We looked back to the days of Patrick O'Ryan to identify one of the historical and religious roots of economism, evangelicalism in Great Britain in the early 19th century. We next went even farther back, to the days of Josiah Benson, to track the other root, American Puritanism in the early 18th century.

We saw that economism often operates by Reverse Robin Hood policies, but that its advocates seldom come clean about this aspect of their ideology and often operate by stealth. We traced the important parallels between economism and intelligent design, as two examples of religious dogma being disguised as science. We looked deeper into the problem of layoffs to see how economism-type policies have worsened job security and generally reduced the quality of life for the American middle class. We next saw how economism led directly to the Great Recession, a fact which its devotees conveniently deny, just as they ignore all facts that disagree with their religious faith.

Stan and Carol Wyzansky thought they knew what sort of world they were leaving behind for their children and grandchildren. By the time their grandchildren's generation reached adulthood, as Shelly and Darin Graham discovered, something in that picture was seriously out of whack. We can now see how that dysfunction was produced, during the intervening years, by the rise of economism, and the capture of public policy in America by those committed to its cause.

What, then, ought we to do? Step one is to return to the central task of this book, which has all along been to sort out what belongs under what proper category—science or religion. Step two would then be to see what sorts of positive ideas for the future could emerge, once the fog of economism has lifted and we can see our way clearly.

Is Economism Victorious?

We concluded the previous chapter with an image of economism triumphant following the November, 2010 elections. As I write this, it is too soon to determine any longer-term trends. Both conservatives and liberals are busily trying to spin their analyses of the voting to favor whatever pet messages they want to cling to. If Bill Moyers is right, the forces of plutocracy— government of and by the rich—are so deeply entrenched that nothing short of massive organization and activism at the grass roots level, followed by years of patient struggle, will dislodge them.[1] On the other hand, it seems at least possible that the voters who acted in 2010 mostly out of anger and frustration will soon see ample evidence that the Republicans they elected actually have no coherent alternative program to offer except for a deep-seated hatred of anything Obama. That could drive enough of the electorate back into the pro-Obama camp to assure his re-election in 2012, even with solid majorities in both houses of Congress such as he enjoyed in 2008.

It would be wrong, also, to chalk up the election results in 2010 solely to the triumph of economism without holding Obama and the Democrats responsible for their role. I personally concur with the charges that the Democrats, despite important accomplishments, managed to present to the American public no persuasive vision for the future of the country. Obama also clung far too long (and still at this writing is clinging) to a failed attempt at bipartisanship. One cannot have bipartisanship so long as the other party insists that the only posture that is truly bipartisan is handing them whatever they ask for, and giving nothing back in exchange. (We'll see a bit later what true bipartisanship consists of.)

Yet whatever the failures of the Democrats, it cannot be denied that economism is everywhere. To mention just one example, at least a few Republican politicians in my state of Texas appeared serious early in 2011 about withdrawing the state from the federal Medicaid program. They claimed that without the cumbersome Federal restrictions, Texas could make for itself a far more efficient program of health care, so that no one would be turned away. Consider, first, that Texas currently has more uninsured citizens than just about any other state, and that Texans become ineligible for Medicaid assistance under the current program when they begin to make as much as 25 percent of the federal poverty level. Then consider that if Texas were to split from the Feds over Medicaid, it would lose about two-thirds of the current Medicaid budget.[2]

So supposedly responsible adults appear to be saying that they could provide decent health care for just as many people for just one-third of the funds, if only they did away with Federal regulations and oversight. There is virtually no way that a person could make such a statement based on scientific economic analysis. The only possible way one could make such a statement is if one was captivated by an ideological doctrine of absolute faith in what the "free market" can do when left alone. Yet as we have seen so many times before, the critics who oppose such proposals don't fully get it. They accurately list all the reasons why withdrawing from Medicaid is a terrible idea, but they don't call the advocates of that plan what they are-- religious fanatics.

When Ronald Reagan first ran for president touting the most toxic version of economism, his supply-side theory, George H. W. Bush had the gumption to call it "voodoo economics"—though that accurate label sadly did little to help Bush in the Republican primaries. Today, few Democrats seem to have either the courage or the perception that the elder Bush had in 1980. Economist Paul Krugman prefers the term "zombie economics," because no matter how many times it has been killed by being shown in practice not to work, it refuses to die. One of the reasons it won't die, Krugman adds, is that Barack Obama is helping to give it new life: "President Obama... has consistently tried to reach across the aisle by lending cover to right-wing myths. He has praised Reagan for restoring American dynamism..., adopted G.O.P. rhetoric about the need for government to tighten its belt even in the face of recession....None of this stopped the right from denouncing him as a socialist. But it helped empower bad ideas, in ways that can do quite immediate harm."[3] If the leaders of the Democratic Party won't reveal economism for what it truly is, then the rest of us have to step up.

Exposing Economism

The analogy between economism and intelligent design helps to show us just how we need to expose the true nature of economism. Recall my conclusions about intelligent design. If a person, as a matter of religious faith, believes that God created the different plant and animal species essentially as they now exist, and that Darwin and his followers have simply been wrong about some species evolving from other species, then she is perfectly entitled to those beliefs. But she cannot go on to claim that when she puts forth intelligent design as a better alternative to Darwinism, she is doing science. She cannot reasonably claim that there is a scientific difference of opinion, with some scientists favoring the Darwinian approach and others favoring intelligent design; we are obligated to point out that this represents a misunderstanding and a distortion of science. When our advocate goes farther and insists that intelligent design must be taught in school science classes alongside of, or even instead of evolution, we have every reason to condemn these recommendations. We can, with all reason on our side, insist that this person is trying to force her own religious views on others, and yet call it science rather than religion. Chapter 7 listed all the reasons why we are justified in holding this position.

We now have a recipe for dealing with economism. So long as the economism advocate is willing to admit that his faith in the market is a religious sort of faith, he is fully entitled to his religious views. If he wants to worship at the altar of the marketplace, he's fully entitled to do so. We, on the other hand, are fully entitled to object whenever economistic forms of thinking are put forth as science, or as the only accurate description of the facts of the case. Whenever policies are recommended on the basis of ideas or theories or models that we can trace back to economism, we are entitled to ask whether hidden religious agendas are being forced upon us. When, for instance, a program that would reduce the effects of poverty is denounced based on the theory of "moral hazard," we are right to ask for evidence that this is not simply a repackaged form of evangelicalism, condemning the poor as morally deficient sinners. When we hear a call to privatize some part of Social Security, we are right to ask for evidence that this is not a return to the protestant-ethic thinking that the rich are more worthy than the rest of us, so that programs that transfer wealth from the poor to the rich are a way of increasing the glory of God.

Our call to show us the evidence may, in any particular case, be met. There are times when an assertion that looks at first glance like economism turns out on closer inspection to be a reasonable exercise of economic science, of the sort that Uwe Reinhardt praised (Chapter 3). For example, the welfare reforms initiated by the Clinton administration in the 1990s were probably a mixed bag of economism and sound policy. They were partly motivated by economism, the Republican right program of "shrinking big government" that the neoliberals bought into, eliminating entitlement programs that were unpopular with many voters. But no reasonable critic of the various welfare programs in place in 1990 could deny that some elements of welfare were dysfunctional and created perverse incentives, encouraging people to remain in poverty and on welfare rather than to get a job or go back to school, for instance. When the incentives are truly dysfunctional in that way, the concept of "moral hazard" makes sense and forms a part of a reasonable economic model, showing us the likely consequences of our policy choices. When the same concept of "moral hazard" is adopted uncritically across the board, regardless of evidence or lack of it, we have economism rather than economics. So the take-home message is that we need to be critical about across-the-board slogans and get down to the actual facts and their implications in *specific* circumstances.

For economism, certain things are true as a matter of divine law. Taxes for the rich must be kept low. Government must be kept small both to lower taxes and also to keep it from interfering with the freedom of the rich to make more money in a largely unregulated market. When evidence comes along that challenges the correctness of these dogmas, a scientific, thoughtful person looks at and weighs the evidence. The person in the throes of economism sees this so-called evidence as a test of religious faith, maybe sent by God to test the flock and to see who is truly worthy of God's grace. Those who are among the faithful will therefore deny the evidence and reaffirm their commitment to smaller government and lower taxes, no matter what. We could have another recession, even another depression, and their faith would not waver one iota. The human cost of these economic disasters would not matter, any more than the deaths of the Irish famine sufferers disturbed the most-committed evangelicals in England in 1846-48. These people will continue to look at the snake and insist that it's a pony.

This book, therefore, is not written for economism's true believers, who will view it as a test of faith, and their rejection of its message as proof of their virtue. I have rather two other audiences in mind. One is the large, pragmatic middle of the American voting public. This group has no ideological commitment to economism, but can easily be swayed by its rhetoric, especially when economism invokes such cherished American values as personal responsibility and hard work. My second audience is the leadership cadre of those now called progressives, who, as I have noted, seem far too timid in calling out economism and revealing its true colors.

Finally, saying what's wrong with economism does not mean going off the deep end in the other direction. Columnist Froma Harrop warned liberals that while voters would go along with their proposal to raise taxes for the rich, in the name of basic fairness, they would not go along with bashing the rich as greedy and unworthy, as liberal rhetorical excess often portrays them.[4] We should not go from admiring the rich as God's darlings to hissing at them the way we used to boo the mustached villain in the old melodramas. There are good people and bad people among the rich just as among the poor and the middle-class, and all deserve to be treated as individuals and regarded according to their own merits, not stereotyped. Negative stereotypes about the rich are in their own way just as offensive as the tales of the welfare queen driving up in her Cadillac to spend her food stamps on cake and champagne. When later I speak of "the monied interests," I do not mean all wealthy people, but only those who defend the status quo despite its deleterious effects on American society.

True Bipartisanship?

One advantage of clearing away the fog of economism is that we might once again understand what bipartisanship, and the political center, really mean.

David Frum has (or at least had) impeccable Republican credentials, as the speechwriter who helped to craft the "axis of evil" message delivered by George W. Bush. He gave an interview with National Public Radio after the 2008 election in which he was quite candid in assessing why the Republican party performed badly, and what the party needed to do to regain its status. In the interview he said, "Every country has a center-left party and a center-right party; America shouldn't be any different. The Democrats are the center-left party." He went on to deplore the fact that the Republican Party had lost the allegiance of so many college graduates and talked about the messages that would bring them back to the fold.[5] Of course, had Frum waited two years, he could have seen the Republican party roaring back into power, precisely by ignoring his advice and moving even farther to the right.

Frum was willing to grant "center-left" status to the Democrats. That is clearly at odds with the mainstream Republican rhetoric, which enjoys painting the opposition party as the refuge of a bunch of crazy, far-left radical socialists. So that in itself was an extraordinarily moderate statement coming from a Republican former speechwriter.

There is one thing, however, that I suspect that Frum did not mean to suggest. What exactly does it mean to compare America's two-party system with that of other industrial democracies? The comparison relies heavily on where one locates the "center." And in the US, the "center" has become located well to the rightward of where it can be found in most European nations and comparable societies. As we have seen, this is due in large part to the triumph of economism. When, as Thomas Frank put it, the "opposition [has] literally ceased to oppose," when Democrats and Republicans alike are spouting off formulas that glorify the free market and view "shrinking big government" as the ultimate virtue, then the "center" means something far different than it did in the U.S. in 1970, and that it does now in England, France, or Germany.[6] So a debate in the U.S. between a representative of the political "left" and one from the "right" is highly misleading. We are likely to hear two slightly different versions of economism. Sadly, things get even worse when corporations can donate unlimited campaign cash, so that both Republicans and Democrats come to depend equally on wealthy Wall Street donors.

Therefore, I disagree with Frum. We do not have today in America a center-left and a center-right party. What we have instead is a center-right party and a far-right party.

If political debate in America is going to address the issues as they ought to be addressed, putting forward real solutions to real problems, we are going to have to restore balance. We are going to have to shift the center of the political spectrum back toward the true middle. We can do this so long as we can smoke out economism from all the nooks and crannies where it is presently hiding and expose its fallacies.

An example of the false political center as I write this is the report of the "bipartisan" commission on the federal deficit, which proposed tough measures to balance the Federal budget over time. It was co-chaired by Alan Simpson, a supposedly moderate Republican former Senator, and Erskine Bowles, a former advisor to Bill Clinton. We saw in Chapter 8 how Clinton Administration policies with regard to employment were shot through with economism's assumptions, so it should not surprise us that the report overseen by these two individuals essentially represents an economism platform, despite its reassuring rhetoric that both Republican and Democratic programs must be ruthlessly sacrificed in order to achieve the goals they seek.

A liberal alternative for reducing the deficit, the product of three left-leaning think tanks, instead challenges economism in two basic ways.[7] First, the liberal alternative accepts the appropriateness of using Federal taxation as a means for equalizing income. (We'll see more on why this is a good idea in the next section of this chapter.) Instead of tax cuts for everyone, as the Simpson-Bowles commission suggests, taxes might be raised for the rich and for corporations, leaving more money in the hands of consumers who will spend it and thereby stimulate the economy. Second, the liberal plan buys into the idea that when the economy is in tough shape, there may be no effective alternative to a Federal stimulus package. Simpson-Bowles would place a permanent limit on Federal spending that would tie the President's and Congress's hands in the event of another major recession such as 2008-9. The liberal plan, by contrast, proposes that no Federal spending reduction would be allowed until unemployment has fallen to six percent and has remained there for at least six months.

I do not wish to claim that there is nothing good about the "bipartisan" plan or that the liberal plan ought to be adopted wholesale. I simply would suggest that a truly meaningful debate on the issue would put the two plans out on the table and argue their respective pros and cons. If we did so, then possibly a middle ground position would emerge that truly deserved to be called the "middle" politically. (And just because it's a "middle ground" plan does not automatically mean it's the *best* plan.) So long as the "bipartisan" plan is the only game in town, and no one will give the liberal plan the time of day (as certainly seems to be the case so far in the mainstream media and in Congress), then it's very hard to see how any real "middle" could ever be found.

Is Greater Income Equality the Answer?

A group of public policy experts comes to you with a proposal. They have been doing some research and crunching some numbers. They propose a basic change in an important aspect of American life. They have strong evidence that making this single change would lead to all of these consequences:

- Rates of mental illness would be reduced by two-thirds
- Rates of obesity would be reduced by two-thirds
- Teenage birth rates would be cut in half
- Prison populations could be reduced by 75 percent due to a decrease in overall crime
- People on average would live longer
- People would be able to work, on average, two months less per year in the form of either less overtime or more vacation, while the nation thrives economically
- The number of Americans who believe, in general, that they can trust other Americans would increase by 75 percent

Remember, a *single* change would produce all these varied results. You might imagine, right off, that any change, to be this powerful, would have to be extremely drastic, and hence fundamentally at odds with the American character and culture. The proponents of the change reply that actually, the sort of country that America would be after the change resembles very closely the sort of country that America was between 1948 and 1978, only without the problems of injustices to women and minority groups that afflicted the America of that time. Nor would the U.S. have to engage in overseas wars (like

Vietnam) or an international arms race (like the Cold War with the USSR) in order to achieve these advantages.

Are you interested in this proposal?

Richard Wilkinson and Kate Pickett, British experts on social patterns and public policy, make the proposal in their book, *The Spirit Level*.[8] What would have to happen, they say, for these many goals all to be met, would be to make American society more equal in terms of personal income. Instead of remaining the most unequal among the 22 richest industrialized nations, the U.S. would have to achieve a level of income equality now enjoyed by the most equal countries—Japan, Norway, Finland, and Sweden.

Your next reaction might well be, "I knew it! Another secret plot to socialize us and launch another massive government takeover of American life." To which Wilkinson and Pickett would reply that of the four countries the U.S. would be tasked to emulate in their proposal, three of them have in fact achieved their level of equality by heavy taxation and intrusive government programs. But Japan has become a very equal society, since World War II, almost entirely via the private sector. Japanese businesses pay their workers and executives much more equally, so there does not need to be any heavy hand of government taxation to redistribute the wealth. (Interestingly, many of the social programs that led to this marked equality through the private sector were initially put into place as a result of the role of American civil servants and social planners during the postwar occupation of Japan.) Wilkinson and Pickett insist that their data show that it does not matter what route (government action or private sector) a country chooses to follow to become more equal—as long as in the end it achieves equality, all the consequences on the list are very likely to occur.

I venture to say that the idea, that we could improve all sorts of indicators of social malaise through one relatively simple measure, runs strongly counter to what most of us consider to be common sense. So let's back up a few steps and look at the evidence that Wilkinson and Pickett bring forth. It turns out that if you look at four graphs, you understand pretty much all they have to say.

The first graph (Figure 10.1) compares the national average income in a country with the percentage of people reporting that they are reasonably happy with life in that country. (If you plot life expectancy instead of happiness against average income, you get an almost identical curve.) Wilkinson and Pickett's original graph is very complex because it shows dozens of countries, so I have simplified it to show the basic shape of the curve.

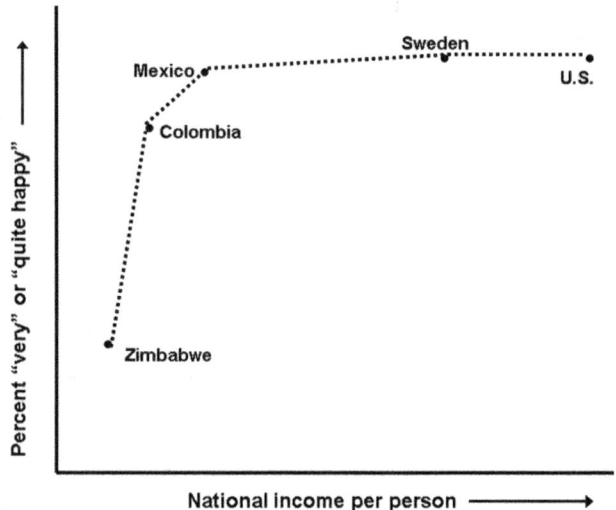

Figure 10.1. Happiness and average incomes in various nations (modified from Wilkinson and Pickett)

The take-home message seems to be that if you start off with an economically underdeveloped nation, you can substantially add to the total happiness of its people with a relatively small degree of economic development. Colombia is not that much richer than Zimbabwe, yet the citizens of Colombia report a much higher level of happiness with their lot than residents of Zimbabwe. Mexico is again a notch richer than Colombia, and again Mexicans seem to be somewhat happier than Colombians (though now the increment is much less than in the Zimbabwe-Colombia comparison).

Once we get to the part of the curve past Mexico, things change dramatically. Economic development proceeds; Sweden has massively more total riches than Mexico, and the U.S. is in turn far ahead of Sweden. But here we find a major disconnect between national wealth and happiness. For all the extra economic productivity, the richer nations seem unable to get much past the middle group of nations in adding to their citizens' overall satisfaction with their lives. Among the select club made up of the world's wealthiest nations, *further economic growth is not the pathway to a better life for all citizens.*

This finding flies in the face of the basic assumptions of economism, and especially of Reagan supply-side economics. Since in the U.S. we have a lot of poor people as well as some rich people, it is an article of faith that the only way to improve overall happiness is to make the poor better off, and that will happen only through economic development. The rising tide, as the old saying goes, lifts all boats. If only the rich keep getting richer, they will invest their money in more productive enterprises that generate jobs, and trickle-down will assure that the poor eventually get their share and become better off. Wilkinson and Pickett show that the available facts simply do not support that picture. If you start off with a very poor country like Zimbabwe or Colombia, the process works; economic development adds to overall happiness. But as soon as you get to the level of the U.S. or Sweden or even Mexico, the equation no longer holds. The nation can become a great deal wealthier without the average person becoming any happier.

Does this mean that if people in a rich nation like the U.S. are miserable, they are fated to remain so? That's where the next set of graphs come in, all looking very much like Figure 10.2. In these graphs we've eliminated Zimbabwe, Colombia and Mexico, and have included only the world's richest 23 nations—the countries where, according to Wilkinson and Pickett, the most reliable comparison figures are available. As we go from those countries where incomes are most equal to those with the greatest income inequality, we see a steady increase in poor health and many bothersome social problems such as crime, teenage pregnancy, drug abuse, distrust, and poor educational outcomes. In virtually every one of these individual graphs the U.S. is an outlier on both scales—it has even worse social problems than you'd expect from the overall international trend line, and it's by far the most unequal in income of all the nations.

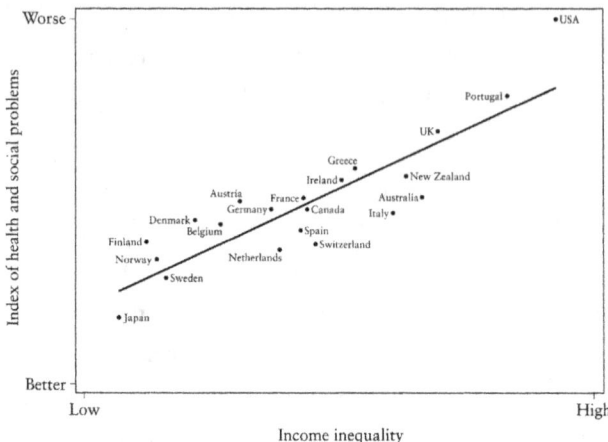

Figure 10.2. General index of health and social problems, compared to income inequality among rich countries

Wilkinson and Pickett, being careful statisticians, make a couple of points about their second set of graphs. First, the way the points cluster closely about the trend line make it virtually impossible that the association between worse social problems and greater income inequality is due to chance. Second, the graphs look identical regardless of which measure of social dysfunction you happen to pick. Whether you use obesity, or mental illness, or teenage pregnancy, or rates of drug abuse, or crime, you get just about the same trend line and just about the same ranking among the various countries. (About all that changes is the precise slope of the trend line; some are relatively shallow and others are very steep.) That makes it hard to imagine that there is some other causal factor out there, that produces all these social problems, and income inequality just happens to be going along for the ride. Rather it is a good deal more likely that income inequality, in addition to being in a reliable statistical association with each social problem, is in fact the common causal factor.

The third graph, Figure 10.3, is one that Wilkinson and Pickett throw in for confirmation. It's the same comparison as the second graph—although instead of comparing 23 different countries, we compare the 50 U.S. states. Yet the same association holds true. *On average,* the social problem gets worse as you move from the states with the highest level of income equality to those with the greatest inequality. Wilkinson and Pickett use the within-U.S. comparisons as a further bit of proof that we are not seeing merely a chance association. If we were to break down other countries by smaller region, we would find the same link between income inequality and worse social problems. The power of income inequality to cause social problems, or the power of income equality to prevent them, seems to show itself whether we look at the world or at entire countries or at smaller regions within countries. (You will notice that the scatter of the states around the trend line, in the third graph, is wider than that of the nations in the second graph. Wilkinson and Pickett explain that a wider scatter usually means that a wider set of other factors may be at work. Thus, income inequality may be far and away the most important reason why the U.S. has more social problems than does France, but only one among several factors why California has more social problems than North Dakota. But income inequality remains firmly associated in all cases, again with a negligible likelihood that the association could be due to chance.)

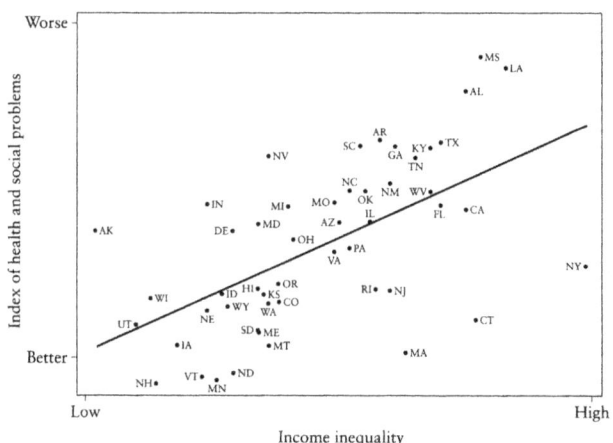

Figure 10.3. General index of health and social problems, compared to income inequality among U.S. states

Finally, Figure 10.4 teaches us a history lesson. It shows that there was a certain gap between the income of the richest 10 percent and the poorest 10 percent of the U.S. population up to the mid-1970s. (If we could follow the graph farther out to the left we'd see that this gap had been pretty steady-state for much of the 1950s and 1960s.) Starting around 1978 (just about the time, as we have seen, that economism-type ideas and policies started to become most entrenched in American thinking), the gap started to widen rapidly, and reached its height around 1994. Since then, the gap has not gotten much wider. In other words, the extreme degree of income inequality that makes the U.S. such an outlier on all the international comparisons, and that is linked with so many social ills, is a product of a relatively short span of time in the history of the nation. It hardly seems graven in stone that that is the way we have to be forevermore.

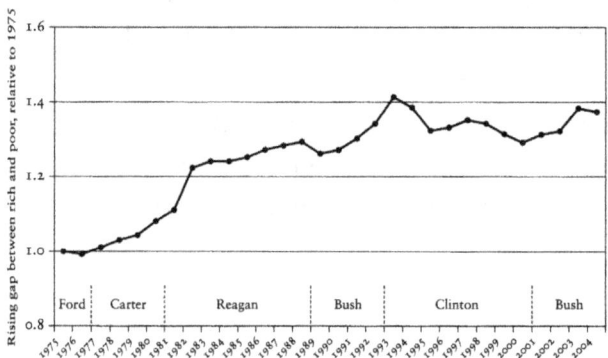

Figure 10.4. The widening gap between the incomes of the richest and poorest 10 per cent in the U.S., 1975 to 2004 (1975 amounts shown as =1)

The other message that Wilkinson and Pickett stress throughout their book is that while many of the social ills that income inequality breeds affect the poor disproportionately, their effects are hardly contained among the poor. Income inequality, it appears, is an equal-opportunity social disease. Its bad effects spread throughout the entire society. Rich Americans have a longer life expectancy than poor Americans, but they have a shorter life expectancy than the poorer members of many societies where income is distributed more evenly. Put the other way around, the benefits of a more equal America would accrue to all Americans, rich and poor alike.

A different way of putting that last point is to note that if we live in a nation that has greater income inequality, and as a result has a raft of serious health and social problems, we generally end up spending more of everyone's tax dollars on programs to compensate for the social dysfunction—even after economism has worked so hard to shred the social safety net. We have to fund Medicaid to provide health care for the poor, and the Medicaid budget is always suffering cost overruns because the poor have such bad health. We need to keep building more prisons and hiring more police to deal with rampant crime. If Wilkinson and Pickett are only partly correct, we could just as well devote the same amount of money to equalizing income. The middle class and the rich would lose that money in either case. If the money goes to more prisons and more drug-abuse treatment programs, it goes to piecemeal, Band-aid solutions that have been shown in the past to do little to solve the problems long-term. If the same money were spent on redistributing income to make all of us more equal—whether through public taxation or through some private market mechanism—there would be a much greater chance that we'd see long-range improvements in our society and in everyone's quality of life.

Offering indirect support for Wilkinson and Pickett's arguments for societal reform is Stephanie Coontz, a historian of family studies and author of the popular book, *The Way We Never Were: American Families and the Nostalgia Trap.* In the first edition of her book in 1992, Coontz listed a number of myths about the American family in the decades 1950-1970 that get in the way of sober analysis of our policy options today. Writing a new introduction for the 2000 edition, Coontz noted that most of the trends she had described in 1992 had been further validated by new data. But she mentioned one area where she regretted her earlier discussion: "In retrospect, however, I now wish that I had focused more on the interaction between socioeconomic inequality and consumerist individualism in explaining many of our social strains." [9] She then went on to cite some of the same sorts of statistics that Wilkinson and Pickett rely on, showing that the worsening income inequality in America after the mid-1970s corresponded to a time of deteriorating social conditions.

Are Wilkinson and Pickett right? Would their proposal actually work? Should the U.S. strive to reduce income inequality as a high national priority? I think that Wilkinson and Pickett, and the many other policy scholars whose work they summarize, have provided enough evidence to make all these questions well worth asking—even were we to decide in the end that their proposal is ill founded. And that is where economism comes in. It seems evident that if economism were not a huge part, and too often a controlling part, of the U.S. political and policy conversation, then a proposal such as Wilkinson and Pickett's could at least get a fair hearing on its merits. So long as economism rules the roost, it is highly unlikely that we'll give the income-equality proposal the time of day. (After all, it cannot be in keeping with God's will that we should try to make others better off when they have not succeeded in making themselves better off through their own individual, responsible behavior.) Our present seduction by economism shuts our minds off from an entire range of much more promising and creative policy options.

Is Michael Moore Right?

I referred in Chapter 8 to Michael Moore's movie, *Capitalism—A Love Story.*[10] As Moore covers a good deal of the same ground that I do in this book, it might be instructive to mention two ways in which I disagree with his ideas.

My larger disagreement is with his attack on *capitalism*. Moore acknowledges that if what the U.S. had during the 1950s, when he was growing up in Flint, Michigan and when Stan and Carol Wyzansky were raising their family, was capitalism—when the middle class was thriving, jobs were plentiful, and the rich were well off but also paid their fair share of taxes—then he's all for it. (He also alleges that the reason we were so successful back then is that our major trading competitors had been bombed to rubble in World War II. If that was what was required for success, then Germany and Japan would not be as successful, and more equitable than the U.S. in their distribution of wealth, today.) I've tried to be more fine-grained by saying that the enemy is not capitalism; it's a peculiar, extreme version of it called economism. We could get rid of economism tomorrow and still be a capitalist society.

My lesser disagreement with Moore is that he portrays the Troubled Asset Relief Program (TARP), the Federal bailout of the big financial institutions in the fall of 2008, as a scam perpetrated on the American people by Wall Street. What we saw of the "shock doctrine" as a tool of economism's policies (Chapter 6) would tend to support Moore's claim, as we saw several international examples of the "Chicago school" cooking up a fiscal crisis as an excuse for a takeover of society and doing away with democratic institutions. My own view, backed by such left-leaning economists as Paul Krugman, is that the bailout was sadly necessary to prevent a complete global financial meltdown, and that the claims that the sky was falling were not exaggerated. I agree that more strings could have been put on those bailout funds. And Moore produced his movie before it could be seen how much of the TARP loans are actually being paid back—a much better deal for the American taxpayers than most initially feared. Here I concur with Charles Ferguson's assessment in his film, *Inside Job*—that the real scam pulled by Wall Street was not with TARP but in the later aftermath, when the investment banks went back to business as usual, and took advantage of the Supreme Court's *Citizens United* decision to buy off Congress and the White House and head off any serious threat of regulation.[11]

Where I agree with Moore is the fundamental lesson that if we want our country back from the forces of economism, it is up to us to take it back. This is why "government of the people, by the people, and for the people" is so critical for our future—and why economism's troops stay up nights trying to figure out ways to be sure we never realize this.

Recovering Government Of, By and For the People

Everyone knows the famous phrase from the last sentence of Lincoln's Gettysburg Address, "government of the people, by the people, and for the people." Chances are good that we have not thought about what that really means. Did Lincoln, for instance, really mean to suggest three distinct ideas, or was he just using fancy rhetoric to say one single thing about government? The taut brevity of the Gettysburg Address strongly suggests that had he meant one thing, he would have said one thing only. In that case, just what are the three distinct ideas? Why does the future of America depend on us rediscovering these ideas and (Lincoln's word again) rededicating ourselves to them?

Government of the people suggests that the people who work in government, who are the government, are people more or less just like the rest of us. Government will not be like us—all of us—unless people who represent all segments of America have an equal opportunity to serve. So long as economism teaches us that certain classes of Americans represent God's chosen people, and that people like them are more worthy than the rest of us to be leaders, economism will subvert "government of the people." This subversion will be even more severe if economism convinces us that all of life is really one big marketplace, so that corporate wheelers and dealers, who seem to be able to rake off the most profits in the market, are therefore natural leaders and are the people we should listen to in governmental affairs.

"Government of the people," of course, does not mean government consisting of just anyone; ideally it means that *the best* people—those most talented and most qualified--will serve the rest of us. Ever since Ronald Reagan cynically framed his campaign to be the head of the U.S. government as a campaign *against* government (or "gumment" as he preferred to pronounce it), it has become fashionable to regard all government as incompetent and all who work in government as crooks or ignoramuses. This economism-inspired view seems a sure recipe for discouraging the most talented and qualified people from seeking careers in government service. If government agencies filled with crooks and ignoramuses can most easily be controlled by lobbyists for the wealthy and the big corporations, then economism says, "Bring it on."

Government by the people suggests that the people of the U.S. are actively involved in the affairs and decisions of their own government. The champions of economism seem quite worried that this might happen. How worried they are is suggested by the model of "American democracy" that our leaders have been promoting around the world. According to that model, "democracy" means holding a presumably free and fair election, and the people all coming out to vote. After that the people are expected to go home and mind their own business until the next election, and leave it to their elected representatives to do all the governing. In Afghanistan, for example, U.S. policy has focused on holding elections for the national government, which many Afghans distrust and from which they feel disenfranchised. U.S. policymakers have been much less concerned about, or even frankly suspicious of, local village councils, despite the possibility that these councils represent more of real democracy in action, in a way more consistent with Afghan culture and history.

Lincoln himself would understand what a minimal conception of democracy the model favored by economism represents. He was elected President because of the fame that he gained through his debates with Stephen Douglas during their 1858 campaign for the U.S. Senate seat in Illinois (which Douglas won). Illinoisans drove wagons or walked many miles to attend these debates. They stood in fields or sat on tree stumps while each candidate spoke for an hour or more. The Illinois newspapers reprinted their speeches verbatim, and for months after, people gathered in taverns or country stores to read over the speeches and to debate the points among themselves. These Illinoisans of 1858 still felt close to the time when their "fathers" (as Lincoln put it at Gettysburg) fought and died for American independence. The level of civic engagement and attention that was required as a matter of duty, for them, seems to have been much greater than we accept today—when far too many of us cannot be bothered even to vote in a presidential election, far less pay close attention to the pressing issues of the day in between elections.

Champions of economism like our present state of apathy just fine. Our apathy allows the government to be run by the special interests, which in practice always means those with the most money. Economism holds that only experts in economics are fit to manage the government, because all of public policy actually boils down to the supposedly "free" marketplace. And of course, the people who are said to be the "experts" are all those who believe that the government should keep its hands off the market. The "plutonomy," the ruling elite who believe that government exists solely to benefit the wealthiest slice of the citizenry, can have their way only so long as the rest of us ignore what they're up to.[12]

For several generations of American workers, their true classroom in local, participatory democracy has been the union hall. Is it too paranoid to imagine that at least a part of the reason why economism is so eager to do away with unions is to eliminate this classroom, and assure that the great mass of the public never gets any ideas about direct participation in the affairs of government?

Both Bill Moyers and Michael Moore are sure that we will not overcome economism's stranglehold on our policies until we organize at the grassroots level and commit ourselves to a long and arduous struggle. We've already seen reasons to doubt that the two major political parties will be of much help. Such a move toward community organizing would constitute a major resurgence of *government by the people.*

Government for the people is the easiest concept to relate to economism. Economism is devoted to government for only one class of people, those whom God has favored; and its advocates believe fervently that God has favored the rich and wants to punish the poor. Moreover, to assure that true participatory democracy, "government by the people," doesn't get off the ground again, these advocates want to keep us divided. They want us to look at others in society and see competitors rather than fellow Americans or fellow human beings. Individual greed, according to economism's creed, is the great lubricator of the free market. Any sense of civic solidarity or responsibility, of true citizenship in the common cause of the American nation, is foreign to economism's way of thinking.

If we were again to take government for the people seriously, we'd start to ask how to make financial markets serve the interests of the public rather than the other way around. We'd have to heed the warning of health economist Robert Evans: "Markets were made for and by men, not vice versa."[13] And if we asked that question, as we saw in Chapter 9, we'd soon discover that some degree of government regulation of markets was a necessary ingredient in our national well-being. Economism has nightmares about our discovering that fact. Its true believers are so worried about our making that discovery that the Republican members of the Fiscal Crisis Inquiry Commission, the "bipartisan" group convened to draw the policy lessons from the Great Recession of 2008, voted as a bloc to refuse to allow the word "deregulation" even to appear in the group's report.[14]

Finally, if we were again to take government of, by, and for the people seriously, we would have to confront the basic fact about economism that we've encountered over and over—that economism is fundamentally anti-democratic. Again economism is slippery, and tries to deny this. According to economism, the market is the ideally democratic institution, with everyone free to choose to buy or sell as he or she wishes. Government by contrast is full of bureaucrats and politicians who think they know better than us what we need and want.

Economism wishes us to worship the Golden Calf. Instead of the true God, which is in this case the democratic American institutions that Lincoln's "fathers" fought for in the Revolution and which Lincoln fought a bitter civil war to maintain, we are supposed to worship the false god of the market that glitters in the sun and that promises that maybe we'll get rich, if we just win the lottery.

Thomas Frank answers the false god in this way:

Markets may look like democracy, in that we are all involved in their making, but they are fundamentally not democratic. We did not vote for Bill Gates; we didn't all sit down one day and agree that we should only use his operating system and we should pay for it just however much he thinks is right. We do not go off to our jobs checking telephone lines or making cold calls or driving a forklift every morning because this is what we want to do; we do it because we have to, because it is the only way we can afford food, shelter, and medicine. The logic of business is coercion, monopoly, and the destruction of the weak, not 'choice' or 'service' or universal affluence.[15]

If we don't like how our government institutions work, we cannot run away and go hide in the market. We must do the hard work that the citizens of Lincoln's time took for granted—we must pay attention, and insist that government be run by and for the people, not by and for monied interests. If we won't take the time and pay attention, we can be sure that the lobbyists who work for the wealthy interests will. And, finally, we will have to undo the damage recently done by the Supreme Court, and change the rules that allow the rich to buy elections, even if it requires a constitutional amendment.

From Lincoln's point of view, one of the most anti-democratic sentiments ever expressed was by Grover Norquist, the anti-tax activist: "I don't want to abolish government. I simply want to reduce it to the size where I can drag it into the bathroom and drown it in the bathtub."[16] As we saw in Chapter 6, from economism's viewpoint, this sentiment is half true. Its devotees would love to drown a part of government in the bathtub—the part that collects taxes from all, with the wealthy and the corporations paying their fair share, and then provides programs that benefit the middle-class and the poor. The part of government that the wealthy and the corporations can take control of, so as to be allowed to continue to manipulate unfree markets for their own advantage, while avoiding paying the costs that their behavior imposes on the rest of society, is the part of government economism hopes will never drown.

New York Times columnist Bob Herbert decided to ring out the old year of 2008 with a comment headlined, "Stop Being Stupid."[17] The events of that ill-fated year, he suggested, pointed the U.S. to the policies that would make us successful in the future.

On the negative side, he said–stop imagining that we could have a government that works and fight two wars while slashing taxes. Stop imagining that you can have a house twice as big as you can afford with no down payment and easy terms. Stop imagining that you can have all the latest expensive gizmos and put it on the credit card. Stop spending money that we don't have. On the positive side–spend real money, that we do have, on things that make us better and stronger, like a solid infrastructure, education, health care, a clean environment, and energy independence.

Along the way, Herbert added, "It didn't require a genius (or even an economics degree) to understand a crucial point that popped up some years ago in a front-page article in *The Wall Street Journal*: 'Markets are a great way to organize economic activity, but they need adult supervision.'"

The man said *adult* supervision. Not *divine* supervision. There's a difference.

Notes

1. Moyers B. Bill Moyers: "Welcome to the plutocracy!" Truthout, http://www.truth-out.org/bill-moyers-money-fights-hard-and-it-fights-dirty64766 (accessed November 28, 2010).

2. Fikac P. Official paints stark image of Medicaid opt-out. *Houston Chronicle*, November 28, 2010; http://www.chron.com/disp/story.mpl/metropolitan/7315107.html (accessed November 29, 2010).

3. Krugman P. When zombies win. *New York Times*, December 19, 2010; http://www.nytimes.com/2010/12/20/opinion/20krugman.html (accessed December 22, 2010).

4. Harrop F. Raising taxes on the rich not waging class warfare. *Houston Chronicle*, November 27, 2010: B7; http://www.chron.com/disp/story.mpl/editorial/outlook/7312808.html (accessed November 29, 2010). Family historian Stephanie Coontz would add a further reason to avoid any personal vilification of the rich, based on her comparisons between the first and second Gilded Ages in U.S. history (Chapter 5). She noted that in the first Gilded Age, it was actually common to encounter personal attacks against the morals of the wealthy, but that these attacks did not result in any meaningful social reform that improved the lot of the lower and middle classes. Rather, the attacks reflected a shrinking of the scope of moral discussion, as a society that used to believe strongly in civic virtue and community-mindedness redefined morality as something restricted to the family and individual realms only. One could criticize a person's morals for cheating on his spouse or neglecting his children, but not for failing to support fair practices that would benefit the entire community. Coontz believes that much of what is wrong with the Gilded Age in which we now live (an age, I believe, of economism) is that our moral language has once again shrunk in this fashion. This puts much too much pressure on the family as the institution that is blamed for all social ills, at the same time that our attention is distracted from those areas of society where we could genuinely make a difference for the better; Coontz S. *The way we never were: American families and the nostalgia trap.* New York: Basic Books, 2000: 93-121. I believe that Coontz is right—else how could one explain a society

that, in the spring of 2011, faced continued unemployment and a stalled economic recovery, and yet seemingly was unable to talk about anything besides a Congressman's sexual peccadilloes?

5. Frum: GOP is the party of the old. Morning Edition, National Public Radio, December 12, 2008; http://www.npr.org/templates/story/story.php?storyId=98174969 (accessed November 29, 2010).

6. Frank T. *One market under God: extreme capitalism, market populism, and the end of economic democracy.* New York, Anchor, 2001: 17.

7. Goozner M. Liberals' deficit plan stresses defense cuts and tax hikes. *Fiscal Times,* November 29, 2010; http://www.thefiscaltimes.com/Blogs/2010/11/29/Vault-Liberal-Deficit-Plan-Stresses-Defense-Cuts-and-Higher-Taxes.aspx (accessed Nov. 29, 2010).

8. Wilkinson R, Pickett K. *The spirit level: why greater equality makes societies stronger.* New York: Bloomsbury Press, 2009. For more on the cause of greater income equality, see their website, http://www.equalitytrust.org.uk/ (accessed December 19, 2010).

9. Coontz S. *The way we never were: American families and the nostalgia trap.* New York: Basic books, 2000:xxvii. I mention Coontz as one example, but a long list of authors whose studies agree with Wilkinson and Pickett's basic message is given in their extensive endnotes.

10. Moore M. *Capitalism—A Love Story* (Overture Films/Paramount Vantage, 2009).

11. Ferguson C. *Inside job.* Sony Pictures Classics, 2010.

12. Moyers B. Bill Moyers: Welcome to the plutocracy! Truthout, http://www.truth-out.org/bill-moyers-money-fights-hard-and-it-fights-dirty64766 (accessed November 28, 2010). Moyers takes the term "plutonomy" from a memo prepared by Citibank. Michael Moore, in his movie *Capitalism—A Love Story* (Overture Films/Paramount Vantage, 2009), cites this same memo, and adds that according to the Citibank experts, the biggest threat to the continued enjoyment of these privileges by the super-wealthy is the American creed of "one man, one vote." The mass of voters, they feared, would take issue with policies that allowed the top one percent of the population to control more wealth than the lower 95 percent.

13. Evans RG. Going for the gold: the redistributive agenda behind market-based health care reform. *Journal of Health Politics, Policy and Law* 22:427-65, 1997, quote p. 429.

14. Krugman P. Wall Street whitewash. *New York Times*, December 16, 2010; http://www.nytimes.com/2010/12/17/opinion/17krugman.html?partner=rssnyt&emc=rss (accessed December 18, 2010).

15. Frank, *One market under God*: 86-87.

16. Norquist's statement apparently occurred during an interview with NPR on May 25, 2001; http://www.npr.org/templates/story/story.php?storyId=1123439 (accessed July 3, 2011).

17. Herbert B. Stop being stupid. *New York Times*, December 27, 2008: A25; http://www.nytimes.com/2008/12/27/opinion/27herbert.html (accessed December 18, 2010).

About the Author

Howard Brody received his MD and his PhD in philosophy from Michigan State University. He is the Director of the Institute for the Medical Humanities at the University of Texas Medical Branch in Galveston, where he also holds the title of John P. McGovern Centennial Chair in Family Medicine. Before moving to Texas in 2006, he was a practicing family physician and a member of the faculty of the College of Human Medicine, Michigan State University, for 26 years. He is the author of numerous books and articles about health care ethics and humanities; he is also co-author of two books on the history of medicine in the 19th century.

The views expressed here (naturally) are those of the author alone, and are not the official views of any of the institutions with which he is now or has been affiliated.

Index

A

Aaron, 10
Afghanistan, 220
AIG, 181
air traffic controllers' union, 162
Alger, Horatio, 121
American Enterprise Institute, 128
American Medical Association
(AMA), 119
American Prospect, 163, 170, 195
Andre, Judy, 19
Anglican church, 62, 83
Appelbaum, Binyamin, 196
Aquinas, Thomas, 142, 149
Argentina, 123, 169
Asia, 184
Atlanta Journal-Constitution, 130-133,
155
Australia, 53
autism, 130
Avida computer program, 150-152

B

Baker, Dean, 119-120, 196-197, 201n37
Bakersfield, California, 191
Bank of America Merrill Lynch, 162
Barker, Randolph, 189, 190

Barnum, P.T., 102
Bartels, Larry, 31
Baucus, Max, 17
Baxter, Richard, 89, 90
Bear Stearns, 181, 190
Benson, Josiah (fictional), 23, 34, 83-
84, 91-92, 202
Berkeley, California, 24
Bernanke, Ben, 196
Bible, 21n1, 92, 112
Book of Job, 92, 133
New Testament, 18, 65-66, 85,
105n8
Old Testament, 10, 63, 93, 105n8
Ten Commandments, 10, 153
Bigelow, Gordon, 19, 51, 64, 66-67,
75-77, 81n22, 137
bioethics, 18, 19, 132
bipartisanship, 203, 207-210, 222
Blitzer, Wolf, 125
BMW, 171
Born, Brooksley, 185-186
Boston, 34, 69, 99
Boston University, 162
Bowles, Erskine, 209
Brazil, 124, 169
Bremer, Paul, 172-173
Britain. *See* Great Britain
Brooks, David, 194-195

bubbles, financial, 101-102, 179-181,
      195, 196
   dot-com, 49, 52, 99, 137, 179
   Dutch tulip bulb, 179
   housing, 29, 33, 181, 186, 188, 192;
      See also subprime mortgages
   South Sea, 179
Buffett, Warren, 99
Burke, Edmund, 110
Bush, George H.W., 180, 192, 204
Bush, George W., 12, 96, 109, 120, 125, 138,
      168, 169, 172, 180, 193, 196, 207
Bushnell, David, 189-190

C

California, 23, 24, 25, 29, 33, 174, 191,
      193, 215
Callahan, Daniel, 18-19, 114
Calvin, John, 87-90, 93, 95
Calvinism, 14, 85-94, 110
Canada, 21n9, 113, 121
Cancun, Mexico, 161
capitalism, 85-86, 90, 93, 96, 112, 124,
      163, 174, 180, 183, 195, 218
Carnegie, Andrew, 98-99, 127
Carrier, John, 21n1, 105n11
Cassidy, John, 81n28
category mistake, 15-16, 50
Cavallo, Domingo, 123
Center for Economic and Policy
      Research, 119, 196
Center for Renewal of Science and
      Culture, 142

Central Valley, California, 23
Chait, Jonathan, 51-52, 108-110, 126, 127
Chalmers, Thomas, 65-66
charity, 65-66, 68, 98-99
Charles I, 83
Charles II, 83
Chicago, 23, 25
"Chicago Boys," 122-124, 169
Chile, 124, 169
China, 44, 122, 170-171
Cho, David, 196
cholera, 36-37
Christianity, 18, 65, 73, 85, 104, 129,
      142-148, 153
Chrysler, 160
Citibank, 226n12
Citicorp, 187
Citigroup, 183, 185-190, 191, 193
Citizens United case, 197, 219
Civil War, American, 222-223
Civil War, English, 83
Clinton, Bill, 120, 162-163, 167, 171, 187,
      192, 196, 206, 209
Cold War, 26, 211
collateralized debt obligations
      (CDOs), 188-189, 193
Colombia, 190-191, 212, 213
Columbia University, 123
Commodity Futures Trading
      Commission, 185
communism, 44, 195
Conwell, Russell, 98, 99
Coontz, Stephanie, 97, 121, 128, 134n2,
      217, 225n4

Cork, County, Ireland, 59, 68-69

Corn Laws (England), 70

corporations, 14, 37, 56n14, 119-125,
159-163, 165-171, 172, 173, 187,
198, 208, 209, 220, 223

    employee ownership of, 173-174

Countrywide Financial, 193

creationism, 137-144; *See also*
intelligent design

Creswell, Julie, 185, 188

culture codes, 100-101

Curry, Boykin, 183

D

Darwin, Charles, 73, 138-141, 143, 146-
147, 152, 155, 156, 205

Dash, Eric, 185, 188

Declaration of Independence, 41

Defense Policy Board
(Pentagon), 125

Democratic Party, 12, 51, 120, 160,
163, 167, 184, 192-193, 195-196,
203-204, 208-209

Depression, *see* Great Depression

deregulation, 123, 166, 192-197, 222

derivatives, 180-189

Dewey, Tim, 165

Dickens, Charles, 72-73, 75, 129

Digital Evolution Laboratory, 151

Discover magazine, 151

Discovery Institute, 142, 156

Dodd, Christopher, 192

Dorsetshire, England, 83

Douglas, Stephen, 220-221

Dover, Pennsylvania, 138-144, 148,
153-154

Dow Jones average, 42, 181, 195

E

Eagle Capital, 183

economic reductionism, 55n4

economics, 11-13, 16-20, 39-41, 44, 52,
53, 64, 74-79, 104, 108, 119,
122, 133, 135n17, 179, 196, 202,
206, 219, 221

    Chicago school, 122-125, 218

    Keynesian, 122

    neoclassical, 51, 53, 58n35, 60, 74-
79, 84, 122, 137, 194-195

    supply-side, 51, 101, 108-110, 116,
120, 126-127, 137, 162-163, 191,
204, 213

    "voodoo," 204

economism:

    advantages of, 41-42

    anti-democratic nature of, 48-50,
112-113, 219-223

    definition of, 13, 20, 38-39, 103-
104, 202

    extent of, 50-52

    flaws of, 42-48

    ideology, viewed as, 103-104

    intelligent design and, 14, 154-
157, 202, 205

    opportunism, viewed as, 103-104

    origins of, 38

stealth campaign of, 52, 104, 108-136, 137, 197, 202, 222

vs. economics, 13, 39-41

Economist, The, 121, 126

Eisenhower, Dwight, 126

Ekins, Paul, 38

Elect (Calvinist doctrine), 88-95

Elizabethan era, 66, 72

England, 13, 19, 23, 51, 59-82, 83-85, 89, 91, 129, 132, 155, 179, 207, 208; *See also* Great Britain

Enlightenment, 62-63, 73, 156

Enron, 101-102, 109, 180-181, 183, 184, 191

ethics, 15, 45, 53, 154

of international development, 19, 36-38

Europe, 17, 23, 36, 51, 59, 86, 161, 164, 208

evangelicalism, 13, 14, 19, 51, 59-82, 84-85, 89, 91, 95, 98-99, 103, 104, 129, 132, 133, 137, 155-156, 202, 205, 207

beliefs of, 61-62

Evans, Robert, 21n11, 57n22, 113-119, 222

evolution, 73, 138-141, 143-145, 146-148, 150-152, 155, 156, 205

Exxon, 184

F

Fannie Mae, 192

Federal Bureau of Investigation (FBI), 193

Federal Deposit Insurance Corporation, 187

Federal Reserve, 186, 196

feminism, 52

Ferguson, Charles, 185, 197, 219

Fiji, 25

financial crisis of 2008-9, *see* Great Recession

Finland, 211

First Amendment, 198

Fiscal Crisis Inquiry Commission, 222

Flint, Michigan, 218

Florence, Italy, 85

Florida, 26, 30, 32, 160, 165

Foley, Duncan, 53, 104, 112

Ford, 160

Fortune magazine, 180

France, 25, 63, 73, 75-77, 87, 100, 156, 208, 215

Frank, Barney, 192

Frank, Thomas, 49-50, 99, 112, 170, 176n15, 208, 223

Franklin, Benjamin, 63, 93-94, 97, 106n25

Freddie Mac, 192

free market, *see* markets

French Revolution, 63, 73, 156

Friedman, Milton, 122-125, 169; *See also* economics, Chicago school

Frum, David, 207-208

G

Galbraith, John, 130
Gasparino, Charles, 185, 187-189, 192, 193
Gasper, Des, 38, 41-47, 48, 51
Gates, Bill, 90, 99, 223
General Electric, 167, 176n15
General Motors, 33-34, 160
Georgia, 130
Georgia State University, 132
Germany, 32, 85, 94-95, 96, 171, 208, 218
Gettysburg Address, 219, 221
GI Bill, 25, 33
Gilded Age, 97-99, 121, 127, 165, 168, 170, 198, 225n4
Gilder, George, 52, 108, 137
Glass-Steagall Act, 187
Glassman, James, 128
Glenview, Illinois, 25
Golden Calf, 9-10, 21n1, 113, 222
Goldman Sachs, 187
Gospels, *see* Bible, New Testament
Graham, Darin (fictional), 28-33, 42, 121, 126, 130, 202
Graham, Shelly (Wyzansky) (fictional), 27-33, 42, 121, 126, 130, 160, 202
Gramm, Phil, 110, 134n2, 186
Gramm-Leach-Bliley Financial Services Modernization Act, 187

Great Britain, 17, 21n9, 25, 60, 71, 79, 122, 173, 202, 211; *See also* England
Great Depression, 12, 18, 23, 26, 27, 126, 129, 161, 187, 196
Great Recession, 14, 18, 29, 32, 81n28, 109, 130, 160, 170, 174, 178-201, 202, 204, 209, 222
Greece, 12
Greenspan, Alan, 186, 196
Greg, William, 73

H

Habitat for Humanity, 42
Hacker, Jacob, 30-33, 120-121, 126-129, 165, 191
Hague, The, 38
Haiti, 36
Harley-Davidson, 162
Harris, Ethan, 162, 168
Harrop, Froma, 207
Hastings Center, 18
Hastings Center Report, 132
Haught, John, 142, 149
health care systems, 19, 39-40, 113-115; *See also* single-payer system
health insurance, 16, 29, 30, 119, 130, 132, 184, 198
health reform, 17, 21n4, 30, 33, 119-120
Health Savings Accounts, 127

hedge funds, 185
Heller, Jan, 80n4, 106n40
Herbert, Bob, 224
Hersh, Seymour, 125
Hilton, Boyd, 61, 63, 74
Hobby, Paul, 183
Holland, 179
Houston, 183
Hurricane Katrina, 169

I

Illinois, 26, 221
income inequality, 17, 31, 99, 121, 173,
    210-218
Indianapolis, 165
Industrial Revolution, 67, 71, 164
Institute of Social Studies, The
    Hague, 38
intelligent design, 14, 52, 137-158,
    202, 205
International Monetary Fund, 36-37,
    123, 186
International Olympic Committee,
    140
invisible hand, 44-45, 74, 155-156,
    194
Iraq, 114, 125, 172-173
Ireland, 12, 23, 34, 59-60, 69-72
Irish potato famine, 13, 59-60, 67,
    69-72, 120, 194, 206
Islam, 104
Israelites, 10
Iwo Jima, 25

J

Jackson Hole, Wyoming, 186
Japan, 211, 218
Jefferson, Thomas, 63
Jesus, 18, 61, 65-66, 68
Jevons, William, 74-75
Jones, John, III, 138-148, 156
*Journal of the American Medical
    Association*, 39

K

Kansas Board of Education, 140
Keen, Steve, 53, 58n35, 130
Kessler, James, 105n8
King Philip's War, 84
Klein, Naomi, 122-123, 169
Kozul-Wright, Richard, 57n23, 104,
    112
Krugman, Paul, 11-14, 52, 115, 195,
    204, 219
Kwazulu-Natal, South Africa, 36

L

Laffer curve, 110
Lake Michigan, 161
Lawrence, William, 98-99
layoffs, 14, 43, 126, 157, 159-177, 202;
    See also unemployment
Lehman Brothers, 181
Lenin, Vladimir, 55n4
leverage, 183, 185-186

Levitation Science (fictitious example), 144-149
Lincoln, Abraham, 219-223
Liverpool, 69
London, 70
Long Beach Financial, 191
Los Angeles, 24
Luther, Martin, 89-90

M

Maheras, Thomas, 189, 190
Malthus, Thomas, 63, 67, 73, 129
market fundamentalism, 48-49, 57n23
market populism, 48-49
markets, 19, 38-50, 67, 72, 74-75, 77-79, 85, 101, 104, 111-116, 120, 121-125, 137, 154-156, 163, 168, 170-172, 174, 178-179, 180, 182-198, 204, 205-208, 217, 220-224
Marxism, 55n4
Massachusetts, 23, 83-84, 91-92, 98, 198
Mather, Cotton, 92
Max-Neef, Manfred, 38
McCain, John, 18
McKinley, William, 168
Medicaid, 203-204, 217
Medicare, 119, 123, 127
Memphis, 19
Methodist church, 62
Mexico, 176n15, 212, 213

Meyerson, Harold, 163, 170-171, 195
Michigan, 160, 218
Michigan State University, 19, 150-152
Middle East, 125
Middleborough, Massachusetts, 84, 91
Misty of Chincoteague, 6
Mondragon Corporation, 174
Moore, Michael, 174, 218-219, 221, 226n12
moral hazard, 98-99, 127-133, 205-206
Morgan Stanley, 81n28
Morris, Charles, 184
Moses, 10
Moyers, Bill, 162, 168, 171, 203, 221, 226n12
Mozilo, Angelo, 193
Murdoch, Rupert, 198
Murphy, Kate, 181
Murray, Charles, 128
My Little Pony, 6

N

National Academy of Sciences, 142
National Defense Education Act, 134n2
National Public Radio, 207
Netherlands, The, *see* Holland
New Deal, 18, 122, 126-127, 129
New Orleans, 169
New Republic, The, 51, 108
New York, 18

New York Times, 11, 115, 185, 194, 195, 201n37, 224

Newman, Katherine, 127

Newsweek, 170, 182

Newtonian mechanics, 75, 77

Nixon, Richard, 126

Nobel Prize, 11, 122

Norquist, Grover, 223

North Dakota, 215

Norway, 175n1, 211

Nussbaum, Martha, 47

O

Obama, Barack, 12, 72, 163, 190, 197, 203, 204

Ofria, Charles, 151

Okun, Arthur, 46

O'Ryan, Bridget (fictional), 59, 69

O'Ryan, Kate (fictional), 59, 69

O'Ryan, Patrick (fictional), 23, 34, 59-60, 68-69, 202

P

Pacific Ocean, 25

Paris, 195

Pauly, Mark, 128

PeachCare for Kids, 130

Pearl Harbor, 25

Peel, Sir Robert, 60, 70

Pennsylvania, 86, 138

Pentagon, 114, 125

Perkins, William, 91

Perle, Richard, 125

Personal Responsibility Crusade, 127-130

Pharaoh, 10

philosophy, 15, 41, 44, 45, 47, 50, 53, 62, 74, 98, 139, 172

Physicians for a National Health Program, 17, 21n4

physics, 10, 74-78, 141, 145-146

Pickett, Kate, 173-174, 211-218

Pinochet, Augusto, 124

plutocracy, 110, 203

plutonomy, 221, 226n12

Plymouth Colony, 83

political economy, 74-75

Poole, England, 83-84

Poor Law (England), 66-67, 71, 72

populism, 49

Post, Cadence, 130-131

Post, Connie, 130-133, 155

Post, Michael, 130-133, 155

poverty, 14, 17, 18, 31, 32, 37, 43, 49, 54, 60, 64-66, 67, 74, 78, 79, 84, 88-89, 91, 93, 95, 98, 99, 110, 115-120, 123-130, 133, 154-155, 192-193, 207, 213, 215-217, 222-223

predestination, 87-90, 95

Prince, Charles, III, 187-190

Princeton University, 31, 39, 51

privatization, 114-124, 138, 169
    of risk, 126-130, 159, 165-167, 182, 191

productivity, 162, 175n1

Protestant Ethic, 13-14, 83-106, 110, 164, 205

Puritanism, 13, 83-106, 110, 133, 155, 181, 202

pyramid scheme, 190

Pythagorean Theorem, 15

Q

Quakers, 91

R

Rajan, Raghuram, 186

Rapaille, Clotaire, 100-101

rationing, of health care, 119

Rayment, Paul, 57n23, 104, 112

Reagan, Ronald, 51-52, 108-109, 122, 134n2, 162, 192, 195, 204, 213, 220

Reformation, 105n11

Reinhardt, Uwe, 39-40, 46, 50, 51, 53, 135n17, 206

religion, 9-15, 18, 53, 54, 75-79, 85, 98, 103-104, 110, 127-133, 137-157, 202, 205-207; *See also specific denominations*

Renaissance, 147

Republican Party, 12, 51, 109, 123, 126, 138, 160, 163, 166, 187, 192-193, 195-198, 199n10, 203-204, 206, 207-209, 222

Reverse Robin Hood Rule, 14, 108-135, 153, 202

Revolution, American, 222

Rhodes College, 19

Rodrik, Dani, 123

Romney, Mitt, 198

Roosevelt, Franklin, 18

Rove, Karl, 168, 198

Rubin, Robert, 187-188, 190

Rumsfeld, Donald, 125

Russell, Lord, 60-61, 71, 72

Russia, 44, 122

Ryken, Leland, 86-87, 89, 90, 92, 105n11, 106n25

S

Sachs, Jeffrey, 182

Salem, Massachusetts, 91

San Diego, 28, 29

San Francisco, 24

Sarasota, Florida, 26

savings and loan crisis, 109, 179, 182

science, 10-11, 15, 50, 52, 53, 73, 75-79, 104, 133, 137-158, 202, 206

Scotland, 44

Scott, Charity, 132

Seattle, 170

Sen, Amartya, 41

shock doctrine, 121-125, 218

Simpson, Alan, 209

single payer system, 17, 21n3, 21n4

Smith, Adam, 44-45, 53, 56n14, 74, 110, 111, 112, 155-156, 198

snake (fable), 6-11, 13, 15, 16, 34, 207

social contract, 33

Social Security, 127, 128, 160, 184, 205
socialism, 21n9, 198, 204, 208
socialized medicine, 21n9
sociology, 48, 85-86, 164
Somers, Margaret, 48-49, 111-113
Soros, George, 48, 57n22
South America, 122, 169
South Carolina, 171
Soviet Union, 26, 211
Spain, 174
Stevens, James, 64
Stevenson, Adlai, 26
stock market, 42, 52, 100, 111, 162, 166, 168, 179-181, 190; *See also* Wall Street
subprime mortgages, 42, 101, 109, 178-182, 188, 190, 192-193, 196
Summers, Larry, 186
Sweden, 211, 212, 213
Switzerland, 87

T

Tea Party, 119
Teivainen, Teivo, 38
Texas, 203-204
Texas A&M University, 134n2
Thatcher, Margaret, 122
theory, scientific, 11, 140-141
Tiananmen Square, 123
Tory Party (England), 60, 70, 80n2
Travelers Group, 187
Trevelyan, Charles, 60-61, 67, 71-72

Troubled Asset Relief Program (TARP), 218-219
Trump, Donald, 90, 97

U

Uchitelle, Louis, 163-168, 171-172
unemployment, 12, 42, 43, 44, 123, 166, 170, 174, 181, 197, 209; *See also* layoffs
Union of Soviet Socialist Republics (USSR), *see* Soviet Union
unions, 123, 161, 162, 164-171, 172, 173, 174, 221
Unitarianism, 74
United Auto Workers, 161
United Nations, 175n1
United States Army, 114-115
United States Army Air Corps, 23
United States Army Medical Corps, 25
United States Congress, 123, 182, 186, 187, 192, 193, 196, 203, 209, 210, 219
United States Department of Defense, 125; *See also* Pentagon
United States House of Representatives, 195
United States Senate, 196, 221
United States Supreme Court, 197, 219, 223
University of British Columbia, 113
University of Chicago, 122
University of Illinois, 26

University of Minnesota, 27

University of North Carolina, 27

University of Wisconsin, 25, 27

utilitarianism, 67, 95, 154

utility, 74

V

Vanderpool, Harold, 80n8

Vietnam, 26, 211

W

Walker, Scott, 123

Wall Street, 162, 184, 185-190, 193, 195, 196, 208, 210, 218-219

Wall Street Journal, 224

Wal-Mart, 34

War Orphans Act, 134n2

Washington, George, 63

Washington, DC, 51-52, 123, 187, 196

Washington Consensus, 124

Washington Post, 196

Wasunna, Angela, 18-19, 114

wealth, 14, 17, 18, 31, 49, 51, 78-79, 84-85, 89-103, 108-110, 112, 113, 115-121, 122, 125, 159, 166, 183, 188, 192, 206, 207, 208, 212-213, 218, 221, 223, 225n4, 226n12

Wealth of Nations, The, 44, 111

Weber, Max, 84-96, 103, 164

Weill, Sanford, 187

Welch, Jack, 167, 176n15

welfare, 66, 128, 206, 207

Wesley, John, 62

Whig Party (England), 60, 71, 72, 80n2

Wikipedia, 179

Wilkinson, Richard, 173-174, 211-218

Winthrop, John, 83

Wired magazine, 100

Wisconsin, 69, 123

Wolfe, Alan, 45

World Bank, 36-37, 123, 124

World War II, 13, 18, 25, 32, 211, 218

Wyzansky, Carol (Benson) (fictional), 23-27, 30-34, 126, 129, 160, 161, 202, 218

Wyzansky, Carolyn (fictional), 27-33, 129

Wyzansky, Frances (fictional), 25-26

Wyzansky, Henry (fictional), 25, 27-35, 129, 160

Wyzansky, John (fictional), 25, 26

Wyzansky, Michael (fictional), 27

Wyzansky, Stanley (fictional), 23-27, 30-34, 126, 129, 160, 161, 202, 218

Y-Z

Yale University, 126

Yeltsin, Boris, 122

Zakaria, Fareed, 182-183, 199n10

Zimbabwe, 212, 213